STUDY GUIDE

Henry Borne

Holy Cross College

SOCIETY

THE BASICS

FOURTH EDITION

John J. Macionis

PRENTICE HALL, *Upper Saddle River, NJ 07458*

© 1998 by PRENTICE-HALL, INC.
Simon & Schuster / A Viacom Company
Upper Saddle River, New Jersey 07458

ISBN 0-13-621228-X
Printed in the United States of America

Contents

Preface

This Study Guide has been written to enhance the foundation of sociological ideas and issues which are presented in the text *Society: The Basics (fourth edition)* by John Macionis. To help you review and think about the material found in the text, the Study Guide has been organized into several sections to accompany each chapter in the text.

A *chapter Outline* provides a basis for organizing segments of information from each chapter in the text. A section on *Learning Objectives* identified the basic knowledge, explanations, comparisons, and understandings students should have after reading and studying each chapter in the text. A section entitled *Chapter Review--Key Points* consists of a brief review of the chapter in paragraph form, following the outline of each chapter. This is followed by a section entitled *Key Terms* in which the important concepts from each chapter are listed, with space provided for you to write out the definition for each of the terms. Next, there is a section called *Important Researchers*. Researchers cited in the text are listed, with space provided for you to write significant ideas, findings, etc. for each researcher. The next section provides *Study Questions*, including true-false, multiple-choice, matching, fill-in, and definition and short-answer type questions. The study questions are followed by a section that provides *Answers to Study Questions*, including a listing of page numbers where the answers to these questions can be found. The final section, *Analysis and Comment*, provides space for you to raise questions and make comments on the *boxes* presented in the text.

This Study Guide is intended to be a concise review and learning tool to accompany the text *Society: The Basics* (fourth edition). It is complementary to this text and is not intended o stand alone as a brief text. It hopefully will provide you with opportunities to more deeply benefit from the knowledge of sociology which the author of the text offers.

On a personal note I want to once again congratulate John Macionis for writing another excellent introductory sociology text. He offers students a very meaningful perspective on many important sociological concepts, ideas, researchers, and issues. I believe students will be both challenged and excited by Dr. Macionis' text. It was once again a pleasure for me to write the Study Guide for this introductory text. I would like to thank the wonderful people at Prentice Hall for this opportunity--especially Nancy Roberts and Stephen Jordan. It is an honor for me to be able to work with such people. To my family--Cincy, Benjamin, and Abigail--thanks again for you patience and support!

Sociology: Perspective, Theory and Method

PART I: CHAPTER OUTLINE

PART II: LEARNING OBJECTIVES

1. To begin to visualize how sociology helps us put our world into global perspective.
2. To be able to define sociology and understand the basic components of the sociological perspective.
3. To be able to provide examples of the way in which social forces affect our everyday lives.
4. To see how research on suicide by Emile Durkheim illustrates how social forces affect an individual's behavior.
5. To begin to recognize factors in society that encourage people to perceive the world sociologically.
6. To begin to consider the interdependence between the U.S. and other nations of the world.
7. To be able to identify important historical factors in the development of the discipline of sociology.
8. To be able to identify and discuss the differences between the three major theoretical paradigms used by sociologists in the analysis of society.
9. To be able to provide illustrative questions raised about society using each of the theoretical paradigms.
10. To review the fundamental requirements for engaging in scientific investigation using the sociological perspective.
11. To become familiar with the basic elements of science and how they are used in sociological investigation.
12. To see how research is affected by gender.
13. To begin to view ethical considerations involved in studying people.
14. To become familiar with research methods used by sociologists in the investigation of society.
15. To gain a sense about how information technology is affecting sociological investigation.
16. To be able to identify and describe each of the ten steps in sociological research.

PART III: CHAPTER REVIEW--KEY POINTS

Our author begins the text with some general demographic patterns found in the college classroom. There are many approaches to the study of humanity, *sociology* is being introduced as one of these.

THE SOCIOLOGICAL PERSPECTIVE

Sociology is defined as *the scientific study of human social activity*. The qualities of the sociological perspective are outlined, with some illustrations for each being presented.

Seeing the General in the Particular

Sociologists look for *general social patterns* in the behavior of *particular individuals*. While not erasing our uniqueness as individuals, sociology studies the social forces that impinge on our lives in so many unseen, yet significant ways.

Seeing the Strange in the Familiar

Sociologist Peter Berger suggests that "things are not always what they seem." Sociology pushes us to questions the assumptions we are making about society, and reveals aspects of our social life that we typically would not claim to be "obvious" facts. The *Social Diversity* box entitled "The Name Game" (p. 4) demonstrates social forces affecting personal choice.

Seeing Individuality in Social Context

In our society we tend to downplay the idea that our lives are *predictable* and *patterned*. Sociologists suggest that while people must take personal responsibility for their actions, the choice and decisions of individuals are made within the context of a myriad of social forces.

Research by Emile Durkheim on suicide clearly show how impersonal forces affect personal behavior. Durkheim showed that certain social categories in central Europe during the later part of the nineteenth century had higher suicide rates than others. The degree of *social integration* experienced by people was found to be a significant factor influencing patterns in suicide rates. *Figure 1-1* (p. 5) provides a contemporary view of suicide rates in the U.S. using the categories of race and sex.

Situations that stimulate sociological thinking are identified, including: *encountering different cultures and people, social marginality,* and *social disruption.*

Applied Sociology

The benefits of sociology for various careers, particularly those involving social programs and social policy creation and implementation, are briefly discussed.

The Importance of Global Perspective

Global perspective is *a view of the larger world and our society's place in it.* In the *Window on the World* box (p. 7), *Global Map 1-1* places *economic development* into global perspective. Three categories of nations are identified based on their relative economic development. These include: The *high-income countries*, or *industrial nations that are relatively rich*, the *middle-income countries*, or *nations characterized by limited industrialization and moderate-to-low personal income*, and the *low-income countries*, or *nations with little industrialization in which severe poverty is the rule.*

Reasons why *global perspective* is so important are introduced, including (1) *Societies all over the world are increasing interconnected, making traditional distinctions between "us" and "them" less and less valid,* (2) *Many human problems that we face in the United States are far more serious elsewhere,* and (3) *Studying other societies is an excellent way to learn more about ourselves.*

THE ORIGINS OF SOCIOLOGY

Sociological thinking is a recent historical phenomenon. The discipline of sociology emerged as a product of particular social forces in Europe during the nineteenth century. French sociologist Auguste Comte coined the term *sociology* in 1838.

Science and Sociology

Prior to the nineteenth century philosophers used only *philosophical* and *theological* perspectives in their studies, concentrating on the imaginary "ideal" rather than on the analysis of what society was really like. Sociology emerged as focus was given to understanding how society actually operates.

3

Auguste Comte argued for a scientific approach in studying society. He divided history into three distinct eras, which he labeled the *theological stage*, the *metaphysical stage*, and the *scientific stage*. The latter be called *positivism*, or *the path to understanding based on science*.

Social Change and Sociology

Sociology emerged after the great transformations in European societies which took place during the seventeenth and eighteenth centuries. Three basic interrelated changes fostered the emergence of the sociological perspective. These included: (1) *Industrial technology*, (2) *Urban growth*, and (3) *Political change*. Each of these is discussed illustrating their respective impact on sociology.

SOCIOLOGICAL THEORY

While the sociological perspective provides us with a unique vantage point from which to observe our social world, theory helps us to meaningfully organize and explain the linkages between specific observations we make. A *theory* is *a statement of how and why specific facts are related*. In the *Seeing Ourselves* box (p. 11), *National Map 1-1* provides data on suicide rate in the United States. This data can be used to do some *theorizing*.

Sociologists are guided by one or more general frameworks, or theoretical paradigms. A *theoretical paradigm* is *a set of fundamental assumptions that guides thinking and research*. There are three principal theoretical paradigms used by sociologists. Each one focuses the researcher's attention on particular types of questions about how society is organized,, and on different explanations about why certain patterns are found in society.

The Structural-Functional Paradigm

The *structural-functional paradigm* is *a framework for building theory based on the assumption that society is a complex system whose parts work together to promote stability*. The two basic components of this paradigm are *social structure*, or *a relatively stable pattern of social behavior*, and *social function*, which refers to *consequences of a social pattern for the operation of society as a whole*. Early sociologists using this perspective included Auguste Comte, Herbert Spencer, and Emile Durkheim.

As sociology developed in the United States during the twentieth century, Robert Merton further applied and developed the thinking of these early social scientists. Merton differentiated between *manifest functions*, or *consequences of social structure both recognized and intended*, and *latent functions*, which are *unrecognized and unintended consequences of social structure*. There may be *undesirable effects on the operation of society*, or *social dysfunctions*.

In critically evaluating this paradigm, it is pointed out that it is a conservative approach to the study of society which tends to ignore tension and conflict in social systems.

The Social-Conflict Paradigm

The *social-conflict paradigm* is *a framework for building theory based on the assumption that society is a complex system characterized by inequality and conflict that generates social change*. Social differences, rather than social integration, are the focus using this paradigm. Educational achievement is discussed to illustrate the unequal distribution of power and privilege.

Karl Marx is perhaps the most famous social scientist associated with this view of society. Three people whose gender or race put them at the margin of society are also identified as contributing to this paradigm, they include Harriet Martineau, Jane Addams, and W.E.B. Du Bois.

Critical evaluation of this paradigm raises concern that social unity is ignored, and that in focusing on change, objectivity may be lost.

The Symbolic-Interaction Paradigm

The structural-functional and social-conflict paradigms focus on a *macro-level orientation*, meaning *a concern with large-scale patterns that characterize society as a whole*. An alternative approach is to take a *micro-level orientation*, meaning *a concern with small-scale patterns of social interaction in specific settings*. The *symbolic-interaction paradigm* is *a framework for building theory based on the view that society is a product of the everyday interactions of individuals*. People are seen as interacting in terms of shared symbols and meanings. This paradigm was greatly influenced by the work of Max Weber, a German sociologist of the late nineteenth and early twentieth centuries. In the United States, during the twentieth century, the work of George Herbert Mead, Erving Goffman, George Homans, and Peter Blau was instrumental in the development of this paradigm.

In critically analyzing this view it must be stressed that the focus is on how individuals personally experience society. This approach does not allow us to generalize findings to establish broad general patterns.

Each of the three paradigms provides a unique perspective for helping to develop our understanding of society. *Table 1-1* (p. 15) reviews each of the paradigms, the respective image of society each offers, and the types of questions asked by researchers using each of the paradigms. The *Exploring Cyber-society* box (pp. 16-17) entitled "Welcome to the Information Revolution!" discusses how these three paradigms help us understand the impact of the Information Revolution.

SCIENTIFIC SOCIOLOGY

Researchers rely on *science, a logical system that derives knowledge from direct, systematic observation*. Science is based on *empirical evidence*--meaning evidence we can verify using our senses. Three common sense statements considered to be true by many people in our society are identified. However, using scientific evidence these statements are contradicted by empirical facts.

Concepts, Variables, and Measurement

Sociologists use concepts to identify elements of society. A *concept* is *a mental construct that represents an aspect of the world, inevitably in a somewhat simplified form*. For example, terms like family and social class are concepts. A *variable* is *a concept whose value changes from case to case*. For example, social class varies, with some people being identified as middle class and others as working class.

Measurement is *a procedure for determining the value of a variable in a specific case*. For example, the factors of family income and occupation can be used to determine the social class of a particular person or family. Variables can be measured in many different ways. *Operationalizing* a variable means to specify exactly what is to be measured in assigning a value to a variable. For example, social class can be measured using income and occupation.

Sociologists must make use of *descriptive statistics*. The three most used descriptive measures are the *mean, median,* and *mode*. The *mode* is defined as the value that occurs most often in a series of numbers. The *mean* is calculated by taking the arithmetic average of a series of numbers. The *median* refers to the value that occurs midway in a series of numbers or, simply, the middle case.

5

Two other important issues concerning the measurement of variables include reliability and validity. *Reliability* concerns *the quality of consistency in measurement*. For example, does a person taking several math achievement tests score equivalently on each test? *Validity* concerns *the quality of measurement gained by precisely what one intends to measure*. For example, are the math tests truly measuring what they purport to measure--skills and knowledge, or are they possibly measuring some other quality like obedience to rules?

Correlation and Cause

Correlation refers to *a relationship between two (or more) variables*. Sociological investigation enables researchers to identify **cause and effect** relationships among variables in which one variable (*independent variable*) causes a change or effect in another variable (*dependent variable*). While variables may be correlated, they may not involve a cause and effect relationship. A *spurious correlation* refers to a "false" or indirect link between two (or more) variables where no cause and effect exists.

In summary, to conclude that a cause and effect relationship exists, at least three conditions must be established: (1) *a correlation exists between the variables*, (2) *the independent variable precedes the dependent variable in time*, and (3) *no evidence exists that a third variable is responsible for a spurious correlation between the two variables*.

The Ideal of Objectivity

Researchers must make every effort to neutralize their personal biases. Complete neutrality, or *objectivity*, is seen as an ideal rather than as a reality in science. Max Weber argued that research may be *value-relevant*, or of personal interest to the researcher, but the actual process of doing research must be *value-free*. Two criticisms value-free science include: (1) researchers must always make some *interpretation* of their data, and (2) any and all research is inevitably *political*.

Research and Gender

Values influence research in terms of gender. Dangers to sound research involving gender include: *Androcentricity* (or its opposite *gynocentricity*), *overgeneralizing, gender blindness, double standards*, and *gender interference*. Each are discussed with examples.

Feminist Research

While still evolving, the feminist approach primarily focuses on the condition of women in society, seeing women as generally experiencing a subordinate position relative to men.

Research Ethics

Yet another issue concerns how research affects the people being studied. The American Sociological Association has a set of formal guidelines for the conduct of social research, including technical competence, awareness of bias, safety and privacy, discussion with subjects concerning risks involved, accurate presentation of purpose of research, full reporting of findings, and identification of any organizational affiliations. There are also global dimensions to research ethics. The *Social Diversity* box (pp. 22-23) offers tips on how outsiders can effectively and sensitively study Hispanic communities. These tips include: (1) *Being careful with terms*, (2) *Anticipating unfamiliar interpersonal dynamics*, (3) *Anticipating different family dynamics*, and (4) *Expecting cultural differences*.

RESEARCH METHODS

A *research method* is *a strategy systematically carrying out research*. Four of the most commonly used methods are introduced, each with particular strengths and weaknesses for the study of social life.

Testing a Hypothesis: The Experiment

Experiments are used to *investigate cause-and-effect relationships under highly controlled conditions*. This type of research is usually explanatory. Experiments are typically designed to test a specific *hypothesis*--or unverified statements of a relationship between two (or more) variables. The ideal experiment involves three steps leading to the acceptance or rejection of the hypothesis. The three steps are: (1) measurement of the dependent variable, (2) exposure of the dependent variable to the independent variable, and (3) remeasurement of the dependent variable.

Asking Questions: The Survey

A *survey* is *a research method in which subjects respond to a series of statements or questions in a questionnaire or an interview*. It is the most widely used of the research methods. A *population* is defined as the people about whom a researcher seeks knowledge. A *sample* is a relatively small number of cases selected to represent an entire population.

A very critical issue concerns the extent to which the sample is representative of the population from which it is taken. Random selection techniques are used to help ensure the probability that inferences made from the results of the sample actually do reflect the nature of the population as a whole.

Two general techniques are used for asking and recording questions. A *questionnaire* is a series of written questions or items to which subjects respond. Two basic types of questions asked are open-ended and closed-ended formats. An *interview* is a series of questions or items a researcher administers personally to respondents. This strategy has advantages, including more depth, but also involves the disadvantages of extra time and money, and the influence of the researcher's presence on the subjects' responses.

In The Field: Participant Observation

Participant observation is *a method in which researchers systematically observe people while joining in their routine activities*. This method is very common among cultural anthropologists who use fieldwork to gather data for their ethnographies. Sociologists typically use the *case study approach*, a type of participant observation, when doing exploratory research. Participant observation is based heavily on subjective interpretation, and is therefore criticized by some for lacking scientific rigor.

The Second Time Around: Existing Sources

This type of research involves the independent analysis of data originally collected by others. Advantages of this approach include considerable savings in terms of time and money. Disadvantages include the possibility that the data was not gathered systematically and that the data may not be directly related to the interests of the researcher. Emile Durkheim's study on suicide is an example of this type of research.

Sociological investigation is a complex process. *Table 1-3* (p. 24) reviews the applications, advantages, and disadvantages of the four major research methods presented.

Cyber-Research

The effects of information technology on the practice of sociological investigation are very significant, particularly in terms of access to data bases and communication with colleagues.

Ten Steps in Sociological Research

The general guidelines for conducting sociological research involve the following steps:

1. Define the topic you want to investigate.
2. Find out what has already been written about the topic.
3. Assess the requirements for carrying out the research.
4. Specify the questions you are going to ask.
5. Consider the ethical issues involved in the research.
6. Choose the research method.
7. Gather your data.
8. Interpret the findings.
9. State conclusions based on your findings .
10. Publish your research!

The *Controversy and Debate* box (p. 25) entitled "Is Sociology Nothing More Than Stereotypes?" provide three reasons why sociology is not a matter of stereotyping. A *stereotype* is *a prejudiced description that one applies to all people in some category.*

PART IV: KEY CONCEPTS

Define each of the following concepts in the space provided or on separate paper. Check the accuracy of your answers by referring to the key concepts section at the end of the chapter in the text as well as referring to italicized definitions located throughout the chapter. Do the same for each chapter as you read through the text during the semester.

androcentricity
cause and effect
concept
control
correlation
dependent variable

empirical evidence
experiment
gynocentricity
high-income countries
hypothesis
independent variable
interview
latent functions
low-income countries
macro-level orientation
manifest functions
mean
measurement
median
metaphysical stage
micro-level orientation
middle-income countries
mode
objectivity
operationalizing a variable
participant observation population
positivism
questionnaire
reliability
research method
sample
science
seeing individuality in social context
seeing the general in the particular
seeing the strange in the familiar
social-conflict paradigm
social dysfunction
social function
social marginality
social structure
sociology
spurious correlation
stereotype
structural-functional paradigm
survey
symbolic-interaction paradigm
theological stage
theory
validity
variable

PART V: IMPORTANT RESEARCHERS

Auguste Comte

Emile Durkheim

Herbert Spencer

Karl Marx

Max Weber

Robert Merton

Peter Berger

C. Wright Mills

PART VI: STUDY QUESTIONS

<u>True-False</u>

1. T F A major component of the sociological perspective is the attempt to seek the *particular in the general.*
2. T F *Encountering people who are different, social marginality,* and *social disruption* are identified as factors that prompt people to view the world sociologically.
3. T F African Americans and females have *higher suicide rates* than whites and males.
4. T F The *middle-income countries* of the world are primarily found in Latin America, Eastern Europe, and the former Soviet Union.

5.	T	F	The discipline of *sociology* first emerged in Europe during the nineteenth century.
6.	T	F	*Positivism* is the belief that science is the path to knowledge.
7.	T	F	A *theory* is a statement of how and why specific facts are related.
8.	T	F	*Latent functions* refer to social processes which appear on the surface to be functional for society, but which are actually detrimental.
9.	T	F	The *symbolic-interaction* and *social-conflict* paradigms both operate from a *micro-level orientation*.
10.	T	F	The *mode* is the statistical term referring to the value which occurs most often in a series of numbers.
11.	T	F	*If two variables are* correlated, by definition one is an *independent variable* and one is a *dependent variable*.
12.	T	F	The first step in the sociological *research process* should be to determine what research design will be used to gather the data.

Multiple Choice

1.   What is the *essential wisdom* of sociology?

(a)   patterns in life are predestined
(b)   society is essentially nonpatterned
(c)   surrounding society guides our actions
(d)   common sense needs to guide sociological investigations
(e)   none of the above

2.   Which sociologist linked the incidence of *suicide* to the degree of *social integration* of different categories of people?

(a)   Emile Durkheim   (d)   C. Wright Mills
(b)   Max Weber   (e)   Karl Marx
(c)   Robert Merton

3.   Which of the following is/are identified as situations that simulate *sociological thinking*?

(a)   encountering people who are different from us
(b)   social marginality
(c)   social disruption
(d)   all of the above
(e)   none of the above

4.   The term *sociology* was coined in 1838 by:

(a)   Emile Durkheim   (d)   Auguste Comte
(b)   Karl Marx   (e)   Max Weber
(c)   Herbert Spencer

5. *Positivism* is the idea that _____, rather than any other type of human understanding, is the path to knowledge.

    (a)   human nature   (d)   optimism
    (b)   faith   (e)   intuition
    (c)   science

6. A set of *fundamental assumptions about society* that guides sociological thinking and research is the definition for:

    (a)   a research design   (d)   paradigms
    (b)   manifest functions   (e)   social integration
    (c)   social marginality

7. Consequences of social structure which are largely *unrecognized* and *unintended* are called:

    (a)   latent functions   (d)   paradigms
    (b)   manifest functions   (e)   social marginality
    (c)   social integration

8. Which of the following theoretical perspectives is best suited for analysis using a *macro-level* orientation?

    (a)   dramaturgical analysis   (d)   ethnomethodology
    (b)   social exchange theory   (e)   social-conflict paradigm
    (c)   symbolic-interactionist paradigm

9. The questions--How is society experienced? and, how do individuals attempt to shape the reality perceived by others? are most likely asked by a researcher using which of the following theoretical paradigms?

    (a)   structural-functional   (d)   social-conflict
    (b)   symbolic-interaction   (e)   none of the above
    (c)   social Darwinism

10. Specifying exactly what is to be measured in assigning a value to a variable is called:

    (a)   validity   (d)   reliability
    (b)   objectivity   (e)   control
    (c)   operationalizing a variable

11. The *descriptive statistics* that represents the value that occurs *midway* in a series of numbers is called the:

    (a)   median   (d)   norm
    (b)   correlation   (e)   mean
    (c)   mode

12. The quality of *consistency* in measurement is known as:

(a) spuriousness   (d) objectivity
(b) reliability   (e) validity
(c) empirical evidence

13. Measuring what one *intends* to measure is the quality of measurement known as:

(a) reliability   (d) control
(b) operationalization   (e) objectivity
(c) validity

14. An unverified statement of a relationship between any facts or variables is a(n):

(a) correlation   (d) logical induction
(b) logical deduction   (e) theory
(c) hypothesis

15. Sociology is not involved in *stereotyping* because:

(a) sociology makes generalizations about categories of people, not stereotypes
(b) sociologists base their generalizations on research
(c) sociologists strive to be fair-minded
(d) all of the above
(e) none of the above

Matching

1. ___ A mental construct that represents an aspect of the world, inevitably in a somewhat simplified way.
2. ___ A framework for building theory based in the assumption that society is a complex system whose parts work together to promote stability.
3. ___ A statement of how and why specific facts are related.
4. ___ A relatively stable pattern of social behavior.
5. ___ The quality of measurement gained by measuring precisely what one intends to measure.
6. ___ A research method in which subjects respond to a series of statements and questions in a questionnaire or interview.
7. ___ A logical system that derives knowledge from direct, systematic observation.
8. ___ Unrecognized and unintended consequences of social structure.
9. ___ A strategy for systematically carrying out research.
10. ___ A procedure for determining the value of a variable in a specific case.

a.	survey	e.	latent functions	i.	structural-functional
b.	measurement	f.	research method	j.	science
c.	theory	g.	social structure		
d.	concept	h.	validity		

Fill-In

1.   Being excluded from social activity as an *outsider* is termed _____.
2.   A _____ _____ is a view of the larger world and or society's place in it.
3.   The United States, Canada, and most of the nations of Western Europe are classified in terms of economic development as being the _____-*income countries.*
4.   Auguste Comte asserted that scientific sociology was a result of a progression throughout history of thought and understanding in *three stages*: the _____, _____, and _____.
5.   The development of sociology as an academic discipline was shaped with the context of three revolutionary changes in Europe during the seventeenth and eighteenth centuries. These included _____ _____, _____ _____, and _____ _____.
6.   A set of fundamental assumptions that guides thinking and research is called a _____ _____.
7.   A concern with small-scale patterns of social interaction, such as *symbolic-interaction theory.* operates through a _____-_____ *orientation.*
8.   _____ *evidence* we are able to verify with our senses.
9.   A _____ is a *mental construct* that represents an aspect of the world, inevitably in a somewhat simplified way.
10. _____ refers to two variable that *vary together,* such as the extent of crowding and juvenile delinquency.
11. When two variables change together but one does not cause the other, sociologists describe this as a "false" or _____ correlation.
12. The state of complete personal *neutrality* in conducting research is referred to as _____.
13. The German sociologist _____ _____ distinguished between *value-relevant* choice of research topics and *value-free* conduct of sociological investigation.
14. The _____ is a *research method* in which subjects respond to a series of statements or questions in a *questionnaire* or an *interview.*
15. A _____ is a prejudiced description that one applies to all people in some category.

Definition and Short-Answer

1.   Differentiate between the concepts *manifest* and *latent functions* and provide an illustration for each.
2.   Discuss Emile Durkheim's explanation of how *suicide rates* vary between different categories of people. Explain how this research demonstrates the application of the *sociological perspective.*
3.   What are the three types of countries identified in the text as measured by their level of *economic development?* What are the characteristics of the countries that represent each of the three types?
4.   What are the three major reasons why a *global perspective* is so important today?
5.   What were three *social changes* in seventeenth and eighteenth century Europe that provided the context for the development of *sociology* as a scientific discipline?

6. What are the three major components of the *sociological perspective*? Describe and provide an illustration for each.

7. What are the three major *theoretical paradigms* used by sociologists? Identify two key questions raised by each in the analysis of society. Identify one weakness for each of these paradigms for understanding the nature of human social life.

8. What are the three factors which must be determined to conclude that a *cause and effect* relationship between two variables may exist?

9. Discuss how *gender* affects sociological research. Be sure to identify and illustrate each of the four major problems involving gender and research.

10. Define the concept *hypothesis*. Further, write your own hypothesis and *operationalize* the variables that you identified.

11. Identify two advantages and two disadvantages for each of the four major *research methods* used by sociologists.

12. What are the basic steps of the sociological *research process*? Briefly describe each.

13. Three illustrations are provided to show that *common sense* does not always guide us to a meaningful sense of reality. What two examples can you give concerning common sense not paving the way toward our understanding of what is really happening in social life?

14. What is meant by the term *cyber-research*? What are the effects of advances in information technology on the practice of sociological investigation.

15. How do the three paradigms help us understand the impact of advancing information technology on society?

16. What are three reasons why sociology is considered nothing more than *stereotyping*?

PART VII: ANSWERS TO STUDY QUESTIONS

True-False

1.	F	(p. 1)		7.	T	(p. 10)
2.	T	(p. 4)		8.	F	(p. 11)
3.	F	(p. 5)		9.	F	(p. 14)
4.	T	(p. 6)		10.	T	(p. 16)
5.	T	(p. 8)		11.	F	(p. 18)
6.	T	(p. 9)		12.	F	(p. 24)

Multiple Choice

1.	c	(p. 1)		9.	b	(p. 15)
2.	a	(p. 3)		10.	c	(p. 15)
3.	d	(p. 4)		11.	a	(p. 16)
4.	d	(p. 8)		12.	b	(p. 16)
5.	c	(p. 9)		13.	c	(p. 16)
6.	d	(p. 10)		14.	c	(p. 21)
7.	a	(p. 11)		15.	d	(p. 25)
8.	e	(p. 14)				

<u>Matching</u>

1.	d	(p. 15)	6.	a	(p. 21)
2.	i	(p. 10)	7.	j	(p. 14)
3.	c	(p. 10)	8.	e	(p. 11)
4.	g	(p. 11)	9.	f	(p. 20)
5.	h	(p. 16)	10.	b	(p. 15)

<u>Fill-In</u>

1.   social marginality (p. 4)
2.   global perspective (p. 5)
3.   high (p. 5)
4.   theological, metaphysical, scientific (p. 9)
5.   industrial technology, urban growth, political change (pp. 9-10)
6.   theoretical paradigm (p. 10)
7.   micro-level (p. 14)
8.   empirical (p. 14)
9.   concept (p. 15)
10. correlation (p. 17)
11. spurious (p. 18)
12. objectivity (p. 18)
13. Max Weber (p. 19)
14. survey (p. 21)
15. stereotype (p. 25)

PART VIII: ANALYSIS AND COMMENT

Go back through the chapter and write down key points from each of the following boxes. Then, for each of the boxes identified, write out three questions concerning the issues raised which you feel would be valuable to discuss in class. Do the same for each chapter as you read through the text.

Social Diversity

"The Name Game: Social Forces and Personal Choice"

Key Points: Questions:

"Conducting Research With Hispanics"

"Key Points"   Questions:

Window on the World--Global Map 1-1

"Economic Development in Global Perspective"

Key Points: Questions:

Seeing Ourselves--National Map 1-1

"Suicide Rates Across the United States"

Key Points: Questions:

Culture

PART I: CHAPTER OUTLINE

I.   What is Culture?
    A.   Culture and Human Intelligence
II.   The Components of Culture
    A.   Symbols
    B.   Language
    C.   Values
    D.   Norms
    E.   "Ideal" and "Real" Culture
III.   Technology and Culture
    A.   Hunting and Gathering
    B.   Horticulture and Pastoralism
    C.   Agriculture
    D.   Industry
    E.   Information Technology
    F.   A Global Culture?
IV.   Cultural Diversity
    A.   High Culture and Popular Culture
    B.   Subculture
    C.   Multiculturalism
    D.   Counterculture
    E.   Cultural Change
    F.   Ethnocentrism and Cultural Relativity
V.   Theoretical Analysis of Culture
    A.   Structural-Functional Analysis
    B.   Social-Conflict Analysis
    C.   Sociobiology
VI.   Culture and Human Freedom
VII.   Summary
VIII.   Key Concepts
IX.   Critical-Thinking Questions

PART II: LEARNING OBJECTIVES

1.   To begin to the understand the sociological meaning of the concept of culture.
2.   To consider the relationship between human intelligence and culture.
3.   To know the components of culture and to be able to provide examples of each.
4.   To consider the current state of knowledge about whether language is uniquely human.
5.   To consider the significance of symbols in the construction and maintenance of social reality.
6.   To identify the dominant values in our society and to recognize their interrelationships with one another and with other aspects of our culture.
7.   To be abe to provide examples of the different types of norms operative in a culture, and how these are related to the process of social control.
8.   To be able to explain the process of sociocultural evolution.
9.   To be able to explain how subcultures and countercultures contribute to cultural diversity.
10.   To begin to develop your understanding of multiculturalism.
11.   To be able to differentiate between ethnocentrism and cultural relativism.
12.   To be able to compare and contrast analyses of culture using structural-functional, social-conflict, and sociobiological paradigms.
13.   To be able to identify the consequences of culture for human freedom and constraint.

PART III: CHAPTER REVIEW--KEY POINTS

This chapter opens with a story of Taiwanese investors who wanted to consult a *feng shui* before purchasing an office building. The great cultural diversity in beliefs that exists in our world is illustrated.

WHAT IS CULTURE?

Culture is defined as *the beliefs, values, behavior, and material objects that constitutes a people's way of life*. Sociologists differentiate between *non-material culture*, or the intangible creations of human society, and *material culture*, or the tangible products of human society. *Society* refers to *people interacting within a limited territory guided by their culture*.

Sociologically, culture is viewed in the broadest possible sense--referring to everything that is part of a people's way of life. Out lifestyles are not determined by *instincts*, or biological forces, as is true in large degree for other species. The fierce and warlike Yanomamo, the peace-loving Semai of Malaysia, the achievement-oriented and cooperative Japanese, and the achievement-oriented and individualistic people of the United States, all attest to the influence of culture on personality and everyday life experiences. *Culture shock*, or *the personal disorientation accompanying exposure to an unfamiliar way of life* is illustrated by anthropologist Napoleon Chagnon's first visit to the territory of the *Yanomamo* culture in the tropical rain forest of southern Venezuela. This situation is described in the **Global Sociology** box (p. 32).

We are the only species whose survival depends on what we learn through culture, rather than by what we are naturally given through biology. For a few animal species, most notably chimpanzees, a limited cultural capacity exists.

Culture and Human Intelligence

The primate order among mammals, of which our species is a part, emerged some 65 million

19

years ago. Humans diverged from our closest primate relatives some 12 million years ago. However, our common lineage remains apparent--grasping hands, ability to walk upright, great sociability, affective and long-lasting bonds for childrearing and protection.

Fossil records indicate the first creatures with clearly human characteristics lived about 2 million years ago. Our species *homo sapiens* (meaning *thinking person*) evolved a mere 40,000 years ago. Civilization--based on permanent settlements--has existed only for the last 12,000 years. Human culture and biological evolution are linked. Over evolutionary time, instincts have been gradually replaced by *mental power*, enabling humans to actively fashion the natural environment.

COMPONENTS OF CULTURE

Even though considerable variation exists, all cultures share five components: symbols, language, values, norms, and material culture.

Symbols

This component underlies the other four. A *symbol* is *anything that carries a particular meaning recognized by people who share culture*. Symbols serve as the basis for everyday reality. Symbols vary within cultures, cross-culturally, and change over time. *Gestures* are discussed as an example.

Language

Language is *a system of symbols that allows people to communicate with one another*. All cultures have a spoken language, though not all have a written language. In the *Window on the World* box (p. 35) *Global Map 2-1* shows regions using the world's three most widely spoken languages. For example, twenty percent of the world's population speak Chinese, while ten percent have English as their primary language. *Cultural transmission* is *the process by which one generation passes culture on to the next*.

Two anthropologists or the early twentieth century, Edward Sapir and Benjamin Whorf, argued that language is more than simply attaching labels to the "real world." The *Sapir-Whorf hypothesis* holds that *we can know the world only in terms of the symbols contained in our language*.

Values

Values are defined as *culturally defined standards of desirability, goodness, and beauty, which serve as broad guidelines for social living*. They support *beliefs*, or *specific statements that people hold to be true*. There are several central values which are widely accepted in American society. These include: equal opportunity, achievement and success, activity and work, material comfort, practicality and efficiency, progress, science, democracy, freedom, and racism and group superiority.

The values people hold vary to some degree by age, sex, race, ethnicity, religion, and social class. Individuals are likely to experience some inconsistency and conflict with their personal values. Further, the dominant values identified above contain certain basic contradictions. Finally, values change over time.

Norms

Norms are *rules by which a society guides the behavior of its members*. Norms can change over time, as illustrated by norms regarding sexual behavior. Norms vary in terms of their degree of importance. *Mores*, often called taboos, refer to *norms that are widely observed and have great moral significance*. *Folkways* are *norms about which people allow one another considerable personal discretion*. through socialization we *internalize* cultural norms and impose constraints on our own behavior. We may then experience *guilt*--the negative judgment we make of ourselves for having violated a norm--and *shame*--the disturbing acknowledgement of others' disapproval.

"Ideal" and "Real" Culture

Values and norms are not descriptions of actual behavior, but rather reflect how we believe members of a culture should behave. Therefore, it becomes necessary to distinguish between *ideal culture*, or expectations embodied in values and norms, and *real culture*, designated by the patterns that typically occur in everyday life.

TECHNOLOGY AND CULTURE

Material and nonmaterial culture are closely related. *Artifacts*, or material objects that society creates, express the values of a culture. For instance, the Yanomamo value militaristic skill, and devote great care to making weapons. In the U.S. we value independence and individuality, and express this in part with our love affair with the automobile. In the *Global Snapshot* box (p. 38), *Figure 2-1* puts car ownership in global perspective.

Material culture also reflects a culture's *technology*, which is *application of knowledge to the practical tasks of living*. Technology is the link between culture and nature. Gerhard and Jean Lenski have researched *sociocultural evolution*, or historical change in culture caused by technological innovation. The Lenskis have identified four major levels of technological development and how each creates distinctive cultural patterns.

Hunting and Gathering

Hunting and gathering societies are those that *use simple tools to hunt animals and gather vegetation*. Examples of such societies include the Semai of Malaysia and the Pygmies of central Africa. Typical characteristics of people using this subsistence strategy include small bands of people, a nomadic lifestyle over large territories, stratification based only on age and sex, and few positions of leadership. A *shaman* may be recognized, as one who presides over spiritual matters of the group. Social organization tends to be simple and equal, being organized around the family. With the encroachment of more technologically advanced societies on their territories, these hunting and gathering peoples' way of life is vanishing.

Horticultural and Pastoral Societies

Approximately 10,000 years ago plants began to be cultivated. *Horticultural* societies are those that *use hand tools to raise crops*. In regions where horticulture is impractical, *pastoralism*, or *the domestication of animals* exists. Often, pastoral and horticultural strategies are combined by a culture. The domestication of plants and animals had a very significant effect on cultural patterns. Examples discussed include population growth, the establishment of material surpluses, and people's conception of God.

Agriculture

Approximately 5000 years ago, **agriculture**, or *large-scale cultivation using plows first drawn by animals*, emerged as a subsistence strategy in the Middle East. This technological change has been cited as the "dawn of civilization." The advancing technology promoted productive specialization, surpluses in goods, and dramatic increases in population and social inequality. Technology provides the opportunity for people to use the *creativity* and to produce great cultural diversity.

Industry

Industry is *the production of goods using sophisticated fuels and machinery*. Productivity expanded tremendously with industrialization. A major shift occurring was from production within families to production within factories. While some negative effects of technological advancement were created, living standards improved, political rights were extended, educational opportunities expanded, and social inequality began to lessen--but for only about 15 percent of the world's population today.

Information Technology

The U.S., along with some other societies, has entered a postindustrial phase of economic development. The information economy being created changes the skills that dominate our way of life. The **Exploring Cyber-Society** box (p. 41) takes a close look at what is being called "The Coming of Virtual Culture."

A Global Culture?

Are we witnessing the birth of a *global culture*? Global connections involve the *flow of goods, information, and people*. However, this global culture thesis has limitation, including: the flow of goods, information, and people is *uneven*, it cannot be assumed that people everywhere *want* and can *afford* various goods and services, and while certain cultural traits found universally around the world, it should not be assumed that the *meaning* attached to them are the same.

CULTURAL DIVERSITY

We are a land of many peoples, given the many immigrants who have come to the United States over the past 150 years. *Figure 2-2* (p. 42) provides data on recorded immigration to the United States by region of birth, 1880-1990 and 1984-1994. Today the majority of newcomers are from Latin America or Asia.

High Culture and Popular Culture

Not all cultural patterns are equally accessible to all members of society. **High society** refers to *cultural patterns that distinguish a society's elite*, while **popular culture** designates *cultural patterns widespread among a society's people*.

Subculture

Sociologists define **subculture** as *cultural patterns that distinguish some segment of a society's population*. Subcultures can be based on age, ethnicity, residence, sexual preference, occupation, and many other factors.

Globally, ethnicity is perhaps the most recognized dimension with which to identify cultural diversity. While the United States is considered by many to be a *melting pot*, great diversity still exists, and is perhaps increasing. However, hierarchy, not merely difference is typically involved.

Multiculturalism

Should our nation stress cultural diversity or the common elements of our people? How do we strike a balance within the Latin phrase *E Pluribus Unum* (out of many, one)? For example, should English be designated as the official language of the United States? In the *Seeing Ourselves* box (p. 45), *National Map 2-2* shows where there are large numbers of children growing up in homes in which the first language is not English.

Multiculturalism is *an educational program recognizing the cultural diversity of the United States and promoting equality of all cultural traditions*. The "singular pattern" focus in our culture is called **Eurocentrism**, *the dominance of European (particularly English) cultural patterns*. An alternative pattern currently being developed by some multiculturalists to counter these biases is called **Afrocentrism**, or *a view that focuses on the dominance of African cultural patterns*.

Multiculturalists suggest that their perspective will help us develop a more meaningful understanding of our own *past*, the ethnic diversity of our *present*, strengthen the academic *achievements* of African American children, and the reality of the current world *interdependence*.

Critics argue that multiculturalism fuels "politics of difference." They question whether such an orientation benefits minorities, and are concerned about its potential for limiting political and economic freedom.

Counterculture

A **counterculture** is defined as *cultural patterns that strongly oppose conventional culture*. Members of countercultures are likely to question the morality of the majority group and engage in some form of protest activities. The Ku Klux Klan is an example of a counterculture in our society.

Cultural Change

Cultural change is continuous, though its rate may vary greatly. *Table 2-1* (p. 47) presents data on the changing attitudes of college students, comparing cohorts from 1968 and 1995. Patterns of both change and consistency are found.

Cultural integration, or *the close relationship among various elements of a cultural system*, is concept relating to the condition of **cultural lag**, or *the fact that some cultural elements change more quickly than others, with potentially disruptive results*.

Cultural change is set into motion by three different causes, *invention, discovery,* and *diffusion*. Illustrations for each are presented.

Ethnocentrism and Cultural Relativity

Ethnocentrism is *the practice of judging another culture by the standards of one's own culture*. It creates a biased evaluation of unfamiliar practices. A comparison between the United States and the Yanomamo illustrates this concept. Using a map, *Figure 2-2* (p. 42) illustrates ethnocentric images of the world. *Cultural relativity* refers to *the practice of evaluating any culture by its own standards*. The issue of cultural sensitivity related to U.S. business ventures overseas is discussed.

THEORETICAL ANALYSIS OF CULTURE

Structural-Functional Analysis

Research using this approach draws on the philosophical doctrine of *idealism*, which holds that ideas are the basis of human reality. Cultures are understood as organized systems devised to meet human needs. Therefore, *cultural universals*, or *traits found in every culture of the world*, are looked for and studied. One example of a cultural universal is the family. This approach operates at the macro-level, holding that *cultural traits* are to be understood in terms of how they *function* to maintain the overall cultural system. George Peter Murdock has identified dozens of universal traits.

A critical analysis of this approach reveals that while providing significant insights into how cultures are organized systems which attempt to meet human needs, it perhaps underestimates the extent of cultural diversity within and between cultures.

Social-Conflict Analysis

The focus among researchers using this paradigm is the social conflict generated by inequality among different categories of people in a culture. Karl Marx, using the philosophical doctrine of *materialism*, argued that the way we deal with the material world (in our case through capitalism) powerfully affects all other dimensions of our culture, for example, our values. Theorists using this approach ask--Why are certain values dominant in a given culture?

A critical evaluation of this approach suggests that while it provides insights into structural inequalities and processes of social change within a cultural system, it minimizes a sense about the integrative properties found within these same systems.

Sociobiology

Sociobiology is *a theoretical paradigm that explores ways in which human biology affects how we create culture*. Sociologists argue that Charles Darwin's theory of *natural selection*, which is based on a four stage process, applies to human evolution as it does to all other species. The four stages include reproduction within the natural environment, random variability in genes within the species, different survival odds for an organism based on its individual genetic characteristics, and changes in the frequencies of particular genes within a species over time. In this way a species *adapts* to its environment.

This approach has been criticized, based on historical patterns, of supporting racism and sexism. Further, to date, there is lack of scientific proof of their assertions.

24

CULTURE AND HUMAN FREEDOM

While being dependent on culture and constrained by our particular way of life, the capacity for creating change, or shaping and reshaping our existence, appears limitless. Culture is a liberating force to the extent we develop an understanding of its complexity and the opportunities available within it for change and autonomy. The burden of culture is *freedom*. Through evolution, culture has become our means of survival. Cultural diversity in our society is significant, and is ever-changing. The *Controversy and Debate* box (p. 53) takes a look at what is being called "culture wars" which represent our nation's latest round of **cultural conflict**, or *political opposition, often accompanied by social hostility, rooted in different cultural values*.

PART IV: KEY CONCEPTS

Afrocentrism
agriculture
beliefs
counterculture
cultural ecology
cultural integration
cultural lag
cultural relativism
cultural transmission
cultural universals
culture
culture shock
discovery
diffusion
ethnocentrism
Eurocentrism
folkways
horticulture
hunting and gathering
ideal culture
idealism
industry
Information Revolution
information technology
invention
language
material culture
materialism
natural selection
nonmaterial culture
norms
pastoralism

real culture
Sapir-Whorf hypothesis
society
sociobiology
sociocultural evolution
subculture
symbol
technology
values

PART V: IMPORTANT RESEARCHERS

Napoleon Chagnon

Edward Sapir and Benjamin Whorf

Charles Darwin

Gerhard and Jean Lenski

George Peter Murdock

Marvin Harris

PART VI: STUDY QUESTIONS

<u>True-False</u>

1. T   F   As used sociologically, the concept of *society* refers to people interacting within a limited territory guided by their culture.
2. T   F   According to anthropologist Marvin Harris, only humans rely on culture *rather than instinct* to ensure the survival of their kind.
3. T   F   According to the evolutionary record, the human line diverged from our closest primate relative, the great apes, some *12 millions years ago*.
4. T   F   *Cultural transmission* is defined as the process by which culture is passed from one generation to the next.
5. T   F   The *Sapir-Whorf hypothesis* concerns the extent to which the dominant values of a culture are affected by its level of technological development.
6. T   F   *Mores* are as norms which have little more significance within a culture.
7. T   F   *Hunting and gathering* societies tend to be characterized by less social inequality than *agrarian* societies.
8. T   F   *Agrarian* societies emerged about 5,000 years ago.
9. T   F   Three major sources of cultural change are *invention, discovery,* and *diffusion*.
10. T   F   The practice of judging any culture by its own standards is referred to as *ethnocentrism*.
11. T   F   *Structural-functionalists* argue that there are no *cultural universals*.
12. T   F   According to the author of our text, culture has diminished human autonomy to the point where we are *culturally programmed* much like other animals are *genetically programmed*.

<u>Multiple-Choice</u>

1. *Culture* is:

    (a)   the process by which members of a culture encourage conformity to social norms
    (b)   the beliefs, values, behavior, and material objects that constitute a people's way of life
    (c)   the practice of judging another society's norms
    (d)   a group of people who engage in interaction with one another on a continuous basis
    (e)   the aspects of social life people admire most

2. The *Yanomamo* are:

    (a)   a small tribal group of herders living in Eastern Africa
    (b)   a technologically primitive horticultural society living in South America
    (c)   a nomadic culture living above the Arctic circle as hunters
    (d)   a small, dying society living as farmers in a mountainous region of western Africa
    (e)   a people who until very recently were living in complete isolation from the rest of the world in a tropical rain forest in Malaysia

3. Studying *fossil records*, scientists have concluded that the first creatures with clearly human characteristics existed about _____ years ago.

    (a) 2 million   (d) 40 million
    (b) 12,000   (e) 60,000
    (c) 10 million

4. *Symbols*, a component of culture, can:

    (a) vary from culture to culture
    (b) provide a foundation for the reality we experience
    (c) vary within a given culture
    (d) all of the above

5. A system of *symbols* that allows people to communicate with one other is the definition of:

    (a) values   (d) cultural relativity
    (b) cultural transmission   (e) language
    (c) norms

6. Culturally defined *standards* of desirability, goodness, and beauty, which serve as broad guidelines for social living, is the definition for:

    (a) norms   (d) mores
    (b) beliefs   (e) sanctions
    (c) values

7. According to the research cited in the text, which of the following is *not* a central cultural value in U.S. society?

    (a) equal opportunity   (c) science
    (b) racism and superiority   (d) friendship

8. The old adage "Do as I say, not as I do" illustrates the distinction between:

    (a) ideal and real culture
    (b) the Sapir-Whorf hypothesis
    (c) cultural integration and cultural lag
    (d) folkways and mores
    (e) subcultures and countercultures

9. The *domestication of animals* is called:

    (a) agriculture   (d) industry
    (b) horticulture   (e) hunting and gathering
    (c) pastoralism

10. Inconsistencies within a cultural system resulting from the unequal rates at which different cultural elements change is termed:

(a) cultural lag
(b) culture shock
(c) ethnocentrism
(d) counterculture
(e) cultural relatively

11. The theoretical paradigm that focuses upon *universal cultural traits* is:

(a) cultural ecology
(b) cultural materialism
(c) structural-functionalism
(d) social-conflict

12. The philosophical doctrine of *materialism* is utilized in the analysis of culture by proponents of which theoretical paradigm?

(a) sociobiologists
(b) structural-functionalism
(c) symbolic-interaction
(d) cultural ecology
(e) social-conflict

Matching

1. ___ Norms that are widely observed and have great moral significance.
2. ___ People interacting within a limited territory guided by their culture.
3. ___ Specific statements that people hold to be true.
4. ___ A theoretical paradigm that explores ways in which human biology affects how we create culture.
5. ___ The practice of judging another culture by the standards of one's own culture.
6. ___ Culturally defined standards of desirability, goodness, and beauty, which serve as broad guidelines for social living.
7. ___ The personal disorientation accompanying exposure to an unfamiliar way of life.
8. ___ The fact that some cultural elements change more quickly than others, with potentially disruptive results.
9. ___ The view that focuses on the dominance of African cultural patterns.
10. ___ A cultural pattern that distinguishes some segment of a society's population.

a. values
b. culture shock
c. society
d. ethnocentrism
e. beliefs
f. cultural lag
g. Afrocentrism
h. sociobiology
i. mores
j. subculture

Fill-In

1. _____ _____ are Chinese words meaning *wind and water*.
2. _____ is the personal disorientation that may accompany exposure to an unfamiliar way of life.
3. The *tangible products* of human society are referred to as _____.

4. A _____ is anything that carries a particular meaning recognized by people who share a culture.
5. The concept _____ is derived from the Latin word meaning *thinking person*.
6. While *Chinese*, spoken by _____ percent of the world's population is the most widely spoken language, English is spoken by _____ percent of the world's population, and Spanish by _____ percent.
7. Our experience of _____, the negative judgement we make of ourselves for having violated a norm and _____, the painful acknowledgement of others' disapproval, shows that we have internalized cultural norms.
8. _____ _____ is defined as the historical process of cultural change that has accompanied technological innovation.
9. _____ is the use of hand tools to raise crops.
10. One key trend of the *Information Revolution* is that more and more of the cultural symbols that frame our lives will be _____.

11. While _____ *culture* refers to cultural patterns that distinguish a society's elite, _____ *culture* designates cultural patterns widespread among a society's people.
12. A _____ is a cultural pattern that distinguishes some segment of a society's population, while a _____ is a cultural pattern that strongly opposes conventional culture.
13. The practice of judging any culture by its own standards is termed _____.
14. *Structural-functionalism* is based on the philosophical doctrine of _____.
15. Charles Darwin's *theory of evolution* states that living organisms change over long periods of time as a result of _____ _____.
16. According to the author, the *burden of culture* is _____.
17. The "culture wars" represent our nation's latest round of _____ _____, political opposition, often accompanied by social hostility, rooted in different cultural values.

Definition and Short-Answer

1. Three *causes of cultural change* are identified in the text. Identify these and provide an illustration of each.
2. Discuss the research presented in the text concerning the uniqueness of *language* to humans. What are your opinions on this issue?
3. Describe the process of *natural selection*.
4. Review the statistics presented in *Table 2-1* concerning changing values among college students. What have been the most significant changes? In which areas have values remained consistent? To what extent do your values fit the picture of contemporary college students? Explain.
5. What are the basic qualities of the *Yanomamo* culture? What factors do you think may explain why they are so aggressive? To what extent are you able to view these people from a *cultural relativistic* perspective?
6. What is the basic position being taken by *sociobiologists* concerning the nature of culture? What are three examples used by sociobiologists to argue that human culture is determined by biology? To what extent do you agree or disagree with their position? Explain.

30

7. Define the philosophical doctrine of *idealism*?
8. What is the *Sapir-Whorf hypothesis*? What evidence supports it? What evidence is inconsistent with this hypothesis?
9. What are the four basic *types of societies* identified by the Lenkis on the basis of sociocultural evolution? Briefly describe each.
10. Write a paragraph in which you express your opinions about the issue of multiculturalism in our society. Address the benefits of this perspective being suggested by proponents of multiculturalism, as well as the potential problems with this perspective suggested by its critics.
11. Provide two examples of how culture *constrains* us (limits our freedom).
12. What conclusions do you make about immigration concerning the data presented in *Figure 2-2*.
13. What are the basic arguments being made by *sociobiologists* in terms of how the nature of society and human interaction?
14. Differentiate between *values* and *norms*, providing two illustrations for each.
15. Review the list of *core values* of our culture in the United States. Rank order the ten identified in the text in terms of how important they are in our society from your point of view. What values, if any, do you believe should be included in the "top ten" list? Do you feel any of those listed should not be on the list?

PART VII: ANSWERS TO STUDY QUESTIONS

True-False

1.	T	(p. 30)
2.	T	(p. 30)
3.	T	(p. 32)
4.	T	(p. 34)
5.	F	(p. 34)
6.	F	(p. 37)

7.	T	(p. 40)
8.	T	(p. 40)
9.	T	(p. 47)
10.	F	(p. 48)
11.	F	(p. 50)
12.	F	(p. 52)

Multiple Choice

1.	b	(p. 30)
2.	b	(p. 32)
3.	a	(p. 32)
4.	d	(p. 34)
5.	e	(p. 34)
6.	c	(p. 34)

7.	d	(pp. 36-37)
8.	a	(p. 37)
9.	c	(p. 40)
10.	a	(p. 47)
11.	c	(p. 50)
12.	e	(p. 50)

Matching

1.	i	(p. 37)
2.	c	(p. 30)
3.	e	(p. 36)
4.	h	(p. 50)
5.	d	(pp. 48-49

6.	a	(p. 34)
7.	b	(p. 30)
8.	f	(p. 47)
9.	g	(p. 46)
10.	j	(p. 44)

Fill-In

1.	feng shui (p. 30)	11.	high, popular (p. 44)
2.	culture shock (p. 30)	12.	subculture, counterculture (pp. 44, 46)
3.	material culture (p. 30)	13.	cultural relativism (p. 48)
4.	symbol (p. 33)	14.	idealism (p. 49)
5.	homo sapiens (p.33)	15.	natural selection (p. 50)
6.	20, 10, 6 (p. 34)	16.	freedom (p. 52)
7.	guilt, shame (p. 37)	17.	cultural conflict (p. 53)
8.	sociocultural evolution (p. 38)		
9.	horticulture (p. 39)		
10.	created (p. 41)		

PART VIII: ANALYSIS AND COMMENT

Global Sociology

"Confronting the Yanomamo: The Experience of Culture Shock"

Key Points: Questions:

Window on the World--Global Map 2-1

"Language in Global Perspective"

Key Points: Questions:

Seeing Ourselves--National Map 2-1

"Who's "Upper Crust"? High Culture and Popular Culture across the United States"

Key Points: Questions:

"Language Diversity across the United States"

Key Points: Questions:

Exploring Cyber-Society

"The Coming of Virtual Culture"

Key Points: Questions:

Controversy and Debate

"What are the Culture Wars?"

Key Points: Questions:

Socialization: From Infancy to Old Age

PART I: CHAPTER OUTLINE

PART II: LEARNING OBJECTIVES

1. To understand the "nature-nurture" debate regarding socialization and personality development.
2. To become aware of the effects of social isolation on humans and other primates.
3. To become aware of the key components of Sigmund Freud's model of personality.
4. To be able to identify and describe the four stages of Jean Piaget's cognitive development theory.
5. To be able to identify and describe the stages of moral development as identified by Lawrence Kohlberg.

6.	To analyze Carol Gilligan's critique of Kohlberg's moral development model.
7.	To consider the contributions of George Herbert Mead to the understanding of personality development.
8.	To be able to compare the spheres of socialization (family, school, etc.) in terms of their effects on an individual's socialization experiences.
9.	To develop a life-course perspective of the socialization experience.
10.	To begin to understand the cross-cultural and historical patterns of death and dying as part of the life course.
11.	To be able to discuss the sociological perspective on socialization as a constraint to freedom.

PART III: CHAPTER REVIEW--KEY POINTS

THE IMPORTANCE OF SOCIAL EXPERIENCE

The chapter begins with the story of *Anna*, a young girl who was raised in a context devoid of meaningful social context. Kingsley Davis, a sociologist, studied the six year old girl, and described her as being more an object than a person. What Anna was deprived of was *socialization*, or *the lifelong experience by which individuals develop their human potential and learn culture*. Socialization is the foundation of *personality*, referring to *a person's fairly consistent patterns of acting, thinking, and feeling*.

Nature and Nurture

Naturalists during the later nineteenth century, applying Charles Darwin's theory of evolution, claimed that all human behavior was instinctive. In the early part of this century, psychologist John Watson challenged this perspective and developed an approach called *behaviorism*, claiming that all human behavior was learned within particular social environments and rooted in *nurture*. The work of anthropologists illustrating the great cultural variation existing around the world supports Watson's view. Contemporary sociologists do not argue that biology plays no role in shaping human behavior. The current position among sociologists is that nature and nurture are not so much in opposition as they are inseparable.

Social Isolation

Classic research by Harry and Margaret Harlow using rhesus *monkeys* has illustrated the importance of social interaction for other primates besides humans. Using various experimental situations with "artificial" mothers for infant monkeys they determined that while physical development occurred within normal limits, emotional development and social growth failed to occur. Monkeys who experienced short-term isolation (3 months or less) recovered to normal emotional levels after rejoining other monkeys. Long-term separation appears to have irreversible negative consequences.

The cases of Anna and Isabelle both of whom suffered years of isolation and neglect as young *children*, are reviewed. While humans are resilient creatures, extreme social isolation results in irreversible damage to emotional, cognitive, and behavioral domains of personality development.

UNDERSTANDING THE SOCIALIZATION PROCESS

Sigmund Freud: The Elements of Personality

Sigmund Freud's most important contribution was the development of psychoanalysis. Freud saw biological factors having a significant influence on personality, though he rejected the argument that human behavior reflected biological instinct. He conceived instincts as general *urges* and *drives*. He claimed humans had two basic needs. One he labeled *eros*--or a need for bonding. Another he called the death instinct, or *thanatos*, which related to an aggressive drive.

Freud's perspective combined both these basic needs and the influence of society into a unique model of personality. He argued the personality is comprised of three parts. One is the *id*, rooted in biology and representing *the human being's basic drives*, which are unconscious and demand immediate satisfaction. Another, representing *a person's conscious efforts to balance innate pleasure-seeking drives with demands of society*, he labeled the *ego*. Finally, the human personality develops a *superego* which is the *presence of culture within the individual in the form of internalized values and norms*. There is basic conflict between the id and the superego which the ego must continually try to manage. If the conflict is not adequately resolved personality disorders result.

The controlling influence on drives by society is referred to as *repression*. Often a compromise between society and the individual is struck, where fundamentally selfish drives are redirected into socially acceptable objectives. This process is called *sublimation*.

While being controversial, Freud's work highlights the internalization of social norms and the importance of childhood experiences in the socialization process and the development of personality.

Jean Piaget: Cognitive Development

A prominent psychologist of the twentieth century, Jean Piaget's work centered on human *cognition*--how people think and understand. He was concerned with not just what a person knew, but how the person knows something. He identified four major stages of cognitive development which he believed were tied to biological maturation as well as social experience.

The *sensorimotor stage* is described as *the level of development at which individuals experience the world only through sensory contact*. This stage lasts for about the first two years of life.

The *preoperational stage* was described by Piaget as *the level of development at which individuals first use language and other symbols*. This stage extends from the age of two to the age of seven. Children continue to be very egocentric during this time, having little ability to generalize concepts.

The third stage in Piaget's model is called the *concrete operations stage* and is described as *the level of development at which individuals perceive causal connections in their surroundings*. This period typically covers the ages of seven to eleven. The ability to take the perspective of other people emerges during this stage.

The fourth stage is the *formal operational stage* and is described as *the level of development at which individuals think abstractly and imagine*. This stage begins about age twelve. The ability to think in hypothetical terms is also developed.

Piaget viewed the human mind as active and creative. Research now is focusing on the cross-cultural relevance of this model and to what extent males and females develop differently through these stages. Further, some evidence suggests that almost one-third of the adults in the U.S. do not reach stage four.

Lawrence Kohlberg: Moral Development

Lawrence Kohlberg identifies three stages of moral development, including the *preconventional, conventional,* and *postconventional.* In the first stage moral reasoning is tied to feelings of pleasure and avoidance of pain. In the second stage, specific cultural norms dominant moral reasoning. In the third stage more abstract ethical principles are involved.

Many of the same criticisms raised about Piaget's model apply to Kohlberg's work. Also, he only used males in his research which limits generalizability.

Carol Gilligan: The Gender Factor

Carol Gilligan's research focuses on a systematic comparison of moral development for females and males. Her work indicates that the moral reasoning of girls and boys is different. Girls tend to use a *care and responsibility perspective*, while boys tend to use a *justice perspective.* An important question is whether the differences are the result of nature or nurture.

George Herbert Mead: The Social Self

Questions such as--What exactly is social experience? and, how does social experience enhance our humanity? were central to his research on the socialization process. George Herbert Mead's analysis is often referred to as *social behaviorism.*

Mead understood the basis of humanity to be the *self--a dimension of personality composed of an individual's self-awareness.* For Mead, the self was a totally social phenomenon, inseparable from society. The connection between the two was explained in a series of steps--the emergence of the self through *social experience*, based on the exchange of *symbolic interaction*, and occurring within a context in which people *take the role of the other*, or take their point of view into account during social interaction. A fourth argument of Mead's was that people become *self-reflective* in this process of taking the role of the other.

The process of taking the role of the other can be more clearly seen using Charles Horton Cooley's concept of the **looking-glass self**--or *a conception of the self based on the responses of others.*

An important dualism is suggested by Mead's idea that the self thinks about itself. The two components include: (1) the self as subject by which we initiate social action--the *I*, and (2) the self as object, or objective part, concerned how we perceive ourselves from the perspective of others--the *Me*.

Mead minimized the importance of biology in personality development. The key was social experience, not maturation. Mead also saw infants as responding to others only in terms of *imitation*, or mimicking behavior without understanding. As the use of symbols emerges the child enters a *play stage* in which roletaking occurs. Initially, the roles are modeled after *significant others*, especially parents. Through further social experience children enter the *game stage* where the simultaneous playing of many roles is possible. The final stage involves the development of a *generalized other*, or widespread cultural norms and values used as a reference in evaluating ourselves. *Figure 3-1* (p. 64) illustrates the development of the self as a process of gaining social experience.

AGENTS OF SOCIALIZATION

The Family

The family is identified as the most important agent of socialization. The process of socialization within this institution is discussed as being both intentional and unconscious. The social life of the family has been shown to have a considerable bearing upon the values and orientations children learn. This point is elaborated using research by Melvin Kohn, who found that middle-class and working-class parents stress different values for their children.

The School

It is within the context of school that children begin to establish contact with people from a diversity of social backgrounds. The expressed objective purpose of the school experience is imparting knowledge--math, reading, etc. However, there exists a *hidden curriculum* which also teaches children important cultural values. Schooling is critical for obtaining the knowledge and skills necessary for adult roles.

The Peer Group

A *peer group* is *a group whose members have interests, social position, and age in common*. Some research provides evidence suggesting that the conflict between parents and their adolescent children is more apparent than real. A major feature operative during adolescence is *anticipatory socialization*, or *social learning directed toward gaining a desired position*.

The Mass Media

The *mass media* are *impersonal communications directed to a vast audience*. This includes television, newspapers, radio, etc. . In the *Global Snapshot* box (p. 66), *Figure 3-2* shows data on television ownership per 100 people for different countries. The influence of television on thought and behavior is discussed.

In the *Seeing Ourselves* box (p. 67), *National Map 3-1* provides a graphic comparison of television viewing and newspaper reading across the United States, while the *Social Diversity* box (p. 68) illustrates an example of advertising which offends because of racial and ethnic biases. While it attempts to be factual, many sociologists have argued that the mass media offer a biased perspective on society. *Figure 3-3* (p. 69) shows data concerning the politics of Hollywood's elite. Finally, the *Exploring Cyber-Society* box (p. 70) takes a look at what it is like growing up in the Information Age.

SOCIALIZATION AND THE LIFE COURSE

While focus is given to childhood, the significance of socialization is lifelong. Social experience is viewed in this section as being structured during different stages of the life course.

Childhood

In industrial societies, *childhood* lasts roughly the first twelve years. It is a period characterized by freedom from responsibilities. It is an expanding period in technologically advanced societies. Some historians suggest that in medieval Europe, childhood as we know it did not exist. Such research is used to suggest that childhood is far from just being an issue of biological maturation. In the *Window on the World* box (p. 71), *Global Map 3-1* shows the pattern of child labor worldwide. In the less industrialized countries of the world, children serve as a vital economic asset.

Adolescence

The *adolescent* period emerged as a distinct life course stage during industrialization. This period corresponds roughly to the teen years. The emotional and social turmoil often associated with this stage appears to be the result of inconsistencies in the socialization process as opposed to being based on physical changes. Examples concerning sexuality, voting, and drinking are discussed to illustrate these inconsistencies.

Adulthood

Adulthood begins somewhere between the late teens and early thirties, depending on social background. *Early* and *middle-adulthood* are differentiated. Differences between males and females are discussed, including changes in relationship to the family, work, health, and physical appearance.

Old Age

This period begins during the mid-60s. The issue of the *graying* of U.S. society is discussed. *Figure 3-4* (p. 72) shows the proportion of the U.S. population over the age of sixty-five over the course of this century. While about one in eight people is now over the age of sixty-five, by the middle of the next century one in four will be. The consequences of this demographic trend are great.

Gerontology, refers to *the study of aging and the elderly*. Both *biological* and *cultural* patterns of the aged are addressed within this field.

Physical decline during this period is a reality for most people. Examples, such as decline in strength, sensory impairments, and chronic illnesses are briefly reviewed. The vast majority of the aged are not disabled by physical illnesses.

The status of the aged varies greatly cross-culturally. The aged typically have higher status than people in other age groups in industrial societies. In modern cultures the status of the aged tends to be more marginal. *Gerontocracy* is defined as *a form of social organization in which the elderly have the most wealth, power, and privileges.*

Old age in the U.S. seems to be becoming a time of uncertainty. A problem of industrial societies is *ageism*, or *prejudice and discrimination against the elderly*. The economic status of the aged is discussed. The *Sandwich Generation*, referring to the Baby Boom generation who are simultaneously facing the demands of their children and demands of their parents at the same time.

Death and Dying

Elizabeth Kubler-Ross has written extensively on the process of death as an orderly transition involving five distinct stages--*denial, anger, negotiation, resignation,* and *acceptance*.

The Life Course: An Overview

Our author makes three general conclusions: (1) although linked to the biological process of aging, the essential characteristics of each stage of socialization are constructions of society, (2) each period provides different problems and transitions, and (3) the process varies by social background, race, ethnicity, and sex. A key concept identified is **cohort**, referring to *a category of people with a common characteristic, usually their age.*

RESOCIALIZATION: TOTAL INSTITUTIONS

A **Total institution** is *a setting in which individuals are isolated from the rest of society and manipulated by an administrative staff.* Erving Goffman has identified three distinct qualities of total institutions: (1) they control all aspects of the daily lives of the residents, (2) they subject residents to standardized activities, and (3) they apply formal rules and rigid scheduling to all activities. This structure is designed to achieve the policy of **resocialization**--or *deliberate socialization intended to radically alter the individual's personality.* The process of *institutionalization* often occurs whereby residents become dependent on the structure of the institution and are unable to function outside the institution.

While society affects both our outward behavior and innermost feelings, we are not merely puppets. The process of socialization affirms the capacity for choice and *freedom*. The **Controversy and Debate** box (p. 77) takes a closer look at the question--Are we free within Society?

PART IV: KEY CONCEPTS

adolescence
adulthood
ageism
anticipatory socialization
behaviorism
childhood
cognition
cohort
concrete operations stage
ego
eros
formal operations stage
game stage
generalized other
gerontocracy
gerontology
I
id

looking-glass self
hidden curriculum
institutionalized
mass media
me
old age
peer group
personality
preoperational stage
resocialization
repression
sandwich generation
self
sensorimotor stage
significant other
social behaviorism
socialization
sublimation
superego
taking the role of the other
thanatos
total institution

PART V: IMPORTANT RESEARCHERS

Kingsley Davis

John Watson

Harry and Margaret Harlow

Sigmund Freud

Jean Piaget

Lawrenece Kohlberg

Carol Gilligan

Charles Horton Cooley

George Herbert Mead

Elizabeth Kubler-Ross

PART VI: STUDY QUESTIONS

True-False

1. T   F   John Watson was a nineteenth-century psychologist who argued that human behavior was largely determined by *heredity*.
2. T   F   The Harlow's research on rhesus monkeys concerning *social isolation* illustrates that while short-term isolation can be overcome, long-term isolation appears to cause irreversible emotional and behavioral damage to the monkeys.
3. T   F   The cases of *Isabelle* and *Anna* support the arguments made by naturalists that certain personality characteristics are determined by heredity.
4. T   F   *Sigmund Freud* envisioned *biological factors* as having little or no influence on personality development.
5. T   F   *Jean Piaget's* research centered on human *cognition*.

6.	T	F	According to *Jean Piaget*, it is during the *preoperational stage* of cognitive development that a child begins to use language and other symbols.
7.	T	F	*Carol Gilligan's* research focuses on how *gender* affects *moral reasoning*.
8.	T	F	*George Herbert Mead* argued that *biological factors* played *little or no* role in the development of the self.
9.	T	F	*George Herbert Mead's* concept of the *generalized other* refers to widespread cultural norms and values used as a reference in evaluating ourselves.
10.	T	F	The concept *hidden curriculum* relates to the important cultural values being transmitted to children in school.
11.	T	F	*Gerontocracy* is defined as the study of aging and the elderly.
12.	T	F	A *cohort* is defined as a category of people with a common characteristic, usually their age.

Multiple Choice

1. The story of *Anna* illustrates the significance of _____ in personality development.

   (a) heredity
   (b) social interaction
   (c) physical conditions
   (d) ecological forces
   (e) historical processes

2. Culture existing within the individual *Sigmund Freud* called:

   (a) thanatos
   (b) eros
   (c) the ego
   (d) the id
   (e) the superego

3. *Sigmund Freud's* model of personality does *not* include which of the following elements?

   (a) superego
   (b) id
   (c) self
   (d) ego

4. Which of the following is representative of *Sigmund Freud's* analysis of personality?

   (a) biological forces play only a small role in personality development
   (b) the term instinct is understood as very general human needs in the form of urges and drives
   (c) the most significant period for personality development is adolescence
   (d) personality is best studied as a process of externalizing social forces

5. According to *Jean Piaget*, which of the following best describes the *preoperational stage* of cognitive development?

    (a)   the level of human development in which the world is experienced only through sensory contact
    (b)   the level of human development characterized by the use of logic to understand objects and events
    (c)   the level of human development in which language and other symbols are first used
    (d)   the level of human development characterized by highly abstract thought
    (e)   none of the above

6. According to research by *Carol Gilligan*, males use a _____ perspective concerning moral reasoning.

    (a)   justice   (c)   independent
    (b)   visual   (d)   mechanical

7. *George Herbert Mead's* perspective has often been described as:

    (a)   psychological pragmatism   (d)   behaviorism
    (b)   psychoanalysis   (e)   naturalism
    (c)   social behaviorism

8. The concept of the *looking-glass self* refers to:

    (a)   Freud's argument that through psychoanalysis a person can uncover the unconscious
    (b)   Piaget's view that through biological maturation and social experience individuals become able to logically hypothesize about thoughts without relying on concrete reality
    (c)   Watson's behaviorist notion that one can see through to a person's mind only by observing the person's behavior
    (d)   Cooley's idea that a person's self-conception is based on responses of others

9. The process of social learning directed toward assuming a desired status and role in the future is called:

    (a)   resocialization   (c)   socialization
    (b)   looking-glass self   (d)   anticipatory socialization

10. *Gerontocracy* means:

    (a)   the discrimination of the aged in modern society
    (b)   the study of the elderly
    (c)   a form of social organization in which the elderly have the most wealth, power, and privileges
    (d)   the caring of the elderly by society

1. ___ A person's fairly consistent patterns of acting, thinking, and feeling.
2. ___ The presence of culture within the individual in the form of internalized values and norms.
3. ___ Deliberate socialization intended to radically alter the individual's personality.
4. ___ A category of people with a common characteristics, usually their age.
5. ___ The conception of the self based on the responses of others.
6. ___ A group whose members have interests, social position, and age in common.
7. ___ Prejudice and discrimination against the elderly.
8. ___ A setting in which individuals are isolated from the rest of society and manipulated by an administrative staff.
9. ___ Impersonal communications directed to a vast audience.
10. ___ In Piaget's theory, the level of development at which individuals perceive causal connections in their surroundings.

a.	looking-glass self	e.	resocialization	i.	personality
b.	ageism	f.	superego	j.	total institution
c.	mass media	g.	cohort		
d.	concrete operational stage	h.	peer group		

Fill-In

1. A _____ is defined as a person's fairly consistent pattern of acting, thinking, and feeling.
2. The approach called _____ developed by *John Watson* in the early twentieth century provided a perspective which stressed learning rather than instincts as the key to personality development.
3. According to *Sigmund Freud*, the _____ represents a person's conscious efforts to balance the innate pleasure-seeking drives of the human organism and the demands of society.
4. *Sigmund Freud* termed society's controlling influence on the drives of each individual as _____, whereas he called the process of transforming fundamentally selfish drives into more socially acceptable objectives _____.
5. *Jean Piaget's* work centered on human _____.
6. *Lawrence Kohlberg* identifies three stages in moral development, these include the _____, the _____, and the _____.
7. *Carol Gilligan's* suggests that boys tend to use a *justice perspective* in moral reasoning, relying on formal rules in reaching a judgement about right and wrong. On the other hand, says Gilligan, girls tend to use a _____ and _____ *perspective* in moral reasoning, which leads them to judge a situation with an eye toward personal relationships.
8. *George Herbert Mead* explained that infants with limited social experience respond to others only in terms of _____.
9. The process of social learning directed toward gaining a desired position is called _____ *socialization*.

10. The attitudes of people throughout a society about one or more controversial issues is termed _____.
11. _____ is the study of aging and the elderly.
12. Prisons and mental hospitals are examples of _____ institutions.

Definition and Short-Answer

1. How did the work of *Charles Darwin* influence the understanding of personality development in the last nineteenth century?
2. What was *John Watson's* view concerning personality development?
3. Review the research by *Harry* and *Margaret Harlow* on social isolation. What were the important discoveries they made?
4. Discuss the cases of *childhood isolation* presented in the text. What are the important conclusions being drawn from these cases?
5. Identify and define the parts of personality as seen by *Sigmund Freud*.
6. What are the four stages of cognitive development according to *Jean Piaget*? Briefly describe the qualities of each stage. What is one major criticism of his theory?
7. Define the concept *looking-glass self*. Provide an illustration of this concept from your own personal experience.
8. Define and differentiate between the terms *generalized other* and *significant other*. Further, what are the four basic arguments being made by *George Herbert Mead* concerning personality development?
9. According to the text, what are the four important *agents of socialization*? Provide an illustration of how each is involved in the socialization process.
10. What are the stages of *adulthood* and the qualities of each?
11. What is the significance of the *graying of the United States*? Review data from *Figure 3-3* to illustrate.
12. What is a *total institution*? What are the typical experiences of a person who is living within a total institution? How do these experiences affect personality development?
13. Based on the sociological research cited in this chapter, to what extent can it be argued that humans are like "puppets" in society?
14. What is meant by the term *Sandwich Generation*? What are three factors which have helped create it?
15. What conclusions are being made by the author concerning the *life course*?

PART VII: ANSWERS TO STUDY QUESTIONS

True-False

1.	F	(p. 58)	7.	T	(p. 62)
2.	T	(p. 59)	8.	T	(p. 63)
3.	F	(p. 59)	9.	T	(p. 63)
4.	F	(p. 60)	10.	T	(p. 66)
5.	T	(p. 61)	11.	F	(p. 74)
6.	T	(p. 61)	12.	T	(p. 76)

1. b (p. 57)
2. e (p. 60)
3. b (p. 60)
4. b (p. 60)
5. c (p. 61)

6. a (p. 62)
7. c (p. 63)
8. d (p. 63)
9. d (p. 66)
10. c (p. 74)

Matching

1. i (p. 57)
2. f (p. 60)
3. e (p. 76)
4. g (p. 76)
5. a (p. 63)

6. h (p. 66)
7. b (p. 74)
8. j (p. 76)
9. c (p. 67)
10. d (p. 61)

Fill-In

1. personality (p. 57)
2. behaviorism (p. 58)
3. ego (p. 60)
4. repression, sublimation (p. 60)
5. cognition (p. 61)
6. preconventional, conventional, postconventional (p. 62)

7. care, responsibility (p. 62)
8. imitation (p. 64)
9. anticipatory (p. 66)
10. gerontology (pp. 73-74)
11. total (p. 76)

PART VIII: ANALYSIS AND COMMENT

Social Diversity

"How Do the Media Portray Minorities"

Key Points: Questions:

47

Controversy and Debate

"Are We Free Within Society?"

Key Points: Questions:

Window on the World--Global Map 3-1

"Child Labor in Global Perspective"

Key Points: Questions:

Seeing Ourselves--National Map 3-1

"Television Viewing and Newspaper Reading across the United States"

Key Points: Questions:

Social Interaction
In Everyday Life

PART I: CHAPTER OUTLINE

I. Social Structure: A Guide to Everyday Living
II. Status
    A.   Ascribed Status and Achieved Status
    B.   Master Status
III. Role
    A.   Conflict and strain
    B.   Role Exit
IV. The Social Construction of Reality
    A.   The Thomas Theorem
    B.   Ethnomethodology
    C.   New Technology and "Virtual Reality"
    D.   Reality-Building in Global Perspective
V. Dramaturgical Analysis: "The Presentation of Self"
    A.   Performances
    B.   Nonverbal Communication
    C.   Gender and Performances
    D.   Idealization
    E.   Embarrassment and Tact
VI. Interaction in Everyday Life: Two Illustrations
    A.   Language: The Gender Issue
    B.   Humor: Playing with Reality
VII. Summary
VIII. Key Concepts
IX. Critical-Thinking Questions

PART II: LEARNING OBJECTIVES

1. To be able to identify the characteristics of social structure.
2. To be able to discuss the relationship between social structure and individuality.
3. To be able to distinguish between the different types of statuses and roles.
4. To be able to describe and illustrate the social construction of reality.
5. To begin to see how the technological capacity of a society influences the social construction of reality.

6. To be able to describe and illustrate the approach known as ethnomethodology.
7. To see the importance of performance, nonverbal communication, idealization, and embarrassment to the "presentation of the self."
8. To be able to describe and illustrate dramaturgical analysis.
9. To be able to use gender and humor as illustrations of how people construct meaning in everyday life.

PART III: CHAPTER REVIEW--KEY POINTS

We are introduced to a couple who are lost in an unfamiliar part of a city while driving to another couple's home. Each of the two people has a different perspective on the situation. The male does not want to ask for directions, the female does. This chapter focuses on *social interaction--the process by which people act and react in relation to others.*

SOCIAL STRUCTURE: A GUIDE TO EVERYDAY LIVING

The argument that we act in patterned ways based on social influences is not meant to suggest our behavior is rigidly *determined* by social structure. Rather, social structure is seen as *guiding* behavior.

STATUS

A *status* refers to *a recognized social position that an individual occupies*. Each involves certain rights, privileges, obligations, and expectations that are widely recognized. Statuses guide the behavior of people in different social situations, and are an important part of how people define themselves. *Status set* relates to *all the statuses a person holds at a given time*. An example would include being a father, accountant, male, and husband.

Ascribed and Achieved Status

An *ascribed status* is *a social position a person receives at birth or assumes involuntarily later in life*. In contrast, an *achieved status* refers to *a social position that a person assumes voluntarily and that reflects a significant measure of personal ability and choice*. Most often there is a combination of ascribed and achieved factors in each of our statuses.

Master Status

A *master status* is *a social position with exceptional importance for identity, often shaping a person's entire life*. A person's occupation often comprises this position. Ascribed statuses such as race, sex, and illness are discussed as other examples.

ROLE

The concept *role* refers to *normative patterns of behavior for those holding a particular status*. Ralph Linton describes it as the dynamic expression of a status. However, sociologists differentiate between *role performance* and *role expectations*.

Generally, a person has many more roles than statuses, as each status typically has multiple roles attached. Robert Merton defines a *role set* as *a number of roles attached to a single status. Figure 4-1* (p. 84) provides an illustration of a status set and role set. In the *Window on the World* box (p. 85), *Global Map 4-1* focuses on housework around the world. Cross-culturally, housework is a major component of women's routines and identities.

Conflict and Strain

The concept *role conflict* refers to *the incompatibility among roles corresponding to two or more statuses. Role strain* refers to *incompatibility among roles corresponding to a single status.* Ways to deal with role strain include prioritizing roles, insulating roles from one another, or discarding roles.

Role Exit

Role exit is *the process by which people disengage from social roles that have been central to their lives.* The process of becoming an "ex" is discussed in research by Helen Ebaugh, herself an ex-nun.

THE SOCIAL CONSTRUCTION OF REALITY

The phrase *social construction of reality*, refers to *the process by which individuals creatively build reality through social interaction.* Examples from literature are discussed to illustrate this process.

The Thomas Theorem

One observation made by sociologists is that *situations defined as real become real in their consequences.* This has become known as the *Thomas theorem*.

Ethnomethodology

One approach to understanding the ways humans shape reality is called *ethnomethodology*, which is based on the symbolic-interaction paradigm. Harold Garfinkel coined the term, which is defined as *the study of the way people make sense of their everyday surroundings.* This approach highlights awareness of many unnoticed patterns of everyday life.

New Technology and "Virtual Reality"

How people construct reality is influenced by a their society's technological capacity. The *Exploring Cyber-Society* box (p. 88) addresses this issue. For example, computer technology has changed our economy, our sense of place, and even our sense of reality.

Reality-Building in Global Perspective

Variation exists between subcultures in any given society, and cross-culturally in terms of how reality is fashioned. What is produced becomes regarded as "natural" or "given." In the *Seeing Ourselves* box (p. 89), *National Map 4-1* identifies areas across the country in terms of fan support for baseball. In the *Global Snapshot* box (p. 90), *Figure 4-2* survey data on measures of happiness from different countries are presented. The *Global Sociology* box (pp. 92-93) presents research which addresses the question whether all human groups share the same feelings.

DRAMATURGICAL ANALYSIS: "THE PRESENTATION OF SELF"

Erving Goffman developed an approach he called ***dramaturgical analysis***, or *the investigation of social interaction in terms of theatrical performance.* Central to this analysis is a process called the ***presentation of self***, meaning *the ways in which individuals, in various settings, try to create specific impressions in the minds of others.* This process is also referred to as *impression management.*

Performances

Erving Goffman referred to the conscious and unconscious efforts of people in conveying information about themselves as performances. Performances will vary by settings, or physical locations in which they occur. An interesting analysis of physicians and their offices is discussed to illustrate this idea, including reference to the *front* and *back* regions of the office setting.

Nonverbal Communication

Novelist William Sansom's description of a fictional character named Mr. Preedy walking across a beach in Spain is used to illustrate the process of ***nonverbal communication***. This concept refers to *communication using body movements, gestures, and facial expressions rather than speech.* Types of *body language*--smiles, eye contact, and hand movements are reviewed. Most nonverbal communication is *cultural-specific*.

Gender and Personal Performances

How societies link human traits to being female or male is very important to take into account when studying personal performances. ***Demeanor*** refers to *general conduct or deportment.* It tends to vary by an individual's power.

The ***use of space*** is also important. Power is a key here as well. Masculinity has been traditionally associated with greater amounts of ***personal space***, or *surrounding area over which a person makes some claim to privacy.* Also, men tend to intrude on a woman's space more often than women intrude on a man's space.

Other significant factors include ***staring, smiling***, and ***touching***. While women tend to maintain interactions through sustaining eye contact longer than men do, men tend to stare more. Meanings associated with smiling also seem to vary with gender. Touching patterns also vary, with men tending to touch women more than women touch men.

Idealization

Erving Goffman suggests that we attempt to *idealize* our intentions when it comes to our performances. The context of a hospital involving physicians is used to illustrate.

Embarrassment and Tact

As hard as we may try to craft perfect performances, slip-ups do occur and may cause *embarrassment*--or the discomfort following a spoiled performance. Oftentimes audiences will ignore flaws in performances, using *tact* to enable the performance to continue. While life is not a scripted play, Shakespeare's "All the world's a stage" idea does portray our relationships within social structure to some extent.

INTERACTION IN EVERYDAY LIFE: TWO ILLUSTRATIONS

Language: The Gender Issue

The content of communication is both manifest, or what is explicitly stated, and latent, which conveys much more information. Language functions to define the sexes in at least three ways. First, there is the *power function of language*. One example of this is that males tend to attach female pronouns to valued objects, consistent with the concept of possession. Another illustration is women changing their name when they marry. Second, there is the *value function of language*. Language conveys different levels of status in many subtle ways. Typically, the masculine terms carry higher status. Third, there is the *attention function of language*. The English language seems to almost ignore what is feminine. This is reflected in our pronoun usage. Recent attempts to correct this absence of gender equality in language are discussed. Further, gender is often a source of miscommunication. The *Social Diversity* box (p. 97) takes a look at this issue.

Humor: Playing With Reality

The issues raised here concern the real "character" of humor. One issue concerns the *foundation of humor*. Humor emerges out of ambiguity and double meanings involving two differing definitions of the situation--a contrasting of the *expected* and the *unexpected*. Examples are discussed. A second issue concerns the *dynamics of humor*, or "getting it." To get a joke the listener must understand two realities, the *conventional* and the *unconventional*. Examples of different levels of complexity of jokes on this dimension are provided. A third issue concerns the *topics of humor*. While humor is universal, what is viewed as funny is not. Yet, humor is everywhere closely tied to what is controversial. There is also a fine line between what is funny and what is "sick." A fourth issue concerns the *functions of humor*. The universality of humor reflects its function as a safety valve. Sentiments can be expressed that might be dangerous to relationships if taken seriously. A final issue involves *humor and conflict*. Humor is often used by different groups in society to question the interests of those they oppose.

PART IV: KEY CONCEPTS

achieved status
ascribed status
demeanor
dramaturgical analysis
ethnomethodology
humor
idealization
master status
nonverbal communication
performance
personal space

presentation of self
role
role conflict
role exit
role expectations
role performance
role set
role strain
social interaction
status
status set
social construction of reality
Thomas theorem

PART V: IMPORTANT RESEARCHERS

Robert Merton   Harold Garfinkel

Erving Goffman

PART VI: STUDY QUESTIONS

True-False

1.	T	F	A *status* refers to a pattern of expected behavior for individual members of society.
2.	T	F	A *status set* refers to all statuses a person holds during his or her lifetime.
3.	T	F	Both *statuses* and *roles* vary by culture.
4.	T	F	*Role strain* refers to the incompatibility among roles corresponding to a single status.
5.	T	F	The phrase *the social construction of reality* relates to the sociologist's view that statuses and roles structure our lives along narrowly delineated paths.
6.	T	F	According to *Erving Goffman*, *performances* are very rigidly scripted, leaving virtually no room for individual adaptation.

7.	T	F	Cross-cultural research suggests virtually all *nonverbal communication* is universally understood.
8.	T	F	According to research on gender and personal performances, men use significantly more space than women.
9.	T	F	According to *Erving Goffman's* research, *tact* is relatively uncommon in our society.
10.	T	F	A foundation of *humor* lies in the contrast between two incongruous realities--the *conventional* and *unconventional*.
11.	T	F	One trait of humorous material which appears to be universal is controversy.

Multiple Choice

1. The relationship between social structure and human behavior is one of:

    (a) providing guidelines   (d) ideal versus real
    (b) rigid determination   (e) none of the above
    (c) predestination

2. Which of the following is *not* a structural component of social interaction?

    (a) master status   (d) role set
    (b) role   (e) ascribed status
    (c) value

3. *Ralph Linton* described _____ as the dynamic expression of a status.

    (a) master status   (d) dramaturgy
    (b) role   (e) nonverbal communication
    (c) performance

4. The incompatibility among the roles corresponding to two or more statuses refers to:

    (a) role conflict   (d) status inconsistency
    (b) role strain   (e) role set
    (c) status overload

5. Methods of reducing *role strain* include which of the following?

    (a) discarding one or more roles
    (b) compartmentalizing roles
    (c) emphasizing some roles than others
    (d) all of the above
    (e) none of the above

6. The *Thomas theorem* states:

   (a) roles are only as important as the statuses to which they are attached
   (b) statuses are only as important as the roles to which they are dependent
   (c) the basis of humanity is built upon the dual existence of creativity and conformity
   (d) common sense is only as good as the social structure within which it is embedded
   (e) situations defined as real become real in their consequences

7. The approach used by *ethnomethodologists* to study everyday interaction involves:

   (a) conducting surveys   (d) breaking rules
   (b) unobtrusive observation   (e) laboratory experiments
   (c) secondary analysis

8. The process of the *presentation of the self* is also known as:

   (a) ethnomethodology   (d) ascribed status
   (b) achieved status   (e) impression management
   (c) idealization

9. *Mr. Preedy*, the fictional character introduced in the text, provides an example of:

   (a) role conflict   (c) nonverbal communication
   (b) role strain   (d) status inconsistency

10. Which of the following is *not* an example provided in the text to illustrate how *language* functions to define the sexes?

    (a) the attention function   (c) the power function
    (c) the value function   (d) the affective function

Matching

1. ___ Normative patterns of behavior for those holding a particular status.
2. ___ Incompatibility among roles corresponding to two or more statuses.
3. ___ A social position a person receives at birth or assumes involuntarily later in life.
4. ___ The process by which people act and react in relation to others.
5. ___ The study of the way people make sense of their everyday surroundings.
6. ___ The investigation of social interaction in terms of theatrical performance.
7. ___ General conduct or deportment.
8. ___ Situations defined as real become real in their consequences.
9. ___ A recognized social position that an individual occupies.
10. ___ Incompatibility among roles corresponding to a single status.

a.	ascribed status	f.	role
b.	ethnomethodology	g.	demeanor
c.	Thomas theorem	h.	status
d.	role strain	i.	dramaturgical analysis
e.	social interaction	j.	role conflict

Fill-In

1. _____ _____ refers to the process by which people act and react in relation to others.
2. _____ refers to a recognized social position that an individual occupies in society, while _____ refers to patterns of expected behaviors attached to a particular status.
3. _____ refers to the incompatibility among the roles corresponding to two or more statuses.
4. The study of everyday, common-sense understandings that people within a culture have of the world around them is known as _____.
5. _____ *analysis* is the investigation of social interaction in terms of theatrical performance.
6. _____ refers to ways in which individuals, in various settings, attempt to create specific impressions in the minds of others.
7. Props in a doctor's office, like books and framed diplomas, are examples of the _____ *region* of the setting.
8. According to *Erving Goffman,* _____ refers to general conduct or deportment.
9. When people try to convince others that what they are doing reflects ideal cultural standards rather than less virtuous motives, *Erving Goffman* said they are involved in _____.
10. *Humor* stems from the contrast between two incongruous realities, the _____ and the _____.

Definition and Short-Answer

1. Review the story of the physician's office and *performances* in the text. Using this account as an example, select a social situation you have been involved in and do a dramaturgical analysis to describe its context.
2. Provide an illustration of *nonverbal communication* using the story of *Mr. Preedy* as a model.
3. What are some different types of information provided by a *performer* in terms of nonverbal communication which can be used to determine whether or not a person is telling the truth? Provide an illustration.
4. Refer to *Figure 4-1* (p. 84) and using it as a model diagram your own status and role sets. Identify points of *role conflict* and *role strain*.
5. What are three ways in which language functions to define the sexes differently? Provide an illustration for each.
6. What is *ethnomethodology*?
7. Define the concept *idealization*. Provide an illustration using the doctor's office account as a model.

8.   Provide an illustration of the *Thomas theorem* from experiences you have had either at home or in school.
9.   What are the basic characteristics of *humor*? Write out a joke and analyze how it manifests the characteristics discussed in the text..

PART VII: ANSWERS TO STUDY QUESTIONS

True-False

1.	F	(p. 82)	7.	F	(p. 91)
2.	F	(p. 83)	8.	T	(p. 93)
3.	T	(p. 84)	9.	F	(p. 95)
4.	T	(p. 84)	10.	T	(p. 97)
5.	F	(p. 86)	11.	T	(p. 99)
6.	F	(p. 90)			

Multiple Choice

1.	a	(p. 81)	6.	e	(p. 87)
2.	c	(pp. 82-84)	7.	d	(p. 87)
3.	b	(p. 83)	8.	e	(p. 90)
4.	a	(p. 84)	9.	c	(p. 91)
5.	d	(p. 84)	10.	d	(p. 96)

Fill-In

1.	social interaction (p. 81)	6.	presentation of self (p.90)
2.	status, role (pp. 82-83)	7.	back (p. 90)
3.	role conflict (p. 84)	8.	demeanor (p. 92)
4.	ethnomethodology (p. 87)	9.	idealization (p. 94)
5.	dramaturgical (p. 90)	10.	conventional, unconventional (p. 97)

Matching

1.	f	(p. 83)	6.	i	(p. 90)
2.	j	(p. 84)	7.	g	(p. 92)
3.	a	(p. 82)	8.	c	(p. 87)
4.	e	(p. 81)	9.	h	(p. 82)
5.	b	(p. 87)	10.	d	(p. 84)

PART VIII: ANALYSIS AND COMMENT

Social Diversity

"Gender and Language: You Just Don't Understand!"

Key Points: Questions:

Global Sociology

"Emotions in Global Perspective: Do We All Feel the Same?"

Key Points: Questions:

Window on the World--Global Map 4-1

"Housework in Global Perspective"

Key Points: Questions:

Seeing Ourselves--National Map 4-1

"Baseball Fans Across the United States"

Key Points: Questions

Exploring Cyber-Society

"How New Technology Is Changing Reality"

Key Points: Questions:

Groups and Organizations

PART II: LEARNING OBJECTIVES

1. To be able to identify the differences between primary groups, secondary groups, aggregates, and categories.
2. To be able to identify the various types of leaders associated with social groups.
3. To be able to compare and contrast the research of several different social scientists on group conformity.
4. To be able to recognize the importance of reference groups to group dynamics.
5. To be able to distinguish between ingroups and outgroups.

6. To understand the relevance of group size to the dynamics of social groups.
7. To be able to identify the types of formal organizations.
8. To be able to identify and describe the basic characteristics of bureaucracy.
9. To become aware of both the limitations of and informal side of bureaucracy.
10. To be able to consider ways of humanizing bureaucracy.
11. To consider the issue of the McDonaldization of society.
12. To analyze formal organizations from a cross-cultural perspective.

PART III: CHAPTER REVIEW--KEY POINTS

The amazing success story of *McDonald's* is recounted. In 1954 Ray Kroc bought the interests of the McDonald brother's restaurants in California. This chapter gives insight into the extent to which *social groups*, from families to *formal organizations*, have meaning in our lives.

SOCIAL GROUPS

A *social group* is defined as *two or more people who identify and interact with one another*. Not all collections of individuals are social groups. People who share a status in common are defined as a *category*. People who are together but who interact very little are termed a *crowd*.

Primary and Secondary Groups

Charles Horton Cooley studied the extent to which people have personal concern for each other in social interaction settings. *Primary groups* are *small social groups in which relationships are personal and enduring*. Relationships in such groups have a *personal orientation*. *Secondary groups* are *large and impersonal social groups based on a specific interest or activity*. The distinction between these types of groups are not always clear in real life. *Table 5-1* (p. 105) provides a summary of the key differences between primary and secondary groups. In the *Seeing Ourselves* box (p. 106), *National Map 5-1* examines the quality of social relationships across the United States by looking at people's willingness to sue each other.

Group Leadership

Some research reveals that there are usually two *types of leaders* in social groups held by separate individuals. *Instrumental leadership* refers to *group leaders who emphasize the completion of tasks*. If successful, such leaders gain a distant *respect*. The other, *expressive leadership*, emphasizes *collective well-being*. If successful, such leaders enjoy more personal *affection*. This differentiation is also linked to gender.

Leaders also vary in the ways in which they include others in the decision-making process. Three *decision-making styles* are identified. One is *authoritarian leadership*, which focuses on instrumental concerns. This type of leader makes decisions independently, demanding strict compliance from subordinates. Another type is the *democratic leader* who takes a more expressive approach, seeking to include all members in the decision-making process. A third type is labeled *laissez-faire*. Leaders using this approach tend to downplay their power, allowing the group to function on its own.

Group Conformity

Three research projects illustrate the importance of group conformity to the sociological understanding of group processes. Solomon Asch conducted an experiment in which "naive" subjects were asked to answer questions concerning the length of lines. Five to seven secret accomplices of the experimenter comprised the rest of the group. They purposely gave incorrect answers. Often the naive subject would give a "wrong" answer in order to conform. *Figure 5-1* (p. 107) illustrates an example of the lines used in this experiment.

Stanley Milgram conducted an experiment which naive subjects believed was about learning and memory. The experiment was actually measuring obedience to authority. Naive subjects played the part of "teachers," who thought they were giving electric shock to "learners" when wrong answers were given.

Irving Janis studied three factors which he believed affected decision-making processes and create *groupthink*, or *group conformity that limits understanding of an issue*. The Kennedy administration's decision to invade Cuba is used as an example of this phenomenon.

Reference Groups

The term *reference group* signifies *a social group that serves as a point of reference for making evaluations and decisions*. These groups can be primary or secondary. They are also important in anticipatory socialization processes. Samuel Stouffer conducted research on morale and attitudes of soldiers in World War II in order to investigate the dynamics of reference groups. Stouffer found what appeared to be a paradox: Soldiers in branches with higher promotion rates were more pessimistic about their own chances of being promoted than soldiers in branches with lower rates of promotion. In relative terms, those soldiers in branches with higher rates felt deprived. This research suggests specific social groups are used as standards in developing individual attitudes.

Ingroups and Outgroups

An *ingroup* is *an esteemed social group commanding a member's loyalty*. This group exists in relation to *outgroups*, or *a scorned social group toward which one feels competition or opposition*. This dichotomy allows us to sharpen boundaries between groups and to highlight their distinctive qualities.

Group Size

Group size significantly influences how members socially interact. As a group's membership is added to arithmetically, the number of possible relationships increases in a geometric progression. *Figure 5-2* (p. 109) provides an illustration. Georg Simmel studied social dynamics in small social groups. He differentiated between the *dyad*, *a social group with two members*, and the *triad*, *a social group with three members*. Each is identified as having certain unique qualities resulting in particular patterns of stability, intensity, and other socially significant variables.

Social Diversity

Race, ethnicity, and gender also affect group dynamics. Peter Blau identifies three factors which influence group dynamics. These include: group size, internal heterogeneity, and physical characteristics.

Networks

The term **network** refers to *a web of weak social ties*. Little sense of membership is felt by individuals in the network and only occasionally do they come into contact. Most are secondary in nature. Demographic characteristics, such as age, education, and residence influence the likelihood of a person's involvement in networks. The **Exploring Cyber-Society** box (p. 112) takes a look at the Internet. In the **Window on the World** box (p. 113), *Global Map 5-1* shows the global reach of the Internet.

FORMAL ORGANIZATIONS

Today our lives seem focused around **formal organizations**, or *large, secondary groups organized to achieve specific goals*.

Types of Formal Organizations

Amitai Etzioni uses the variable of how members relate to the organization as a criterion for distinguishing three types of formal organizations. The first is termed a *normative organization*. People join this type or organization to pursue some goal they consider morally worthwhile. These are sometimes also called *voluntary associations*. In the **Global Snapshot** box (p. 111), *Figure 5-3* takes a cross-cultural look at data concerning membership in cultural and educational organizations. The second type is referred to as a *coercive organization*. These serve as a form of punishment (prisons) and treatment (mental hospitals). The third type identified are *utilitarian organizations*. These organizations provide material benefits in exchange for labor.

Origins of Bureaucracy

Formal organizations date back thousands of years. Max Weber suggested that **tradition**, referring to *sentiments and beliefs about the world passed from generation to generation*, dominated the world view in preindustrialized societies. Focus was on the past, and so organizational efficiency was not of great concern. *Table 5-2* (p. 115) compares small groups and formal organizations on several variables.

Modern society, according to Weber, is dominated by a world view dominated by **rationality**, or *deliberate, matter-of-fact calculation of the most efficient means to accomplish a particular task*. The key to the "organization society," according to Weber, lies in the process of **rationalization**, or *the change from tradition to rationality as the dominant mode of human thought*.

Characteristics of Bureaucracies

Bureaucracy is *an organizational model designed to perform tasks efficiently*. The telephone system in the United States is discussed to illustrate a bureaucratic system. Max Weber identified six basic characteristics or elements of the ideal bureaucracy. These include: *specialization, hierarchy of offices, rules and regulations, technical competence, impersonality, and formal written communications*. Each of these characteristics is defined.

The Informal Side of Bureaucracy

While in principle bureaucracy has a highly formal structure, in reality not all behavior in bureaucracies fits precisely the organizational rules. While it is the office which is supposed to carry the power, the personalities of the occupants are important factors.

Problems of Bureaucracy

Alienation is a problem within bureaucracies as they tend to *dehumanize* those they serve through their impersonal operation. *Bureaucratic ritualism* signifies *a preoccupation with rules and regulations to the point of thwarting an organization's goals*. *Bureaucratic inertia* refers to *the tendency of bureaucratic organizations perpetuating themselves*. Other features of bureaucracies include *waste and incompetence*. *Parkinson's Law,* for example, states that "*work expands to fill the time available for its completion.*" This creates *bureaucratic bloat*. Also, the *Peter Principle* states that "*bureaucrats are promoted to their level of incompetence.*"

Oligarchy

Robert Michels observed the fact that *oligarchy*, or *the rule of the many by the few*, was a typical outgrowth of bureaucracy. He suggested that individuals in high levels within a bureaucratic hierarchy tend to accumulate power and use it to promote their own objectives.

Gender and Race in Organizations

Rosabeth Moss Kanter points out that gender and race often determine who holds power and who is given the most opportunities in bureaucratic hierarchies. She finds that such a system has important consequences for on-the-job performance. *Figure 5-4* (p. 118) provides information on U.S. managers by race, sex, and ethnicity.

Deborah Tannen claims that women have a greater *information focus,* and men have a greater *image focus* in organizations. In a similar vein, Sally Helgesen has found that women tend to place greater value on *communication skills*, are more *flexible*, and are more attentive to the *interconnectedness* or all organizational operations than are men. *Humanizing* organizations refers to organizational efforts to develop human resources. This seems to produce happier employees and better profits.

Self-Managed Work Teams

Self-managed work teams are becoming more popular in U.S. corporations. Employees are being given more autonomy and a broader understanding of organizational operations. Such a strategy appears to boost productivity while overcoming worker alienation.

Organizational Environment

Besides an organization's structure, its organizational environment--or any external factors that affect its operation need to be considered. *Technology, political and economic trends, population patterns,* and *other organizations* are discussed as examples.

The McDonaldization of Society

McDonald's organizational principles are steadily coming to dominate society. The basic principles include: *efficiency, calculability, predictability, and control through automation.* Max Weber warned in the early part of this century of the price paid for efficiency--*dehumanization.* George Ritzer, who developed the concept of the McDonaldization of society, echoes Weber's concern asserting that the rationality of McDonaldization may be the ultimate irrationality. In the *Seeing Ourselves* box (p. 122), *National Map 5-2* indicates where in the U.S. people are most concerned about the growing loss of privacy.

Japanese Organizations

Japan's formal organizations reflect their culture's *collective identity* and *solidarity.* In the U.S., on the other hand, we have stressed *individuality.* Five distinctions between Japanese and Western formal organizations are highlighted by William Ouchi. These include: *hiring and advancement, lifetime security, holistic involvement, nonspecialized training,* and *collective decision making.* In the U.S. the focus is on *individual achievement,* while Japan focuses on *success by the group.*

The *Global Sociology* box (p. 123) discusses the Japanese model of organizations and whether such a system would work in the U.S.

GROUPS AND ORGANIZATIONS IN GLOBAL PERSPECTIVE

In recent years there has been a shift in focus from organizations themselves to organizational environments in which they operate. The Japanese success with more humanized and personal organizational environments has illustrated that organizations need not be impersonal. Collective identity and responsibility seems to be compatible with high organizational productivity. Max Weber's analysis of bureaucracy, rooted as it was in nineteenth century Europe, and so focused on impersonal, secondary relationships, may not tell of the whole range of organizational realities.

PART IV: KEY CONCEPTS

aggregates
authoritarian leadership
bureaucracy
bureaucratic ritualism
category
coercive organization
democratic leadership
dyad
expressive leadership
formal organizations
groupthink
humanizing bureaucracy
ingroup
instrumental leadership
laissez-faire leadership

McDonaldization
network
normative organization
oligarchy
organizational environment
outgroup
Parkinson's law
Peter principle
primary group
rationality
rationalization
reference group
secondary group
social group
tradition
triad
utilitarian organization

PART V: IMPORTANT RESEARCHERS

Max Weber   George Simmel

Charles Horton Cooley   Amitai Etzioni

Stanely Milgram   Solomon Asch

Irving Janis   Samuel Stouffer

Rosabeth Moss Kanter   Robert Michels

William Ouchi   Deborah Tannen

Sally Helgesen   George Ritzer

PART VI: STUDY QUESTIONS

<u>True-False</u>

1.   T   F   While members of *categories* could potentially become transformed into a social group, by definition members of *crowds* cannot be transformed into social groups.

2.   T   F   *Expressive leadership* emphasizes the completion of tasks.

3.   T   F   *Stanley Milgram's* research on group conformity patterns illustrated that most individuals are skeptical about the legitimacy of authority for people in positions of power.

4.   T   F   *Samuel Stouffer's* research on soldiers' attitudes toward their own promotions during World War II demonstrates the significance of reference groups in making judgments about ourselves.

5.   T   F   According to research by *Georg Simmel*, large groups tend to be more stable than small groups, such as dyads.

6.   T   F   *Networks* tend to be more enduring and provide a greater sense of identify than most other types of social groups.

7.   T   F   *Normative organizations* are defined as those which impose restrictions on people who have been labeled as deviant.

8.   T   F   According to *Max Weber*, diffusion of responsibility is a major element of bureaucratic organizations.

9.   T   F   *Parkinson's Law* and the *Peter Principle* relate to processes of bureaucratic waste and incompetency.

10.   T   F   Research on *self-managed work groups* demonstrates that those members of a bureaucracy who have restricted opportunities often are the people who demonstrate the most creativity and have the highest aspirations for achievement.

11.   T   F   A basic organizational principle involved in the *McDonaldization of society* is efficiency.

12.   T   F   Worker participation programs, like those traditionally found in *Japan*, have been openly accepted by union leaders and workers here in the United States.

Multiple Choice

1. A social group characterized by long-term personal relationships usually involving many activities is a _____.

   (a) primary group   (d) aggregate
   (b) secondary group   (e) normative organization
   (c) category

2. Which of the following is *not* true of *primary groups*?

   (a) they provide security for their members
   (b) they are focused around specific activities
   (c) they are valued in and of themselves
   (d) they are viewed as ends in themselves

3. Which of the following theorists differentiated between *primary* and *secondary* groups?

   (a) Max Weber   (d) Charles Horton Cooley
   (b) Amitai Etzioni   (e) George Herbert Mead
   (c) Emile Durkheim

4. Which of the following is *not* identified in the text as a *leadership style*?

   (a) laissez-faire   (c) authoritarian
   (b) democratic   (d) utilitarian

5. Crisis situations in social groups are least adequately resolved when the *leader* is:

   (a) instrumental
   (b) laissez-faire
   (c) authoritarian
   (d) democratic

6. Which researcher concluded that people are not likely to question authority figures even common sense dictates that they should?

   (a) Solomon Asch
   (b) Irving Janis
   (c) Stanley Milgram
   (d) Charles Horton Cooley

7. The Kennedy administration's decision to invade Cuba is used as an example of:

   (a) ingroups and outgroups
   (b) reference groups
   (c) bureaucracy
   (d) oligarchy
   (e) groupthink

8. *Amtitai Etzioni* constructed a typology of *formal organizations*. Organizations such as the PTA, the Red Cross, and United Way illustrate the type of organization he called:

   (a) utilitarian
   (b) coercive
   (c) normative
   (d) utilitarian

9. Which of the following is *not* a type of formal organization as identified by *Amitai Etzioni*?

   (a) coercive
   (b) normative
   (c) hierarchial
   (d) utilitarian

10. *Bureaucratic ritualism* is:

    (a) the process of promoting people to their level of incompetence
    (b) the tendency of bureaucratic organizations to persist over time
    (c) the rule of the many by the few
    (d) a preoccupation with rules and regulations to the point of thwarting an organizations goals

11. *Robert Michels* identified one of the limitations of bureaucracy which involves the tendency of bureaucracy to become dominated by *oligarchy* because:

    (a) technical competence cannot be maintained
    (b) bureaucrats abuse organizational power
    (c) bureaucrats get caught up in rule-making
    (d) specialization gives way to generalist orientations

70

12. According to *Rosabeth Moss Kanter's* research:

    (a) proper application of technology in bureaucracy is critical for success
    (b) oligarchy is effective in bureaucratic structures during times of rapid change
    (c) race and gender issues must be addressed as they relate to organizational hierarchies
    (d) humanizing bureaucracies would diminish productivity
    (e) none of the above

13. Which of the following is *not* identified by *Sally Helgesen* as a gender-linked issue in organizations?

    (a) attentiveness to interconnections
    (b) flexibility
    (c) worker productivity
    (d) communication skills

14. According to *George Ritzer*, which of the following is/are characteristic of the *McDonaldization* of society?

    (a) efficiency   (d) control through automation
    (b) calculability   (e) all are identified as characteristics
    (c) predictability

15. According to *William Ouchi* which of the following highlights the distinctions between formal organizations in Japan and the United States?

    (a) hiring and advancement, lifetime security, holistic involvement, nonspecialized training, and collective decision making
    (b) predictability, calculability, control through automation, and efficiency
    (c) oligarchy, ritualism, privacy, and alienation
    (d) competence, tasks, inertia, and networks

Matching

1. ___ Group conformity that limits understanding of an issue.
2. ___ A social group that serves as a point of reference for making evaluations and decisions.
3. ___ A small social group in which relationships are personal and enduring.
4. ___ Two or more people who identify and interact with one another.
5. ___ People who share a status in common.
6. ___ Group leaders who emphasize the completion of tasks.
7. ___ Large and impersonal groups based on a specific interest or activity.
8. ___ A social group with two members.
9. ___ Large. secondary groups organized to achieve specific goals.
10. ___ An organizational model designed to perform tasks efficiently.

71

a.	secondary	f.	reference group
b.	formal organization	g.	dyad
c.	groupthink	h.	bureaucracy
d.	instrumental leadership	i.	primary group
e.	social group	j.	category

Fill-In

1. A _____ _____ is defined as two or more people who identify and interact with one another.
2. Political organizations and college classes are examples of _____ *groups*.
3. While *primary* relationships have a _____ orientation, *secondary* relationships have a _____ orientation.
4. _____ *leadership* refers to group leadership that emphasizes the completion of tasks.
5. _____ *leaders* focus on instrumental concerns, make decisions on their own, and demand strict compliance from subordinates.
6. *Irving Janis* studies the process he called _____ that reduces a group's capacity for critical reflection.
7. A social group which consists of *two* members is known as a _____.
8. A _____ is an organizational model designed to perform tasks efficiently.
9. Preoccupation with rules and regulations to the point of thwarting an organization's goals is called *bureaucratic* _____.
10. *Bureaucratic* _____ is the term used to describe the tendency for bureaucratic organizations to persist over time.
11. *Deborah Tannen's* research on management styles suggests that women have a greater _____ *focus* and men have greater _____ focus.
12. The success of Japanese organizations is due to their foundation of social solidarity and emphasis on _____ *success* rather than individual achievement.

Definition and Short-Answer

1. Differentiate between the qualities of *bureaucracies* and *small groups*. In what ways are they similar?
2. What are the three factors in decision-making processes in groups that lead to *groupthink*?
3. What are three major *limitations* of bureaucracy? Define and provide an illustration for each.
4. In what ways do bureaucratic organizations in *Japan* differ from those in the *U.S*? What are the consequences of these differences? Relate this comparison to the issue of *humanizing* organizations.
5. Differentiate between the concepts of *aggregate* and *category*.
6. Identify the basic *types of leadership* in groups and provide examples of the relative advantages and disadvantage for each type.
7. What are the general characteristics of the *McDonaldization* of society? Provide an illustration of this phenomenon in out society based on your own experience.

True-False

1.	F	(p. 103)
2.	T	(p. 105)
3.	F	(p. 107)
4.	T	(p. 108)
5.	T	(p. 109)
6.	F	(p. 110)

7.	F	(p. 111)
8.	F	(p. 115)
9.	T	(p. 118)
10.	F	(p. 120)
11.	T	(p. 121)
12.	F	(p. 123)

Multiple Choice

1.	a	(p. 103)
2.	b	(p. 104)
3.	d	(p. 104)
4.	d	(p. 106)
5.	b	(p. 106)
6.	c	(p. 107)
7.	e	(p. 108)
8.	c	(p. 111)

9.	c	(p. 111)
10.	d	(p. 116)
11.	b	(p. 117)
12.	c	(p. 118)
13.	c	(p. 119)
14.	e	(p. 121)
15.	a	(p. 122)

Matching

1.	c	(p. 108)
2.	f	(p. 108)
3.	i	(p. 104)
4.	e	(p. 103)
5.	j	(p. 103)

6.	d	(p. 105)
7.	a	(p. 106)
8.	g	(p. 109)
9.	b	(p. 111)
10.	h	(p. 114)

Fill-In

1.	social group (p. 103)
2.	secondary (p. 104)
3.	personal, instrumental (p. 105)
4.	instrumental (p. 105)
5.	authoritarian (p. 106)
6.	groupthink (p. 108)

7.	dyad (p. 109)
8.	bureaucracy (p. 114)
9.	ritualism (p. 117)
10.	inertia (p. 117)
11.	information, image (p. 119)
12.	group (p. 123)

PART VIII: ANALYSIS AND COMMENT

Global Sociology

"The Japanese Model: Will It Work Over Here?"

Key Points: Questions:

73

Seeing Ourselves--National Map 5-1

"The Quality of Relationships: Lawsuits Across the United States"

Key Points: Questions:

Seeing Ourselves--National Map 5-2

"Concerns About Privacy Across the United States"

Key Points: Questions:

Window on the World--Global Map 5-1

"Cyberspace: A Global Network"

Key Points: Questions:

Exploring Cyber-Society

"The Internet: Welcome to Cyberspace"

Key Points: Questions:

Deviance

PART I: CHAPTER OUTLINE

    I.   What is Deviance?
        A.   The Biological Context
        B   Personality Factors
        C.   The Social Foundations of Deviance
    II.   The Functions of Deviance: Structural-Functional Analysis
        A.   Durkheim's Basic Insight
        B.   Merton's Strain Theory
        C.   Deviant Subcultures
   III.   The Label of Deviance: The Symbolic Interaction Approach
        A.   Stigma
        B.   Labeling and Mental Illness
        C.   The Medicalization of Deviance
        D.   Sutherland's Differential Association Theory
        E.   Hirschi's Control Theory
   IV.   Deviance and Inequality: Social Conflict Analysis
        A.   Deviance and Power
        B.   Deviance and Capitalism
        C.   White-Collar Crime
    V.   Deviance and Social Diversity
        A.   Deviance and Gender
        B.   Hate Crimes
   VI.   Crime
        A.   Types of Crime
        B.   Criminal Statistics
        C.   The "Street" Criminal: A Profile
        D.   Crime in Global Perspective
  VII.   The Criminal Justice System
        A.   The Police
        B.   The Courts
        C.   Punishment
 VIII.   Summary
   IX.   Key Concepts
    X.   Critical-Thinking Questions

PART II: LEARNING OBJECTIVES

1. To be able to explain how deviance is interpreted as a product of society.
2. To be able to identify and evaluate the biological explanations of deviance.
3. To be able to identify and evaluate the psychological explanation of deviance.
4. To be able to identify and evaluate the sociological explanations of deviance.
5. To be able to compare and contrast different theories representative of the three major sociological paradigms.
6. To be able to evaluate empirical evidence used to support these different sociological theories of deviance.
7. To be able to distinguish among the types of crime.
8. To become more aware of the demographic patterns of crime in our society.
9. To be able to identify and describe the elements of our criminal justice system.

PART III: CHAPTER REVIEW--KEY POINTS

WHAT IS DEVIANCE?

Deviance is *the recognized violation of cultural norms.* One familiar type of deviance is *crime*, or *the violation of norms formally enacted into criminal law.* Deviance encompasses a wide range of other acts of nonconformity, from variations in hair styles to mental illness. As pointed out by Howard Becker, the key to deviance is *difference*, either positive of negative, which causes people to react to others as "outsiders."

Deviant people are subject to *social control*, or *attempts by society to regulate the thought and behavior of individuals.* A more formal and multifaceted system of social control, the *criminal justice system*, refers to *the lawful response to alleged crimes using police, courts, and state-sanctioned punishment.* Social control is executed by society through positive reactions to conformity and negative reactions to deviance.

The Biological Context of Deviance

During the later part of the nineteenth century, Caesare Lombroso, an Italian physician who worked in prisons, suggested that criminals have distinctive physical traits. He viewed them as "evolutionary throwbacks to lower forms of life." His research was scientifically flawed. Several decades later, Charles Goring, a British psychiatrist, more scientifically conducted a comparison of prisoners and people living in society and found no overall physical differences.

During the middle of this century, William Sheldon suggested that body structure was a critical link to criminal behavior. Subsequent research by Sheldon and Eleanor Glueck supported this argument; however, they suggested body structure was not the cause of the delinquency.

Since the 1960s new knowledge in the field of *genetics* has rejuvenated interest in the study of biological causes of criminality. The connection between a specific pattern of chromosomes has been shown to be related to deviant behavior. However, in its attempt to explain crime in terms of physical traits alone, this approach provides a limited understanding of its causes. Overall, research findings suggest genetic and social influences are significant in affecting the patterns of deviant behavior in society.

Personality Factors

Psychological explanations of deviance concentrate on *individual abnormalities* involving personality. *Containment theory* posits the view that juvenile delinquency (among boys) is a result of social pressure to commit deviant acts in the absence of moral values and a positive self-image. Longitudinal research conducted by Walter Reckless and Simon Dintz during the 1960s supported this conclusion.

Weaknesses to psychological research are pointed out. First, most serious crime is committed by people who are not psychologically abnormal. Second, cross-cultural differences in what is deemed normal and abnormal tends to be ignored. And third, the fact that people within similar psychological qualities are not equally as likely to be labeled deviant is not considered.

The Social Foundations of Deviance

Both conformity and deviance are shaped by society. This is evident in three ways: (1) de exists only in relation to cultural norms, (2) people become deviant as others define them that way, and (3) both norms and the way people define situations involve social power.

THE FUNCTIONS OF DEVIANCE: STRUCTURAL-FUNCTIONAL ANALYSIS

Durkheim's Basic Insight

Emile Durkheim asserted that deviance is an integral part of all societies and serves four major functions. These include: (1) affirming cultural values and norms, (2) clarifying moral boundaries, (3) promoting social unity, and (4) encouraging social change.

Merton's Strain Theory

According to Robert Merton, deviance is encouraged by the day-to-day operation of society. Analysis using this theory points out imbalances between socially endorsed means available to different groups of people and the widely held goals and values of society. This structured inequality of opportunity makes some people prone to anomie. This leads to higher proportions of deviance in those groups experiencing anomie. Four adaptive strategies are identified by Merton: *innovation, ritualism, retreatism,* and *rebellion. Figure 6-1* (p. 132) outlines the components of this theory. *Conformity*, or the acceptance of both cultural goals and means, is seen as the result of successful socialization and the opportunity to pursue these goals through socially approved means.

There are some inadequacies of this approach. First, it is difficult to measure precisely how much deviance is actually caused by strain. Second, some kinds of deviance, like mental illness and homosexuality, are not adequately explained. Third, Merton is not precise about why one response to strain is chosen over another. And fourth, the extent to which the variability of cultural values creates different concepts of personal success is not adequately incorporated.

Deviant Subcultures

Researchers Richard Cloward and Lloyd Ohlin have attempted to extend the work of Merton utilizing the concept of *relative opportunity structure*. They argue criminal deviance occurs when there is limited opportunity to achieve success. They further suggest that *criminal subcultures* emerge to organize and expand systems of deviance. In poor and highly transient neighborhoods *conflict subcultures* (i.e., violent gangs) are more often the form this process takes. Those who fail to achieve success using illegitimate means are likely to fall into *retreatist subcultures* (i.e., alcoholics).

Albert Cohen found that deviant subcultures occur more often in the lower classes and are based on values that oppose the dominant culture. Walter Miller argued, but also suggested that the values which emerge are not a reaction against the middle-class way of life. Rather, he suggested that their values emerge out of daily experiences with contexts of limited opportunities. He described six focal concerns of these delinquent subcultures--*trouble, toughness, smartness, excitement, fate,* and *autonomy.*

Three limitations of the functionalist approach are pointed out. First, functionalists assume a single, dominant culture. Second, the assumption that deviance occurs primarily among the poor is a weakness of subcultural theories. Third, the view that the definition of being deviant will be applied to all who violate norms is inadequate.

THE LABEL OF DEVIANCE: THE SYMBOLIC-INTERACTION APPROACH

The symbolic-interaction paradigm focuses attention on the creation of different social realities in society and the extent to which these create distinguishable understandings of what deviance is. *Labeling theory, the assertion that deviance and conformity result, not so much from what people do, as from how others respond to those actions,* stresses the relativity of deviance.

Edwin Lemert has distinguished between the concepts of *primary deviance*, relating to activity that is initially defined as deviant, and *secondary deviance*, corresponding to a person who accepts the label of deviant.

Stigma

Erving Goffman suggested secondary deviance is the beginning of a *deviant career*. This typically results as a consequence of acquiring a *stigma*, or *a powerfully negative label that radically changes a person's self-concept and social identity.* Some people may go through a *degradation ceremony*, like a criminal prosecution.

Retrospective labeling, is *the reinterpretation of someone's past in light of some deviance.* The argument being used is that all the evidence was there that the "deviant" would become a problem.

Labeling and Mental Illness

Thomas Szaz has argued that the concept "mental illness" should stop being applied to people. He says only the "body" can become ill and therefore mental illness is a myth. He argues this concept is applied to people who are different and who concern the status quo of society. It acts as a justification for forcing people to comply to cultural norms. Erving Goffman concurs to the extent that oftentimes a person is sent to a mental institution for the benefit of the status quo. The label of mental illness becomes an extremely powerful stigma and can act as a self-fulfilling prophecy.

The Medicalization of Deviance

The *medicalization of deviance* relates to *the transformation of moral and legal issues into medical matters.* Our society's view of alcoholism in recent years is a good illustration of this process. Whichever approach is used, moral or medical, will have considerable consequences for those labeled as deviant. Issues include *who responds, how people respond,* and what assumptions will be held about the *personal competence* of the deviant.

Sutherland's Differential Association Theory

Edwin Sutherland suggest that deviance is learned through association with others who encourage violating norms. This is known as *differential association theory*. A survey research study is reviewed supporting this view.

Limitations of the social-interaction approach concern a lack of focus on why society defines certain behavior as deviant and other behavior as not deviant. Unlike other theories which focus on the act of violence, the focus of labeling theory is on the reaction of people to perceived deviance. It provides a relativistic view of deviance and overlooks certain inconsistencies in the actual consequences of deviant labeling. Further, the assumption that all people resist the deviant label, and the fact that there is limited research on actual response patterns of members of society to people labeled as deviant are weaknesses to this approach.

Hirschi's Control Theory

Travis Hirschi pointed out that what really requires explanation is conformity. He suggested conformity results from four types of social controls: *attachment, commitment, involvement,* and *belief.*

DEVIANCE AND INEQUALITY: SOCIAL-CONFLICT ANALYSIS

Deviance and Power

Social inequality serves as the basis of social-conflict theory as it relates to deviance. Certain less powerful people in society tend to be defined as deviant. This pattern is explained in three ways. First, the norms of society generally reflect the interests of the status quo. Second, even if the behavior of the powerful is questioned they have the resources to resist deviant labels. And third, laws and norms are usually never questioned as being inherently unfair, being viewed as "natural."

Deviance and Capitalism

Steven Spitzer suggested that deviant labels are attached to people who interfere with capitalism. Four qualities of capitalism are critical in determining who is labeled as deviant. This list includes: private ownership, production labor, respect for authority, and acceptance of the status quo.

White-Collar Crime

The concept **white-collar crime**, or *crimes committed by people of high social position in the course of their occupations*, was defined by Edwin Sutherland in the 1940s. While it is estimated that the harm done to society by white-collar crime is greater than street crime, most people are not particularly concerned about this form of deviance.

Research has found that *crime in the suites*, as white-collar crime is often called, is typically dealt with in terms of *civil law* instead of *criminal law*--the former referring to general regulations involving economic losses between private parties, and the latter encompassing specific laws that define every individual's moral responsibility to society.

Social-conflict theory focuses our attention on the significance of power and inequality in understanding how deviance is defined and controlled. However, there are several weaknesses to this approach. The assumption that the rich and powerful directly create and control cultural norms is questionable, given the nature of our political process, Further, the approach seems to overgeneralize the cost of white-collar crime relative to street crime. Finally, the approach suggests that only when inequality exits is there deviance, yet all societies exhibit types of deviance, and as Durkheim has pointed out, deviance can be functional.

Table 6-1 (p. 139) summarizes the major contributions of each of the sociological explanations of deviance.

DEVIANCE AND SOCIAL DIVERSITY

Deviance and Gender

The significance of gender in the study of deviant behavior has historically been ignored in sociological research. The behavior of males and females has tended to be evaluated using different standards and the process of labeling has been sex biased. A brief application of the three sociological paradigms is presented. The *Critical Thinking* box (pp. 140-141) discusses the myths surrounding the problem of date rape which perpetuate a double standard.

Hate Crimes

A *hate crime* is *a criminal act motivated by racial or other bias*. While having a long history in our society, the government has only been tracking hate crimes since 1990. In the *Seeing Ourselves*, *National Map 6-1* (p. 142) shows us how different states have mandated legislation with harsher penalties for hate crimes.

CRIME

What is viewed as criminal varies over both time and place. What all crime has in common is that perceived violations bring about response from a formal criminal justice system. Crime contains two elements, the *act* and the *criminal intent*.

Types of Crime

Two major types of crime are recorded by the FBI in is statistical reports as *index crime*. One, *crimes against the person*--or violent crimes--are defined as *crimes against people that involve violence or the threat of violence*. Examples are murder, rape, aggravated assault, and robbery. And two, *crimes against property*--or property crimes--defined as *crimes that involve theft of property belonging to others*. Examples are burglary, larceny-theft, auto theft, and arson. A third category, *victimless crimes*, is defined as *violations of law in which there are no readily apparent victims*. Examples are gambling, prostitution, and the use of illegal drugs.

Criminal Statistics

The FBI statistics indicate that crime rates have generally risen since 1960, however in recent years rates have remained roughly equivalent. *Figure 6-2* (p. 144) shows trends and relative frquencies for types of both violent and property crime for the years 1960-1995. It is pointed out that these official statistics are far from accurate. First, they only include cases known by the police. People sometimes may not know they have been victimized, or may be reluctant to report a crime to the police. *Victimization surveys* suggest that the actual crime rate may be three times higher than official statistics show.

The "Street" Criminal: A Profile

Four variables, *age*, *sex*, *social class*, and *race*, are focused on in this section. While only 14 percent of the population is between the ages of 15-44, this age group accounts for over 50 percent of all arrests.

Statistics indicate that crime to be predominately a male activity. Males are four times more likely than women to be arrested. However, recent evidence suggests the disparity is shrinking.

While most people believe that poor people commit more crime, the situation is actually more complex. Crime rates are relatively equivalent across social strata; it is the types of crime committed which vary. Victimization rates for different crimes also vary by social class.

The relationship between race and crime is complex. While African-Americans, proportionally speaking, are arrested more for "index crime" more than whites, three factors make this connection between race and crime very tenuous. First, arrest records are not statements of proven guilt. Second, race is closely related to social class. And third, white-collar and other crimes more representative of the white population are not counted in the statistics.

Crime in Global Perspective

Relative to European societies, the United States has a very high crime rate. *Figure 6-3* (p. 146) compares rates of handgun deaths from societies around the world. Several reasons for these relatively high crime rates in the United States have been offered. First, our culture emphases individual economic success. Second, the United States is characterized by extraordinary cultural diversity. Third, the United States has a very high level of economic inequality. Fourth, our society encourages private ownership of guns. Finally, the process of "globalization" is linking the world's societies more closely, allowing crime to more readily cross borders. The illegal drug trade is an example of this last point. In the *Window on the World* box (p. 147) *Global Map 6-1* shows the extent of prostitution worldwide, indicating how social conditions give rise to certain types of crime.

THE CRIMINAL JUSTICE SYSTEM

The criminal justice system is comprised of three component parts--the police, the courts, and the punishment of convicted offenders.

The Police

The police represent the point of contact between the public and the criminal justice system. They are responsible for maintaining public order by uniformly enforcing the law. However, particularly because of the relatively small number of police in our population, they must exercise much discretion about which situations receive their attention.

The Courts

Within this component of the system where guilt or innocence is determined, ***plea bargaining*** is a major practice in resolving cases. This refers to *a legal negotiation in which the prosecution reduces a charge in exchange for a defendant's plea of guilty.* This saves both time and expense, but is a very controversial element within our court system.

Punishment

Four justifications for using punishment as part of our criminal justice system are given. These include: ***Retribution***, or *inflicting on an offender suffering comparable to that caused by the offense.* ***Deterrence***, or *the attempt to discourage criminality through punishment.* ***Rehabilitation***, or *reforming the offender to preclude subsequent offenses.* ***Social protection***, or *rendering an offender incapable of further offenses either temporarily through incarceration or permanently through execution.* These justifications of punishment are summarized in *Table 6-2* (p. 148). Further, *Figure 6-4* (p. 149) in the **Global Snapshot** box provides cross-cultural data on incarceration rates for 1993.

The relative effectiveness of these justifications are brought into question given the high ***criminal recidivism*** rates, or *subsequent offenses by people previously convicted of crimes.* Further, the police, courts, and prisons can never effectively end crime.

The ***Controversy and Debate*** box (p. 151) discusses the ideas of Travis Hirschi concerning our criminal justice system. He points out two key characteristics that define the population of criminal offenders--*age* and *self-control*. Early intervention is critical according to his view.

PART IV: KEY CONCEPTS

civil law
containment theory
conflict subculture
conformity
control theory
crime
crimes against property
crimes against the person
criminal justice system
criminal law
criminal recidivism
criminal subculture
deterrence
deviance
differential association
ectomorph
endomorph
index crime
juvenile delinquency
labeling theory

medicalization of deviance
mesomorph
plea bargaining
primary deviance
rebellion
rehabilitation
retreatism
retreatist subculture
retribution
retrospective labeling
secondary deviance
social control
social protection
stigma
white-collar crime
victimless crime
victimization survey

PART V: IMPORTANT RESEARCHERS

Caesare Lombroso   William Sheldon

Steven Spitzer   Richard Cloward and Lloyd Ohlin

Charles Goring   Albert Cohen and Walter Miller

Walter Reckless and Simon Dintz   Edwin Sutherland

Thomas Szaz   Emile Durkheim

Robert Merton   Travis Hirschi

Howard Becker   Erving Goffman

PART VI: STUDY QUESTIONS

Truc-Falsc

1.   T   F   Using the sociological perspective, *social control* is broadly understood, including the criminal justice system as well as the general socialization process.

2.   T   F   *Containment theory* focuses our attention on how certain behaviors are linked to, or contained by, our genes.

3.   T   F   One of the *social foundations of deviance* is that deviance exists only in relation to cultural norms.

4.   T   F   In Robert Merton's *strain theory* the concept deviance is applied by linking deviance to certain social imbalances between *goals* and *means*.

5.   T   F   Walter Miller's *subcultural theory* of deviance points out that deviant subcultures have *no focal concerns*, and therefore have no social norms to guide the behavior of their members.

6.   T   F   *Primary deviance* tends to be more harmful to society than *secondary deviance*.

7.   T   F   Thomas Szaz argues that *mental illness* is a *myth* and is a label used by the powerful in society to force people to follow dominant cultural norms.

8.   T   F   Our author suggests that during the last fifty years there has been a trend away from what is known as the *medicalization of deviance*.

9.   T   F   Edwin Sutherland's *differential association theory* suggests that certain individuals are incapable of learning from experience and therefore are more likely to become deviant.

10. T   F   The *social-conflict* perspective links deviance to social inequality and power in society.

11. T   F   What qualifies an offense as a *hate crime* is not so much a matter of the race or ancestry of the victim as it is the *motivation* of the offender.

12. T   F   Most *index crimes* in the United States are committed by white people.

13. T   F   Using *index crimes*, the crime rate in the United States is relatively high compared to European societies.

14. T   F   *Criminal recidivism*, while relatively high historically in the United States, has in recent years shown a significant decline.

1.   *Containment theory* is an example of a(n) _____ explanation of deviance.

      (a)   biological   (d)   sociological
      (b)   psychological   (e)   none of the above
      (c)   anthropological

2.   Which of the following is *not a social foundation* of deviance?

      (a)   deviance exists in relation to cultural norms
      (b)   people become deviant in that others define them that way
      (c)   both norms and the way people define social situations involve social power
      (d)   all are identified as foundations of deviance

3.   *Emile Durkheim* theorized that all but which of the following are *functions of deviance*?

      (a)   it clarifies moral boundaries
      (b)   it affirms cultural values and norms
      (c)   it encourages social stability
      (d)   it promotes social unity

4.   *Robert Merton's stain theory* is a component of which broad theoretical paradigm?

      (a)   social-conflict   (c)   symbolic-interaction
      (b)   structural-functional   (d)   social-exchange

5.   Which of the following is *not* an example of a *deviant subculture* identified in *Richard Cloward* and *Lloyd Olhin's* research on delinquents.

      (a)   criminal   (c)   residual
      (b)   retreatist   (d)   conflict

6.   Which of the following theories is *not derived* from the *structural-functional paradigm*?

      (a)   labeling theory   (c)   strain theory
      (b)   deviant subculture theory   (d)   control theory

7.   Skipping school for the first time as an eighth grader is an example of:

      (a)   recidivism   (c)   a degradation ceremony
      (b)   primary deviance   (d)   secondary deviance

8. Sometimes an entire community formally stigmatizes an individual through what *Harold Garfinkel* called a:

(a) hate crime
(b) retrospective label
(c) recidivism process
(d) conflict subculture
(e) degradation ceremony

9. The statements: While what is deviant may vary, deviance itself is found in all societies. Deviance and the social response it provokes serve to maintain the moral foundation of society. Deviance can direct social change. All help to summarize which sociological explanation of deviance?

(a) structural-functional
(b) symbolic-interaction
(c) social exchange
(d) social-conflict
(e) labeling

10. Which contribution below is attributed to the *structural-functional theory* of deviance?

(a) nothing is inherently deviant
(b) deviance is found in all societies
(c) the reactions of others to deviance are highly variable
(d) laws and other norms reflect the interests of the powerful in society

11. Which of the following are included as part of the FBI *index crimes*?

(a) white-collar crime and property crime
(b) victimless crime and federal crime
(c) crime against the state and civil crime
(d) crime against the person and crime against property
(e) violent crime and white-collar crime

12. Which of the following is *not listed* as a *justification for punishment* in our criminal justice system?

(a) retribution
(b) deterrence
(c) rehabilitation
(d) social protection
(e) all are listed as justifications

Matching

1. ___ According to Robert Merton's *strain theory*, these are different ways of responding to the inability to succeed through conformity.
2. ___ The assertion that deviance and conformity result, not so much from what people do, as from how others respond to those actions.
3. ___ Violations of law in which there are no apparent victims.
4. ___ Types of *social controls* according to Travis Hirschi.
5. ___ Crime in the *suites*.

6. ___ Types of *deviant subcultures* identified by Richard Cloward and Lloyd Ohlin's theory of relative opportunity structure.
7. ___ A legal negotiation in which the prosecution reduces a charge in exchange for a defendant's guilty plea.
8. ___ The recognized violation of cultural norms.
9. ___ Attempts by society to regulate the thought and behavior of individuals.
10. ___ A powerfully negative label that radically changes a person's self-concept and social identity.

a. criminal, conflict, retreatist   f. attachment, involvement, belief, commitment
b. victimless crime   g. stigma
c. plea bargaining   h. social control
d. labeling theory   i. retreatism, rebellion, ritualism, innovation
e. deviance   j. white collar crime

Fill-In

1. The _____ is the lawful response to alleged crimes using police, courts, and state-sanctioned punishment.
2. *William Sheldon* argued that _____ might predict criminality.
3. A *psychological explanation* of deviance which posits the view that if boys have developed strong moral values and a positive self-image they will not become delinquents is called _____ theory.
4. The *strain theory* of deviance is based on the _____ paradigm.
5. *Richard Cloward* and *Lloyd Ohlin* explain deviance and conformity in terms of the _____ _____ structure young people face in their lives.
6. Activity that is initially defined as deviant is called _____ *deviance*. On the other hand, a person who accepts the label of deviant may then engage in _____ *deviance*, or behavior caused by the person's incorporating the deviant label into their self-concept.
7. *Social-conflict theory* links deviance with social _____. This approach suggests that *who* or *what* is labeled as deviant is based largely on the relative _____ of categories of people.
8. _____ *crime* is defined as crimes committed by persons of high social position in the course of their occupations.
9. _____ *law* refers to general regulations involving economic affairs between private parties.
10. _____ *surveys* show that the actual level of crime is three times as great as that indicated by official reports.
11. The *criminal justice system* in the U.S. consists of three elements: _____, _____, and _____.
12. Subsequent offenses by people previously convicted of crimes is termed *criminal* _____.
13. According to *Travis Hirschi*, the two key characteristics that define the population of *criminal offenders* are _____ and _____ _____.

87

Definition and Short-Answer

1. According to *Travis Hirschi's control theory* there are four types of social controls. What are these? Provide an example of each.
2. According to *Robert Merton's strain theory*, what are the four deviant responses by individuals to dominant cultural patterns when there is a gap between *means* and *goals*? Provide an illustration of each.
3. According to *Emile Durkheim*, what are the *functions of deviance*?
4. *Social-conflict* theorist *Steven Spitzer* argues that deviant labels are applied to people who impede the operation of *capitalism*. What are the four reasons he gives for this phenomenon?
5. How do researchers using *differential association theory* explain deviance?
6. What is meant by the term *medicalization of deviance*? Provide two illustrations.
7. According to *Elliot Currie*, what factors are responsible for the relatively high crime rates in the United States?
8. What are the four *justifications* for the use of punishment against criminals? What is the effectiveness of these approaches?
9. *Richard Cloward* and *Lloyd Ohlin* investigated delinquent youth and explain deviance and conformity in terms of the *relative opportunity structure* young people face in their lives. Identify and define the three types of *subcultures* these researchers have identified as representing the criminal lifestyles of delinquent youth.
10. Describe *Thomas Szaz's* view of mental illness and deviance. Your opinions of his arguments?
11. Briefly review the demographic *profile* of the *street criminal*.
12. Critique the official statistics of crime in the United States. What are the weaknesses of the measures used in the identification of *crime rates*?
13. What are the three consequences for the deviant person depending on whether a *moral model* or *medical model* is applied?

PART VII: ANSWERS TO STUDY QUESTIONS

True-False

1.	T	(p. 128)	8.	F	(p. 135)
2.	F	(p. 129)	9.	F	(p. 135)
3.	T	(p. 130)	10.	T	(p. 137)
4.	T	(p. 131)	11.	T	(p. 137)
5.	F	(p. 132)	12.	T	(p. 145)
6.	F	(p. 134)	13.	T	(p. 145)
7.	T	(p. 134)	14.	F	(p. 150)

Multiple Choice

1.	b	(p. 129)	7.	b	(p. 133)
2.	d	(p. 130)	8.	e	(p. 134)
3.	c	(p. 131)	9.	a	(p. 139)
4.	b	(p. 131)	10.	b	(p. 139)
5.	c	(p. 132)	11.	d	(p. 142)
6.	a	(p. 133)	12.	e	(p. 150)

<u>Matching</u>

1.   i   (p. 132)
2.   d   (p. 133)
3.   b   (p. 142)
4.   f   (pp. 135-136)
5.   j   (p. 138)

6.   a   (p. 132)
7.   c   (p. 148)
8.   e   (p. 128)
9.   h   (p. 128)
10.   g   (p. 134)

<u>Fill-In</u>

1. criminal justice system (p. 128)
2. body structure (p. 128)
3. containment (p. 129)
4. structural-functional (p. 131)
5. relative opportunity (p. 132)
6. primary, secondary (pp. 133-134)
7. inequality, power (p. 137)

8. white-collar (p. 138)
9. civil (p. 138)
10. victimization (p. 143)
11. police, courts, punishment (p. 146)
12. recidivism (p. 150)
13. age, low self-control (p. 151)

PART VIII: ANALYSIS AND COMMENT

Critical Thinking

"Date Rape: Exposing Dangerous Myths"

Key Points: Questions:

Controversy and Debate

"What Can Be Done About Crime?"

Key Points: Questions:

Window on the World--Global Map 6-1

"Prostitution in Global Perspective"

Key Points: Questions:

Seeing Ourselves--National Map 6-1

"Hate Crimes Legislation across the United States"

Key Points: Questions:

Social
Stratification

PART I: CHAPTER OUTLINE

I.   What is Social Stratification
II. Caste and Class Systems
    A.   The Caste System
    B.   The Class System
    C.   Classless Societies?
    D.   Ideology: Stratification's "Staying Power"
III. The Functions of Social Stratification
    A.   The Davis-Moore Thesis
    B.   Meritocracy
IV. Stratification and Conflict
    A.   Karl Marx: Class Conflict
    B.   Why No Marxist Revolution?
    C.   Max Weber: Class, Status, and Power
V.   Stratification and Technology in Global Perspective
VI. Inequality in the United States
    A.   Income, Wealth, and Power
    B.   Occupational Prestige
    C.   Schooling
    D.   Ancestry, Race, and Gender
VII. Social Classes in the United States
    A.   The Upper Class
    B.   The Middle Class
    C.   The Working Class
    D.   The Lower Class
VIII. The Difference Class Makes
IX. Social Mobility
    A.   Myth Versus Reality
    B.   Mobility by Income Level
    C.   Mobility by Race, Ethnicity, and Gender
    D.   Waking Up From the American Dream
    E.   The Global Economy and the U.S. Class Structure

PART II: LEARNING OBJECTIVES

1.   To understand the four basic principles of social stratification.
2.   To be able to differentiate between the cast and class system of stratification.
3.   To know the relationship between culture and stratification.
4.   To be able to differentiate between the structural-functional and social-conflict perspectives of stratification.
5.   To be able to describe the views of Max Weber concerning the dimensions of social class.
6.   To be able to describe the approach to understanding social stratification as presented by the Lenskis.
7.   To develop a sense about the extent of social inequality in the United States.
8.   To consider the meaning of the concept of socioeconomic status and to be aware of its dimensions.
9.   To be able to review the role of economic resources, power and occupational prestige, and schooling in the U.S. class system.
10.   To be able to identify and trace the significance of various ascribed statuses for the construction and maintenance of social stratification in the United States.
11.   To begin to see the significance of the global economy and its impact on our economic system.
12.   To be able to generally describe the various social classes in our social stratification system.
13.   To become aware of how health, values, family life, and gender are related to the social-class system in our society.
14.   To begin to develop a sociological understanding about the nature of social mobility in the United States.
15.   To develop a general understanding of the demographics of poverty in the United States.
16.   To become aware and critical of different explanations of poverty.

PART III: CHAPTER REVIEW--KEY POINTS

WHAT IS SOCIAL STRATIFICATION

    This chapter opens with the story of the sinking of the *Titanic* to illustrate the consequences of social inequality as evidence by who survived this disaster and who did not. Social inequality, the unequal distribution of valued resources, is found in every society. *Social stratification* refers to *a system by which society ranks categories of people in a hierarchy.* Four fundamental principles explain why social stratification exists: (1) social stratification is a characteristic of society, not simply a function of individual differences, (2) social stratification persists over generations, (3) although universal, social stratification also varies in form, and (4) social stratification involves not just inequality but beliefs.

CASTE AND CLASS SYSTEMS

The Caste System

A *caste system* is *social stratification based on ascription*. Pure caste systems are "closed" with no social mobility. The Hindu social system of rural India is an example. In such systems four factors underlie social life: birth determines one's occupation, the hierarchy is kept intact through *endogamous marriages*, powerful cultural beliefs support the system, and members of different categories are kept apart. In the *Global Sociology* box (p. 158) apartheid in South Africa is discussed as having been a caste-type system along the line of race.

The Class System

Representative of industrial societies, *class systems* are defined as *social stratification based on individual achievement*. Open social mobility is critical to this type of system. Other factors of such a system include migration to cities, democratic principles, and high immigration rates. *Status consistency*, or *the degree of consistency in a person's social standing across various dimensions of inequality*.

The United Kingdom represents a society where caste qualities of its agrarian past still are interwoven within the modern day industrial-class system. Their agrarian caste-like *estate* system consisted of three estates, the first (nobles), the second (primarily clergy), and third (commoners). The law of *primogeniture*, by which property of parents could only be inherited by the eldest son, helped maintain this system. Aspects of their feudal past persist (the monarchy). However, power in government resides in the House of Commons, comprised of people who have achieved their status. Today, about 25 percent of Great Britain's population falls into the middle class, and 50 percent fall into the working class. Almost 25 percent are poor. Their system reflects a class system. Opportunities for social mobility are not as great as in the United States.

Classless Societies?

The former Soviet Union, created through the 1917 revolution, claimed itself to be a classless society because of the elimination of private ownership of the productive components of society. Yet, it remained socially stratified as occupations generally fell into four major categories--high government officials, the intelligentsia, manual laborers, and rural peasantry. Elite standing was based on *power* not wealth. The extremes of wealth and poverty, evident in the West, did not occur in the Soviet Union. *Figure 7-1* (p. 161) puts economic inequality into global perspective over the years 1980-1992. Further, research suggested that there was more upward social mobility in the Soviet Union than in Japan, Great Britain, or the United States over the last century. A major reason for this is what sociologists call *structural social mobility*, or *a shift in the social position of large numbers of people due less to individual efforts than to changes in society itself*. Mikhail Gorbachev's economic restructuring--*perestroka* is discussed.

Ideology: Stratification's "Staying Power"

For the ancient Greek philosopher Plato, a peoples' sense of stratification formed the basis of justice. For Karl Marx, it created social injustice. The role of culture in promoting values that support the stratification system is critical in ensuring acceptance. *Ideology--cultural beliefs that justify social stratification*, is the link between culture and stratification. Inevitably people begin to question cultural "truths."

THE FUNCTION OF SOCIAL STRATIFICATION

Structural-functionalists argue that social stratification is universal and has basic functional consequences for society.

The Davis-Moore Thesis

The *Davis-Moore thesis* asserts that some degree of social stratification actually serves society and is even a social necessity. Certain tasks are understood as being of more value than others, and in order to ensure the most qualified people fill these positions they must be rewarded better than others.

Meritocracy

As society approaches a *meritocracy--social stratification based on personal merit--*becomes more productive. Melvin Tumin, a critic of the Davis-Moore thesis, argues that certain highly rewarded occupations seem no more intrinsically important than other less-valued jobs. Also, functionalists seem to exaggerate the consequences of social stratification for the development of individual talents. Finally, social stratification creates conflict as well, so it is not merely functional.

STRATIFICATION AND CONFLICT

Social-conflict analysis holds that social stratification ensures some people gain advantages at the expense of together.

Karl Marx: Class Conflict

Karl Marx's view of social stratification is based on his observations of industrialization in Europe during the second half of the nineteenth century. He saw a class division dominated by *capitalists*, or *people who own factories and other productive businesses*, and the *proletariat*, or *people who sell their productive labor*. At the core of Marx's analysis of capitalism is social conflict, or the struggle among segments of society over valued resources. According to Marx, a major element of the worker's condition was *alienation*, or *the experience of powerlessness in social life*. He envisioned *socialism* as a system which would embrace the social needs of all people.

As influential as Marx's thinking has been for sociological understanding of social stratification, it does overlook its motivating value. The insight provided by the Davis-Moore thesis perhaps explains, in part, the low productivity characteristic of Eastern Europe under socialism.

94

Why No Marxist Revolution?

The overthrow of the capitalist system has not occurred for a least four central reasons: (1) the fragmentation of the capitalist class, (2) a higher standard of living, (3) more extensive worker organization, and (4) more extensive legal protections.

For example, referring to (2) above, a century ago most U.S. workers were in **blue-collar occupations**, or *lower-prestige work that involves mostly manual labor*. Today, most workers hold **white-collar occupations**, or *higher-prestige work that involves mostly mental activity*. *Table 7-1* (p. 167) summarizes the structural-functional and social-conflict explanations of social stratification.

Max Weber: Class, Status, and Power

Max Weber viewed Marx's ideas of social class as being too simplistic. Weber theorized that there were three dimensions of social inequality--*class, status,* and *power*. These create a *socioeconomic status hierarchy*. These dimensions are continuous in quality. Weber also theorized that a single individual's rankings on the three dimensions might be quite different. The term used today to reflect Weber's model is **socioeconomic status (SES)** referring to *a composite social ranking based on various dimensions of inequality*.

Viewing *inequality in history*, unlike Marx, who focused on economics and believed social stratification could largely be eliminated, Weber doubted that the overthrow of capitalism would significantly diminish stratification, and might even increase social inequality. Recent polarization within our social-stratification system has increased the favor of Marx's model to some degree.

STRATIFICATION AND TECHNOLOGY IN GLOBAL PERSPECTIVE

Gerhard and Jean Lenski's sociocultural evolutionary model of historical change concerning social stratification combines both structural-functional and social-conflict perspectives. In technologically simple societies age and sex tend to be the only basis of social stratification. As technology advances and surpluses in valued resources occur, social inequality increases. They further propose that as technology continues to develop in industrial societies social inequality tends to diminish. The *Kuznets Curve*, diagrammed in *Figure 7-2* (p. 168) illustrates the pattern discussed by the Kenskis. In the **Window on the World** box, *Global Map 7-1* (p. 169) illustrates income disparity in global perspective.

INEQUALITY IN THE UNITED STATES

Income, Wealth, and Power

An important dimension of economic inequality is **income**, or *wages or salary from work and earnings from investments*. The median U.S. family income in 1995 was $40,611. *Table 7-2* (p. 171) presents data on U.S. family income for 1995. **Wealth**, *an individual's or family's total financial assets*, is distributed more unequally than income. *Figure 7-3* (p. 170) illustrates the distribution of income and wealth in the United States. The richest 20 percent of our population owns over three-fourths of the country's entire wealth. The average wealth of a U.S. family is about $40,000. However, some 40 percent of U.S. families have little or no wealth. When assets and liabilities are balanced, the lowest 20 percent of people in the United States are actually in debt.

95

Occupational Prestige

One's occupation is a primary factor in determining social prestige. *Table 7-3* (p. 172) presents a rank ordering of prestige scores for various occupational categories based on the responses of a random sample of U.S. adults. High income and advanced education and training requirements are positively correlated with higher prestige occupations. White-collar occupations tend to have higher prestige than blue-collar ones. Women tend to be concentrated in pink-collar occupations--service and clerical--which tend to be low in prestige.

Schooling

Formal education significantly influences occupational opportunities and income. Great variation exists in terms of how much formal education different groups of people in our society receive. *Table 7-4* (p. 173) indicates this fact. While 80 percent of adults in the U.S. have a high-school education, only about 25 percent have a college degree.

Ancestry, Race, and Gender

Several ascribed statuses influence our position in our stratification system. Perhaps nothing affects our social standing more than "the accident of birth." African American family income, for example, is only about 60 percent of that for whites. Ethnicity and gender are also important factors. In general, people of English heritage have higher status than other people in the United States. On average, women have lower incomes, educational levels, and occupational prestige than men.

SOCIAL CLASSES IN THE UNITED STATES

Many different criteria can be used to place an individual or family into a particular social class, with precise placement not being possible. Nevertheless, patterns do exist. Four general social classes are identified.

The Upper Class

Approximately 3-4 percent of Americans fall into this class. Even among this group there is stratification. A difference is typically made between the *upper-upper class*, or "old money" rich, and the *lower-upper class*, or "new money" rich. The former group represent about 1 percent of our population and obtain their standing through ancestry and inheritance. The latter group obtains their wealth more typically through earnings. Both groups have tremendous power in society, controlling most of our nation's productive property.

The Middle Class

Roughly 40-45 percent of U.S. citizens fall into this category. Given its size alone, the middle class has a significant influence on patterns of U.S. culture. An important quality in the middle class is a diversity of family backgrounds. The upper third of this category is referred to as the upper-middle, being characterized by prestigious white-collar occupations, relatively high educations, nice homes, and an accumulation of property and wealth during their lifetime.

The Working Class

This category comprises about one-third of our population. It is characterized by blue-collar families, vulnerable to unemployment and illness to a greater extent than families in the middle and upper classes. People in this category also have lower levels of personal satisfaction.

The Lower Class

The remaining 20 percent of our population is identified as the lower class. Roughly 13.8 percent of the U.S. population is officially classified as being poor.

THE DIFFERENCE CLASS MAKES

People with higher incomes are more than two times as likely to describe themselves as healthy than are poor people. Social class is also positively correlated with life expectancy. Mental health patterns also vary with social class. Poorer people seem more exposed to stressful events leading to emotional distress.

The values and attitudes people support are closely associated with the types of lifestyles they live. The working class has less security than the middle and upper classes and are more characterized as emphasizing conformity to conventional beliefs and practices. Their greater economic security seems to make middle-class people more tolerant than working-class people as well. Orientation to time also seems to vary by social class. The variation by political orientation is complicated. Generally, however, conservative views on economic issues and liberal views on social issues are found among those of higher social standing. Finally, family life is shaped by social class. Who one marries, how many children are in the family, styles of childrearing, and spousal relationships are also influence by social class.

SOCIAL MOBIITY

The United States is characterized by relatively high levels of social mobility. Social mobility can be *upward* or *downward*. **Intragenerational social mobility** refers to *a change in social position occurring during a person's lifetime.* **Intergenerational social mobility** is defined as *the social standing of children in relation to their parents.*

Myth Versus Reality

Studies on intergenerational social mobility, which have focused almost exclusively on men, do show high rates of upward mobility in the U.S., especially when *horizontal social mobility*, or changes of occupation at one class level, are included. Four general conclusions are made about social mobility in the U.S. These include: (1) social mobility, at least among men, has been fairly high, (2) the long-term trend in social mobility has been upward, (3) within a single generation, social mobility is usually incremental, not dramatic, and (4) the short-term trend has been stagnation, with some income polarization.

Mobility by Income Level

Figure 7-4 (p. 196) shows how families during the 1980s and 1990s fared according to their income level. Families are divided into quintiles based on income. Only the top fifth showed any real improvement.

Mobility by Race, Ethnicity, and Gender

African Americans showed a decline relative to whites by income since 1980. Latino families have also dropped relative to whites. The earnings gap between men and women appears to be closing. Data for each comparison are given.

Waking Up From the "American Dream"

Historically, our society and its economy has been characterized by growth and expansion. Four important trends are identified that suggest stagnation. These include: (1) for many workers, earnings have stalled, (2) multiple job holding is up, (3) more jobs offer little income, and (4) young people are remaining at home. *Figure 7-5* (p. 178) shows median family income for U.S. families for the years 1950-1995 in constant 1995 dollars. While rising for the first half of this time period, family income has remained fairly stable since 1973.

The Global Economy and the Class Structure

Many of the industrial jobs which were the basis of our expanding economy in recent decades have been transferred overseas. Current patterns of change in our economy have undermined many people's expectations about improving their standard of living. This is so even with over one-half of our families having more than one breadwinner. High-paying manufacturing jobs employ only 15 percent of our work force today, with employment opportunities being found primarily in lower-paying "service work."

POVERTY IN THE UNITED STATES

Relative poverty is *the deprivation of some people in relation to those who have more*. By definition this type of poverty is universal and inevitable. A more serious from of poverty is termed *absolute poverty*, defined as *a deprivation of resources that is life-threatening*. Roughly one-fifth of the world's population lives in such conditions.

The Extent of Poverty

The poverty rate in the United States has generally decreased since official measurements were first taken in 1959. At present, about 36 million people, or 13.8 percent of our population are classified as being poor. In 1995 the official poverty line for an urban family of four was $15,569. This standard approximates three times the estimated expense of food.

Who are the Poor?

Age--Children are more likely to be poor than any other age group in our nation. About 21 percent of the children in the United States are poor. Some 40 percent of the people living in poverty are under the age of eighteen.

Race and ethnicity--About two-thirds of all people living in poverty are white, but a disproportionate percentage of African Americans and Latinos are represented among the poor, while only about 9 percent of whites are poor, 30 percent of African Americans and Latinos are living in poverty.

Gender and family patterns--Poverty rates for women and men are considerably different. Of all poor people, about two-thirds are female. Over one-half of all families are headed by women. The widening gap in poverty rates between women and men has been labeled the *feminization of poverty*, referring to *the trend by which women represent an increasing proportion of the poor*.

Area of residence--The highest rates of poverty are found in the central cities. In the *Seeing Ourselves* box (p. 180) *National Map 7-1* provides a visual picture of income levels across the United States, indicating where poverty is most pronounced.

Explaining Poverty

Two distinct views about who is responsible for poverty are debated. Edward Banfield is a proponent of the view that poor people are primarily responsible for their own poverty. He believes a subculture of poverty, with a "present-time" orientation, dominates the lives of the poor. This view is an extension of the *culture of poverty* theory developed by Oscar Lewis.

The idea that society is primarily responsible for poverty is held by one-third of adults in the United States. William Ryan argues that the culture of poverty perspective leads people to "blame the victim." He suggests poverty results from the unequal distribution of resources in society. Any lack of ambition among the poor is seen by Ryan as a *consequence* rather than a *cause* of poverty.

Empirical evidence exists to support both views. For example, while over one-half of the heads of poor families do not work, about one-fifth work full-time, but because of low wages cannot climb out of poverty. Further, inadequacies in child care programs make it difficult for many single-parent women to work.

Homelessness

Though no precise count of the homeless exists, estimates range from 500,000 to several million. The stereotype of the homeless population has been brought into question recently. It is a diverse population. One characteristic shared by the homeless, though, is *poverty*. Both *personal traits* and *societal factors* are discussed as causes of homelessness.

Class and Welfare, Politics and Values

Our values support individual responsibility. For many, the idea of welfare programs undermines initiative. This attitude leads to the *hidden injury of class*, a phenomenon which lowers the self-image of the poor person. At the same time *wealthfare* is such a major part of our value system. In the *Global Snapshot* box (p. 183), *Figure 7-6* shows that people in the U.S. are more likely than people in other industrialized countries to blame individuals rather than society for poverty. The *Controversy and Debate* box (pp. 184-185) looks at our fascination with the idea of personal merit by examining the "Bell Curve" debate. The issue concerns whether poor people are less intelligent than richer people.

PART IV: KEY CONCEPTS

absolute poverty
alienation
blue-collar occupation
capitalists
caste system
class system
culture of poverty
Davis-Moore thesis
femininization of poverty
horizontal social mobility
ideology
income
intergenerational social mobility
intragenerational social mobility
lower-class
marginal poor
meritocracy
middle-class
prestige
primogeniture
proletariat
relative poverty
social inequality
social mobility
social stratification
socioeconomic status
status consistency
structural social mobility
upper-class
wealth
white-collar occupation

PART VI: IMPORTANT RESEARCHERS

Karl Marx   Max Weber

Gerhard and Jean Lenski   Melvin Tumin

William Ryan   Edward Banfield

Oscar Lewis

PART VI: STUDY QUESTIONS

<u>True-False</u>

1.	T	F	Social inequality is *universal*--found in all societies.
2.	T	F	*Ascription* is fundamental to social-stratification systems based on *castes*.
3.	T	F	*Caste* systems tend to be characterized by *endogamous marriages*.
4.	T	F	The *working class* is the largest segment of the population in *Great Britain*.
5.	T	F	The *Davis-Moore thesis* is a component of the social-conflict perspective of social stratification.
6.	T	F	*Structural-functionalists* argue that social stratification encourages a matching to talents and abilities to appropriate positions in society.
7.	T	F	*Max Weber* developed a unidimensional model of social stratification which was dominant earlier this century.
8.	T	F	*Gerhard* and *Jean Lenski* argue that hunting and gathering societies have greater social inequality than agrarian or horticultural societies.
9.	T	F	The *Kutznets curve* projects greater social inequality as industrial societies advance technologically.
10.	T	F	*Wealth* refers to an individual's or family's total financial assets.
11.	T	F	Less than 35 percent of U.S. adults have a college degree.
12.	T	F	The *working class* is the largest social class in the United States.
13.	T	F	Parents in *working-class* families are characterized by an emphasis on *conformity* to conventional beliefs and practices, more so than are middle-class families.

14.   T   F   Compared to the period of 1950-1973, the period 1974-1995 provided greater growth in *median family income*, particularly with more dual earner families in existence.

15.   T   F   The official *poverty rate* in the United States in 1995 was approximately 13.8 percent.

16.   T   F   People in the U.S. are more likely to blame individuals rather than society for poverty compared to people in other industrialized societies.

Multiple Choice

1.   A system by which categories of people within a society are ranked in a hierarchy is called:

(a)   social inequality   (c)   meritocracy
(b)   social stratification   (d)   social mobility

2.   Which of the following principles is *not* a basic factor in explaining the existence of social stratification?

(a)   although universal, social stratification also varies in form
(b)   social stratification persists over generations
(c)   social stratification rests on widely held beliefs
(d)   social stratification is a characteristic of society, not simply a function of individual differences
(e)   all are factors in explaining social stratification

3.   *Apartheid* became law in South Africa in:

(a)   1948   (d)   1875
(b)   1916   (e)   it was never law
(c)   1971

4.   Which characteristics that follow are most accurate of *class systems*?

(a)   they are more clearly defined than castes
(b)   they have variable status consistency
(c)   they have occupations based on ascription
(d)   all of the above
(e)   none of the above

5.   In the text, contemporary *Great Britain* is identified as a(n):

(a)   neomonarchy   (d)   caste system
(b)   estate system   (e)   open estate system
(c)   class society

6. Which society is identified in the text as having experienced the most upward social mobility this century?

   (a)   the United States   (c)   Japan
   (b)   Great Britain   (d)   the former Soviet Union

7. The Soviet Union was:

   (a)   decidedly open
   (b)   socially stratified
   (c)   a society with greater extremes between the wealthy and the poor than the United States
   (d)   more caste-like than the United States

8. Cultural beliefs that justify social stratification is the definition for:

   (a)   meritocracy   (c)   ideology
   (b)   social stratification   (d)   status inconsistency

9. According to *Gerhard* and *Jean Lenski*, social stratification is at its peak in:

   (a)   hunting and gathering societies
   (b)   postindustrial societies
   (c)   horticultural, pastoral, and agrarian societies
   (d)   industrial societies

10. *Education* is distributed unequally in the U.S. as evidenced by the fact that:

   (a)   only 25 percent of U.S. adults are college graduates
   (b)   only 56.6 percent of U.S. adults are high-school graduates
   (c)   only 24.5 percent of U.S. adults have some college
   (d)   all of the above
   (e)   none of the above

11. The *middle class* includes approximately what percentage of the U.S. population?

   (a)   20-25   (d)   40-45
   (b)   10-15   (e)   70-75
   (c)   30-35

12. A change in social position of children relative to that of their parents is called:

   (a)   horizontal social mobility   (c)   intragenerational social mobility
   (b)   structural social mobility   (d)   intergenerational social mobility

13. Approximately what percentage of the U.S. population is officially classified as being poor?

    (a)   5   (d)   26
    (b)   14   (e)   31
    (c)   19

14. Poverty statistics in the United States reveal that:

    (a)   the elderly are more likely than any other age group to be poor
    (b)   almost 70 percent of all African Americans are poor
    (c)   urban and suburban poverty rates are considerably higher than rural poverty rates
    (d)   about 63 percent of the poor are female

15. The *culture of poverty* view concerning the causes of poverty:

    (a)   holds that the poor are primarily responsible for their own poverty
    (b)   blames poverty on economic stagnation relating to the globalization of the U.S. economy
    (c)   sees lack of ambition on the part of the poor as a consequence, not a cause for poverty
    (d)   views the conservative economic policies of the last two decades in the U.S. as the primary reason for relatively high poverty rates

16. Which of the following is/are arguments being made in the book *The Bell Curve* by Charles Murray and Richard Herrnstein:

    (a)   something called "general intelligence" exists
    (b)   at least one-half the variation in human intelligence is genetic
    (c)   higher education and the work place is being dominated by a cognitive elite
    (d)   increasingly, poor people are individuals with lower intelligence
    (e)   all are arguments being made in this book

Matching

1. ___   According to Karl Marx, the people who own and operate factories and other productive businesses in pursuit of profit.
2. ___   Developed the concept of the *culture of poverty*, or a lower-class subculture that inhibits personal achievement and fosters resignation to one's plight.
3. ___   The assertion that social stratification is universal because it has beneficial consequences for the operation of society.
4. ___   The experience of powerlessness in social life.
5. ___   An economic program, meaning *restructuring*, developed by Mikhail Gorbachev.
6. ___   Argued that *society* is primarily responsible for poverty and that any lack of ambition on the part of the poor is a *consequence* of insufficient opportunity.
7. ___   Cultural beliefs that justify social stratification.

8. ___ Reveals that greater *technological* sophistication is generally accompanied by more pronounced *social-stratification,* to a point.
9. ___ Developed a multidimensional model of social class which included the variables of *class, status,* and *power.*
10. ___ According to Karl Marx, the people who sell their productive labor for wages.

a.	proletariat	f.	the Davis-Moore thesis
b.	perestroika	g.	Max Weber
c.	Kuznets curve	h.	Oscar Lewis
d.	capitalists	i.	William Ryan
e.	alienation	j.	ideology

Fill-In

1. _____ refers to a system by which society ranks categories of people in a hierarchy.
2. A _____ is a system of social stratification based on *ascription.*
3. In feudal Great Britain, the *law of* _____ mandated that only the eldest son inherited property of parents.
4. _____ refers to a shift in the social position of large numbers of people due more to changes in society itself than to individual efforts.
5. _____ refers to cultural beliefs that justify social stratification.
6. Social stratification based on *personal merit* is called a _____.
7. According to *Karl Marx,* _____ is the experience of powerlessness in social life.
8. The three components of *Max Weber's* model of social class are _____, _____, and _____.
9. The idea that social stratification systems reflect the interests of the more powerful members of society is from the _____ paradigm.
10. While _____ is defined as wages or salary from work and earnings from investments, _____ refers to an individual's or family's total financial assets.
11. The median *wealth* of U.S. families is about $ _____.
12. While the relationship between social class and politics is complex, generally, members of high social standing tend to have _____ *views on economic issues* and _____ *views on social issues.*
13. The trend by which females represent an increasing proportion of the poor is called the _____ *of poverty.*
14. *Oscar Lewis* describes the _____ as characterized by resignation to being poor as a matter of fate.
15. *William Ryan* suggests the characteristics associated with a "culture of poverty" are not the _____ of poverty but rather the _____.
16. *Richard Sennet* and *Jonathan Cobb* referred to the lowering of self-image due to poverty as the _____ *of class.*
17. Our cultural tendency to equate privilege with personal merit leads us to nod approvingly at _____ while angrily denouncing _____ for the poor.

Definition and Short-Answer

1. What are the four *fundamental principles* of social stratification?
2. Briefly describe the social-stratification system of *Great Britain*.
3. What are the four reasons given in the text for why the *Marxist Revolution* has not occurred?
4. What are the basic qualities of a *caste system*?
5. What is meant by the concept *structural social mobility*? Provide two illustrations.
6. What are the components of *Max Weber's* multidimensional model of social stratification? Define each.
7. What are three criteria of the *Davis-Moore thesis*? What is your opinion of this thesis and its relevance for helping us understand our social stratification? What evidence exists in support of this thesis? What evidence that contradicts it?
8. What are some of the reasons why people in the United States might tend to underestimate the extent of social inequality in our society?
9. How are *wealth* and *income* distributed throughout the population in the United States?
10. What are the basic components of *socioeconomic status*? How are they measured? How do these components differ from Max Weber's components of social class?
11. To what extent do *ascribed statuses* affect a person's place in our social-stratification system? Provide examples using the variables of race, ethnicity, and gender.
12. Using the factors of health, values, and politics, discuss the difference social class makes in the lives of people within our society.
13. Define *Karl Marx's* concepts of *proletariat* and *capitalists*. What value does Marx's perspective offer to the understanding of modern social stratification?
14. Identify six significant *demographic characteristics* of the poor in our society today.
15. What is meant by the term *culture of poverty*? What policies and programs do you think could be instituted to counteract this phenomenon?
16. What is meant by the terms *femininization of poverty*? What can be done to reverse this trend in our society?
17. Review the basic points being made by *Gerhard* and *Jean Lenski* concerning global inequality in historical perspective.
18. What are the four general conclusions being made about *social mobility* in the United States today?
19. What is the evidence that the *American Dream* is waning in our society?

PART VII: ANSWERS TO STUDY QUESTIONS

True-False

1.	T	(p. 156)	9.	F	(p. 168)
2.	T	(p. 157)	10.	T	(p. 170)
3.	T	(p. 157)	11.	T	(p. 173)
4.	T	(p. 159)	12.	F	(p. 174)
5.	F	(p. 163)	13.	T	(p. 175)
6.	T	(p. 163)	14.	F	(p. 178)
7.	F	(p. 166)	15.	T	(p. 179)
8.	F	(p. 168)	16.	T	(p. 184)

Multiple Choice

1.	b	(p. 156)
2.	e	(p. 156)
3.	a	(p. 158)
4.	b	(p. 159)
5.	c	(p. 159)
6.	d	(p. 161)
7.	b	(p. 161)
8.	c	(p. 162)

9.	c	(p. 168)
10.	a	(p. 173)
11.	d	(p. 174)
12.	d	(p. 176)
13.	b	(p. 179)
14.	d	(pp. 180-181)
15.	a	(p. 181)
16.	e	(p. 184)

Matching

1.	d	(p. 164)
2.	h	(p. 181)
3.	f	(p. 163)
4.	e	(p. 165)
5.	b	(p. 160)

6.	i	(p. 182)
7.	j	(p. 162)
8.	c	(p. 168)
9.	g	(p. 166)
10.	a	(p. 164)

Fill-In

1. social stratification (p. 156)
2. caste (p. 157)
3. primogeniture (p. 159)
4. structural social mobility (p. 161)
5. ideology (p. 162)
6. meritocracy (p. 163)
7. alienation (p. 165)
8. class, status, power (p. 166)
9. social-conflict (p. 167)
10. income, wealth (p. 170)
11. 40,000 (p. 170)
12. conservative, liberal (p. 175)
13. femininization (p. 181)
14. culture of poverty (p. 181)
15. causes, consequences (p. 182)
16. hidden injury (p. 184)
17. wealthfare, welfare (p. 185)

PART VIII: ANALYSIS AND COMMENT

Global Sociology

"Race and caste: A Report from South Africa"

Key Points: Questions:

107

Controversy and Debate

"The Bell Curve Debate: Are Rich People Really Smarter?"

Key Points: Questions:

Window on the World--Global Map 7-1

"Income Disparity in Global Perspective"

Key Points: Questions:

Seeing Ourselves--National Map 7-1

"Median Household Income across the United States"

Key Points: Questions:

Global Stratification

PART I: CHAPTER OUTLINE

I. Global Economic Development
    A. The Problem of Terminology
    B. High-Income Countries
    C. Middle-Income Countries
    D. Low-Income Countries
II. Global Wealth and Poverty
    A. The Severity of Poverty
    B. The Extent of Poverty
    C. Poverty and Children
    D. Poverty and Women
    E. Correlates of Global Poverty
III. Global Inequality: Theoretical Analysis
    A. Modernization Theory
    B. Dependency Theory
IV. Global Inequality: Looking Ahead
V. Summary
VI. Key Concepts
VII. Critical-Thinking Questions

PART II: LEARNING OBJECTIVES

1. To be able to define and describe the demographics of the three "economic development" categories used to classify nations of the world.
2. To begin to understand both the severity and extensiveness of poverty in the low-income nations of the world.
3. To recognize the extent to which women are overrepresented among the poor of the world and the factors leading to this condition.
4. To be able to identify and discuss the correlates of global poverty.
5. To be able to identify and discuss the two major theories used to explain global inequality.
6. To be able to identify and describe the stages of modernization
7. To be able to recognize the problems facing women as a result of modernization in the low-income nations of the world.
8. To be able to identify the keys to combating global inequality over the next century.

PART III: CHAPTER REVIEW--KEY POINTS

The extremes of poverty are emphasized in the account of a visit to the Manila dump in the Philippines. People survive off the garbage of what is called "Smokey Mountain."

GLOBAL ECONOMIC DEVELOPMENT

To truly understand ourselves we must explore how life here fits into the larger global order. The interdependence of the nations of the world is an underlying focus of this chapter. *Figure 8-1* (p. 190) divides global income by fifths of the population. The highest fifth of humanity controls 70 percent of the income.

The Problem of Terminology

Citizens of the U.S. are very well-off relative to people in most other nations. Even our poor have a higher standard of living than most people living in the poorer countries around the world. Over the last half-century societies of the world have been classified into three broad categories based on their level of technological development and their political and economic system. However, this "three worlds" model has lost its validity in recent years. In this model the capitalist West was the First World, the communist East was the Second World, and the rest of the nations represented the Third World.

The new model identifies three categories, focusing on the variable of a nation's *economic development*. This model includes *high-income, middle-income,* and *low-income countries*. Differences do exist within these broad categories. There are 191 nations in the world, each with its own unique history and present way of life.

High-Income Countries

The term *high-income countries* refers to those nations which are industrialized and relatively rich. These nations were the first to go through the Industrial Revolution. Roughly 25 percent of the land surface of the globe and 15 percent of the world's population are identified as being part of this category. Because their economies are all market-driven, economic alliances with other such nations are often made. The roughly thirty-five nations representing this economic level of development control more than one-half of the world's income.

Middle-Income Countries

The *middle-income countries* are composed of nations who have limited industrialization. About ninety of the world's nations fall in this level. Relatively more people, about half, are involved in agricultural production. The old "eastern bloc" nations, the oil-producing countries of the Middle-East, Latin American, and western African nations represent this category. Middle-income countries account for 40 percent of the world's land area and about one-third of humanity.

Low-Income Countries

The *low-income countries* encompass primarily agrarian societies that are poor. Economically these societies are less productive than the rest of the world. These societies comprise about 35 percent of the earth's land area and 52 percent of the world's population.

GLOBAL WEALTH AND POVERTY

The Severity of Poverty

The data presented in *Table 8-1* (p. 194) suggest that poverty is more *severe* in the low-income countries of the world. This table compares the GNP, per capita GDP, and quality of life indices for countries around the world. Significant differences are indicated. *Figure 8-2* (p. 195) show the relative share of global income and population by the three above mentioned categories of countries.

In high-income countries poverty is often viewed as a *relative* matter. In the low-income countries *absolute* poverty is much more critical. The people there typically lack the resources necessary to survive. The *Window on the World* box (p. 196) presents *Global Map 8-1* which shows the median age at death in various part of the word.

The Extent of Poverty

Poverty in low-income countries is also more *extensive*. Most people in these nations live in conditions far worse than the bottom 15 percent of our population. Overwhelming numbers of people are dying from starvation--40,000 people each day.

Poverty and Children

Some 75 million children in low-income countries work on the streets to assist their families. It is estimated that another 25 million have abandoned their families altogether. Many children in urban areas are abused or murdered each year.

Poverty and Women

Hardships of poverty fall harder on women than on men. Much of the work women engage in is "invisible," being outside the paid labor force. Traditions of male dominance in kinship systems further subordinate women. Men in poor societies own 90 percent of the land. These male dominated traditions are clearly illustrated in the *Global Sociology* box (p. 198) in which infanticide and sexual slavery are discussed. About two-thirds of the poor people in the world today are female. In the *Global Snapshot* box (p. 197), *Figure 8-3* show the percent of births attended by trained health personnel for several different countries.

Correlates of Global Poverty

Several factors related to the severity and extent of poverty in low-income countries are discussed. These include: (1) technology, (2) population growth, (3) cultural patterns, (4) social stratification, (5) gender inequalities, and (6) global power relationships.

The "cultural patterns" factor is discussed in the *Global Sociology* box (p. 200) in which India is focused upon as having a "different kind of poverty." The Hindu concept of *dharma*, destiny and duty, dominates people's way of understanding their poverty.

In terms of global power relationships, three key concepts are introduced. First, is the historical factor of **colonialism**, or *the process by which some nations enrich themselves through political and economic control of other nations*. As a result of this, it is argued, many nations were exploited and remain underdeveloped. A second concept is **neocolonialism**, referring to *a new form of economic exploitation involving not direct political control but the operation of multinational corporations*. The argument here is focused on **multinational corporations**, or *huge businesses that operate in many countries*.

GLOBAL INEQUALITY: THEORETICAL ANALYSIS

Modernization Theory

Modernization theory is *a model of economic development that explains global inequality in terms of technological and cultural differences among societies*. A point made by these theorists is that *historical perspective* is very important as until a few centuries ago all people in the world were poor. The development of cities during the Middle Ages and the trade and exploration that emerged, coupled with the influence of the Industrial Revolution in the eighteenth and nineteenth centuries launched certain societies ahead in living standards. Therefore, *affluence*, not deprivation is what requires explanation.

Modernization theorists suggest that new technology is likely to be exploited only in certain *cultural environments*. *Traditionalism* is the greatest barrier to economic development. It is also being suggested that all societies are converging on one general form, the *industrial model*. According to W. W. Rostow, four general stages are followed by all societies. These include: (1) The *traditional stage*, (2) the *take-off stage*, (3) The *drive to technological maturity stage*, and (4) the *high mass consumption stage*.

Rather than seeing the high-income countries as part of the cause for global inequality, modernization theorists see it as part of the solution. They see this to be so in the following respects: (1) assisting in population control through exportation of birth control technologies and the promotion of their use, (2) increasing food production by introducing "high-tech" farming methods (collectively referred to as the *Green Revolution*), (3) introducing industrial technology to increase productivity, and (4) instituting programs of foreign aid, particularly in the form of investment capital.

This theory has helped provide perspective for us in understanding how industrialization affects other dimensions of social life. These theorists point out that several societies have demonstrated significant economic developments with the help of the rich nations. However, others argue that modernization theory is just an attempt to defend and spread capitalism, and in many ways has fallen short in its own standards of success. Further, this approach tends to ignore historical facts that interfere with development. Other limitations involve a failure to make connections between rich and poor societies to see how the development of poor countries affects rich countries. Finally, the fact that this approach holds rich nations as the standard by which to judge all development is ethnocentric.

Dependency Theory

Dependency theory is *a model of economic development that explains global inequality in terms of the historical exploitation of poor societies by rich societies*. Dependency theorists argue that people in poor societies were better off in the past. They believe the economic positions of the rich and poor societies are interdependent. Once again *historical perspective* is critical.

Colonialization in Africa, Asia, and the Americas by European societies gave countries like Great Britain and Spain great power and wealth. Colonialism is no longer a force in the world; however this *political liberation* has not meant *economic autonomy*. A neocolonialism has emerged. *Figure 8-4* (p. 205) presents data on Africa's colonial history.

Immanuel Wallerstein developed a model that attempts to explain modern world inequality. A major point being made is that the world economy, a global system, is beyond the control of traditional nations, and is dominated by capitalism. Dependency of certain nations is created and maintained. This dependency is caused primarily by three factors: (1) narrow, export-oriented economies, (2) lack of industrial capacity, and (3) foreign debt.

Dependency theorists argue that rich societies create new wealth though technological innovation. As opposed to highlighting the *productivity of wealth* as modernization theorists do, dependency theorists cast global inequality in terms of the *distribution of wealth*.

Critics point out weaknesses to this perspective. First, dependency theorists seem to assume all wealth obtained by the rich nations is from the poor countries. Second, while blaming world capitalism, dependency theorists ignore factors within poor nations themselves which lead to poverty. Third, they underestimate the influence of the former Soviet Union on the poor nations. Finally, dependency theory does not produce clear policy-making alternatives.

GLOBAL INEQUALITY: LOOKING AHEAD

Table 8-2 (p. 208) summarizes the viewpoints of modernization and dependency theories in terms of how each provides perspective for understanding historical patterns, primary causes, and the role of rich nations in affecting global inequality. Those poor nations that have surged ahead economically seem to have two qualities in common: (1) they are *relatively small*, and (2) they have *traditions emphasizing individual achievement* and *economic success*.

These approaches have uncovered two keys to success during the next century in combating global poverty. The first, offered by modernization, is understanding poverty as being in part a *problem of technology*. The second, derived from dependency theory, is to see poverty as a *political problem*. The **Controversy and Debate** box (p. 209) asks the question: Will the world survive? Issues of rising population and harmful economic practices are discussed.

PART IV: KEY CONCEPTS

absolute poverty
colonialism
dependency theory
high-income countries
low-income countries
middle-income countries
modernization theory
multinational corporation
neocolonialism
relative poverty
traditionalism

PART V: IMPORTANT RESEARCHERS

Immanuel Wallerstein   W. W. Rostow

PART VI: STUDY QUESTIONS

True-False

1.   T   F   The *high-income countries*, representing 15 percent of humanity, control over one-half of the world's income.
2.   T   F   Approximately 50 percent of the world's population live in *low-income countries*.
3.   T   F   Approximately one-fourth of the population of *low-income countries* live in urban areas.
4.   T   F   *Low-income countries* are plagued by constant hunger, unsafe housing, and high rates of disease.
5.   T   F   *High-income countries* are by far the most advantaged economically, with 55 percent of the world's income supporting just 15 percent of the world's population.
6.   T   F   The death toll stemming from poverty is ten times greater than that resulting from all the world's armed conflicts.
7.   T   F   Only about 20 percent of the people living in *low-income societies* farm the land.
8.   T   F   *Modernization theory* suggests the greatest barrier to economic development is *traditionalism*.
9.   T   F   *Modernization theory* draws criticism for suggesting that the causes of global poverty lie almost entirely in poor societies themselves.
10. T   F   *Immanuel Wallerstein's* capitalist world economy model is used to illustrate and support *dependency theory*.
11. T   F   According to *dependency theory*, global inequality must be seen in terms of the distribution of wealth, as opposed to highlighting the productivity of wealth.
12. T   F   Poor nations that have surged ahead have two factors in common including being *relatively large* and having a strong *traditional* base.
13. T   F   The keys to combating global inequality during the next century lie in seeing it as partly a *problem of technology* and also a *political problem*.

Multiple Choice

1. The nickname of the Manila dump is:

   (a) Rohooven Heights   (d) Smokey Mountain
   (b) Svendoven Mire   (e) Rich Hill
   (c) Swollen Hollow

2. The *high-income countries*, representing 15 percent of the world's population, control over
   _____ percent of the world's income.

   (a) 25   (c) 50
   (b) 35   (d) 80

3. What percentage of the world's population live in the *low-income countries* of the world?

   (a) 50   (d) 85
   (b) 60   (e) 95
   (c) 77

4. The per-capita GDP in the United States is:

   (a) $10,033   (d) $24,680
   (b) $51,300   (e) $35,028
   (c) $15,400

5. Which of the following is *not* discussed as a correlate of *global poverty*?

   (a) cultural patterns   (d) social stratification
   (b) population growth   (e) all are discussed
   (c) technology

6. *Neocolonialism* is:

   (a) primarily an overt political force
   (b) a form of economic exploitation that does not involve formal political control
   (c) the economic power of the low-income countries is being used to control the
       consumption patterns in the high-income countries
   (d) the exploitation of the high-income countries by the low-income countries
   (e) none of the above

7. According to *W. W. Rostow's* modernization model, which stage is Thailand currently in?

   (a) traditional   (d) high mass consumption
   (b) take-off   (e) residual-dependency
   (c) drive to technological maturity

8.	Which of the following is *not* a criticism of modernization theory?

(a)	it tends to minimize the connection between rich and poor societies
(b)	it tends to blame the low-income countries for their own poverty
(c)	it ignores historical facts that thwart development in poor countries
(d)	it has fallen short of its own standards of success
(e)	all are criticisms of this theory

9.	Which of the following is *not* mentioned in *Immanuel Wallerstein's* capitalist world-economy model as a reason for the perpetuation of the dependency of the low-income countries?

(a)	narrow, export-oriented economies	(d)	all are mentioned
(b)	lack of industrial capacity	(e)	none are mentioned
(c)	foreign debt

10.	Which of the following is *not* a criticism of dependency theory?

(a)	it assumes that the wealth of the high-income countries is based solely on appropriating resources from low-income societies
(b)	it tends to blame the low-income countries for their own poverty
(c)	it does not lend itself to clear policy making
(d)	it assumes that world capitalism alone has produced global inequality
(e)	all of these are criticisms of this theory

Matching

1.	___	A model of economic development that explains global inequality in terms of the historical exploitation of poor societies by rich ones.
2.	___	The process by which some nations enrich themselves through political and economic control of other nations.
3.	___	The percentage of people in low-income countries who farm the land.
4.	___	Percentage of the world's income controlled by the poorest fifth of the world's population.
5.	___	Two high-income countries.
6.	___	The percentage of the world's population living in low-income countries.
7.	___	Huge businesses that operate in many countries.
8.	___	The percentage of births attended by trained health personnel in Mexico.
9.	___	A model of economic development that explains global inequality in terms of technological and cultural differences among societies.
10.	___	Two middle-income countries.

a.	South Korea and Greece	f.	52
b.	modernization theory	g.	Canada and Singapore
c.	multinational corporations	h.	77
d.	colonialism	i.	dependency theory
e.	2	j.	two-thirds

<u>Fill-In</u>

1. Compared to the older "three worlds" model, the new classification system used in the text has two main advantages, including a focus on the single most important dimension that underlies social life--_____ _____.

2. The *middle-income countries* of the world represent about _____ nations and _____ of the world's population.

3. According to our author, poverty in *low-income countries* is more _____ and more _____ than it is in the United States.

4. The United States had a GDP in 1993 of over _____ dollars.

5. _____ is a new form of economic exploitation that does not involve formal political control.

6. _____ *theorists* suggest global inequality reflects differing levels of technological development and cultural differences among societies.

7. According to *W. W. Rostow's* stages of modernization, all societies are gradually converging to one general form: the _____ *model.*

8. _____ maintains that global poverty historically stems from the exploitation of poor societies by rich societies.

9. Poor nations that have surged ahead economically have two factors in common. One is they are relatively _____. Another is they have cultural traditions emphasizing _____ and _____.

10. Two key to combating global inequality during the next century will be seeing it partly as a problem of _____ and that it is also a _____ problem.

<u>Definition and Short-Answer</u>

1. Define the terms *high-income, middle-income,* and *low-income countries.* Does this resolve the "terminology" problem?

2. How do the economies in each of the three *levels* or *categories* of countries differ from one another? Make specific reference to *Figures 8-1* and *8-2* in your answer.

3. What factors create the condition of *women* being overrepresented in poverty around the world?

4. What are the *correlates* of global poverty? Describe each.

5. What is *neocolonialism?* Provide an illustration.

6. What are the four stages of *modernization* in Rostow's model of societal change and development?

7. What are the *problems* faced by women in poor countries as a result of modernization?

8. According to *modernization* theorists, in what respects are rich nations part of the solution to global poverty?

9. Differentiate between how *modernization theory* and *dependency theory* view the primary causes of global inequality. Critique each of these theories, identifying the strengths and weaknesses of each in terms of explaining global poverty.

PART VII: ANSWERS TO STUDY QUESTIONS

True-False

1.	T	(pp. 191-192)	8.	T	(p. 201)
2.	T	(p. 192)	9.	T	(p. 203)
3.	T	(p. 193)	10.	T	(p. 204)
4.	T	(p. 193)	11.	T	(p. 206)
5.	T	(p. 195)	12.	F	(p. 208)
6.	T	(p. 196)	13.	T	(p. 208)
7.	F	(p. 199)			

Multiple Choice

1.	d	(p. 189)	6.	b	(p. 199)
2.	c	(p. 192)	7.	b	(p. 202)
3.	a	(p. 192)	8.	e	(p. 203)
4.	d	(p. 194)	9.	d	(p. 205)
5.	e	(p. 199)	10.	b	(p. 207)

Matching

1.	i	(p. 203)	6.	f	(p. 195)
2.	d	(p. 199)	7.	c	(p. 199)
3.	j	(p. 199)	8.	h	(p. 197)
4.	e	(p. 190)	9.	b	(p. 201)
5.	g	(p. 191)	10.	a	(p. 192)

Fill-In

1. economic development (p. 190)
2. 90, one-third (p. 192)
3. severe, extensive (p. 194)
4. 6.2 trillion (p. 194)
5. neocolonialism (p. 199)
6. modernization (p. 201)
7. industrial (p. 201)
8. dependency theory (p. 203)
9. small, individual achievement, economic success (p. 208)
10. technology, political (p. 208)

PART VIII: ANALYSIS AND COMMENT

Global Sociology

"Infanticide and Sexual Slavery: Reports from India and Thailand"

Key Points: Questions:

118

"A Different Kind of Poverty: A Report from India"

Key Points: Questions:

Controversy and Debate

"Will the World Starve?"

Key Points: Questions:

Window on the World--Global Map 8-1

"Median Age at Death in Global Perspective"

Key Points: Questions:

Race and Ethnicity

PART I: CHAPTER OUTLINE

I. The Social Significance of Race and Ethnicity
   A. Race
   B. Ethnicity
   C. Minorities
   D. Prejudice and Stereotypes
   E. Racism
   F. Theories of Prejudice
   G. Discrimination
   H. Institutional Prejudice and Discrimination
   I. Prejudice and Discrimination: The Vicious Cycle
II. Majority and Minority: Patterns of Interaction
   A. Pluralism
   B. Assimilation
   C. Segregation
   D. Genocide
III. Race and Ethnicity in the United States
   A. Native Americans
   B. White Anglo-Saxon Protestants
   C. African Americans
   D. Asian Americans
   E. Hispanic Americans
   F. White Ethnic Americans
IV. Race and Ethnicity: Looking Ahead
V. Summary
VI. Key Concepts
VII. Critical-Thinking Questions

PART II: LEARNING OBJECTIVES

1. To develop an understanding about the biological basis for definitions of race.
2. To be able to distinguish between the biological concept of race and the cultural concept of ethnicity.
3. To be able to identify the characteristics of a minority group.
4. To be able to identify and describe the two forms of prejudice.

5. To be able to identify and describe the four theories of prejudice.
6. Be able to distinguish between prejudice and discrimination.
7. To be able to provide examples of institutional prejudice and discrimination.
8. To be able to see how prejudice and discrimination combine to create a vicious cycle.
9. To be abe to describe the patterns of interaction between minorities and the majority.
10. To be able to describe the histories and relative statuses of each of the racial and ethnic groups identified in the text.

PART III: CHAPTER REVIEW--KEY POINTS

Skin color makes a difference in the United States. The story of Linda Brown and the Supreme Court decision of 1954 historically illustrates this fact.

THE SOCIAL SIGNIFICANCE OF RACE AND ETHNICITY

A *race* is *a category composed of men and women who share biologically transmitted traits that members of a society deem socially significant.* Over thousands of generations, the physical environments that humans lived in created physical variability. In addition, migration and intermarriage spread genetic characteristics throughout the world. During the nineteenth century biologists developed a three-part scheme of racial classification, including *Caucasian, Negroid,* and *Mongoloid.* Research confirms however that no pure races exist.

Ethnicity

Ethnicity is *a shared cultural heritage.* While race is a biological concept, ethnicity is a cultural one. However, the two overlap. Ethnic characteristics are sometimes incorrectly believed to be racial, but while ethnicity is subject to modification over time, racial identity persists over generations.

Minorities

A racial or ethnic *minority* is *a category of people, distinguished by physical or cultural traits, that is socially disadvantaged. Table 9-1* (p. 216) presents 1990 census data on the approximate sizes of different racial and ethnic groups in the United States. Minority groups have two distinctive characteristics: they maintain a *distinctive identity* characterized by endogamy, and are *subordinated* through the social stratification system. While usually being a relatively small segment of a society, there are exceptions, for example blacks in South Africa. In the *Seeing Ourselves* box (p. 217) *National Map 9-1* shows data concerning residence patterns that indicate where minority group members are actually a majority numerically.

Prejudice and Stereotypes

Prejudice is *a rigid and irrational generalization about a category of people.* Prejudices are *prejudgments* that can be positive or negative. A *Stereotype* is *a prejudiced description of a category of people.* They often involve emotions so inaccurate descriptions of a category of people are held even when evidence contradicts the descriptions.

Racism

Racism is *the belief that one racial category is innately superior or inferior to another.* Racism has a long and terrifying history. *Individual racism* involves acts such are whites who prevent a black family from moving into their neighborhood. An even more serious problem though is *institutional racism*, or racism that guides the very operation of institutions such as schools, the work place, and the criminal-justice system. The **Critical Thinking** box (p. 219) provides evidence for the argument that racial differences in mental abilities are due to environment rather than to biology.

Theories of Prejudice

Scapegoat theory suggests that frustration leads to prejudice. It further suggests that prejudice is likely to be more common among people who are themselves disadvantaged. A **scapegoat** is *a person or category of people, typically with little power, whom people unfairly blame for their own troubles.*

Authoritarian personality theory, first suggested by T. W. Adorno at the end of World War II, holds that extreme prejudice is a personality trait linked to personas who conform rigidly to cultural norms and values.

Cultural theory suggests that some prejudice takes the form of widespread cultural values. Emory Bogardus developed the concept of *social distance* to measure the attitudes toward different racial and ethnic groups.

Conflict theory argues that prejudice results from social conflict among categories of people. Prejudice is used as an ideology to legitimate the oppression of certain groups or categories of people. A different argument is also presented in this context, which focused on the climate of *race consciousness* being created by minorities themselves as a political strategy to gain power.

Discrimination

Discrimination refers to *treating various categories of people unequally.* While prejudice concerns attitudes and beliefs, discrimination involves behavior. The interrelationship between prejudice and discrimination is addressed by Robert Merton, whose analysis is reviewed in *Figure 9-1* (p. 220). Four types of people are revealed: *active bigots, timid bigots, fair-weather liberals,* and *all-weather liberals.*

Institutional Prejudice and Discrimination

Institutional prejudice and discrimination refers to *bias in attitudes or actions inherent in the operation of any of society's institutions.* For example, until the Supreme Court's *Brown* decision in 1954, the principle of "separate but equal" legally justified discrimination in education.

Prejudice and Discrimination: The Vicious Cycle

It is argued that these characteristics in our society persist because they are mutually reinforcing. The *Thomas theorem* relates to this situation. Prejudice does not produce *innate* inferiority, but rather *social* inferiority.

MAJORITY AND MINORITY: PATTERNS OF INTERACTION

Pluralism

Pluralism is *a state in which people of all races and ethnicities are distinct but have social parity.* Three barriers exist in our society which results in only limited pluralism. First, only a small proportion of our people maintain distinct racial or ethnic identity. Second, our tolerance for social diversity is limited. And third, racial and ethnic distinctiveness is sometimes forced on people. In global perspective, Switzerland may be the best example of pluralism for a nation.

Assimilation

Assimilation is *the process by which minorities gradually adopt patterns of the dominant culture.* The notion of "melting pot" is linked to the process of assimilation. However, this characterization of the United States is a misleading idealism. Instead of a new pattern emerging, minorities more often adopt the traits of the dominant culture.

The process of assimilation involves changes in ethnicity, but not race. Racial traits may diminish over the generations though *miscegenation,* or *the biological process of interbreeding among racial categories.*

Segregation

Segregation is *the physical and social separation of categories of people.* It is generally an involuntary separation of the minority groups, although voluntary segregation occurs occasionally, such as in the case of the Amish. Racial segregation has a long history in the U.S. *De jure*, or "by law" segregation has ended, however *de facto*, or "by fact" segregation continues. Many blacks live in what researchers call *hypersegregation* conditions in inner city ghettos. Individuals can make significant differences though, as the case of Rosa Parks illustrates.

Genocide

Genocide is *the systematic killing of one category of people by another.* Genocide has existed throughout history. Historical examples from around the world are discussed.

RACE AND ETHNICITY IN THE UNITED STATES

The words of Emma Lazarus, inscribed on the Statue of Liberty, provide us with a cultural ideal for opportunity in the U.S. What is the reality?

Native Americans

The term *Native Americans* refers to many distinct people who migrated from Asia to the Americas thousands of years ago. They were the original inhabitants of the Americas. Several million Native Americans lived in the Americas when the Europeans began to arrive five centuries ago. A brief history or European and U.S. relationships with Native Americans is presented in the text. For example, citizenship was not granted to Native Americans until 1924. *Table 9-2* (p. 225) reviews the social standing of Native Americans along the dimensions of income, poverty rates, and educational attainment.

White Anglo-Saxon Protestants

White Anglo-Saxon Protestants, or WASPS, have traditionally enjoyed the status of the dominant ethnic and racial category in U.S. society. Their ancestry is primarily English. They were the early, skilled, achievement-oriented settlers of American society. Their adherence to the Protestant work ethic motivated them to be productive. WASPS enjoy high income, high-prestige occupations, and memberships in the culturally dominant Protestant churches.

African Americans

African Americans accompanied Spanish explorers to the New World in the fifteenth century and officially arrived in the United States in 1619. Soon after, laws recognizing slavery were passed. Estimates put the number of Africans who were forcibly transported to the western hemisphere at 10 million. About half died in transit. Approximately 400,000 came to the United States. The thirteenth Amendment to the Constitution outlawed slavery in 1865. However, Jim Crow laws perpetuated the racial division in this country. Gunnar Myrdal coined this contradiction the *American dilemma*. In the Dredd Scott case of 1857, the Supreme Court answered whether blacks were citizens by saying no.

Important changes for African Americans have occurred in the twentieth century. Migration to northern cities brought greater work opportunities. A national civil rights movement won crucial battles that resulted in ending legal support for racially segregated schools and civil rights acts improved the opportunities for African Americans in employment and use of public accommodations. Problems persist, though, in the social standing of African Americans. The relative standing of African Americans in the U.S. in 1995 is summarized in *Table 9-3* (p. 227). The median income of African Americans is significant lower than whites. African Americans are more likely to be poor, and continue to be overrepresented in low-paying jobs. Unemployment rates has remained twice as high as for whites. Recently, African Americans have made strides in their acquisition of political power.

Asian American

Asian Americans have great cultural diversity while sharing certain racial characteristics. Asian Americans constitute 3 percent of the U.S. population. Asian Americans of Chinese and Japanese ancestry began immigrating to the West over a century ago. Filipinos, Koreans, and Vietnamese have immigrated to this country in recent years. Immigration rates for Asians are increasing.

Chinese Americans have experienced interactions with the dominant culture that have at times been discriminatory. Prior to the economic depression of the 1870s their labor was highly valued in the expansion of the West. After 1870 the Chinese were barred from some occupations. A legal end to immigration by Chinese created a sex-ratio imbalance among the Chinese population.

Japanese immigrants began to arrive in the United States in the 1860s. The Japanese, perhaps due to their small numbers, escaped the prejudice and discrimination directed at the Chinese. Immigration laws in the 1920s practically ended Japanese immigration. Overt prejudice and discrimination were directed toward the Japanese. However, two important differences between the Japanese and Chinese enhanced the position of the Japanese in the United States. First, the Japanese knew more about U.S. culture and were ready to assimilate. Second, the Japanese began

124

to farm in rural areas as opposed to living and working exclusively in urban enclaves. With World War II and the Japanese destruction of Pearl Harbor, the Japanese were treated with overt discrimination. The policy of internment of the Japanese was instituted at this time. *Table 9-4* (p. 229) review the relative social standing of Chinese, Japanese, Korean, and Filipino Americans.

Recent Asian immigrants include large numbers of Koreans, Filipinos, and Vietnamese. Asian Americans are the fastest growing minority in the U.S., accounting for one-half of all immigration into this country. In sum, the social history of Asians in this country is complex.

Hispanic Americans

Hispanic Americans are typically the descendants of a combination of Spanish, African, and Native American peoples. Hispanic Americans represent three main cultures: Mexican American, Puerto Rican, and Cuban. Hispanic Americans represent roughly 10 percent of our population and this percentage is growing rapidly due to high immigration and birth rates. *Table 9-5* (p. 231) shows data on the relative standing of these three main Hispanic cultures represented in the U.S. Further, in the **Seeing Ourselves** box (p. 232), *National Map 9-2* locates counties across the U.S. favored by Hispanics/Latinos, African Americans, and Asian Americans for residence.

The are about 14 million Mexican Americans in the United States in 1917. Illegal entry into this country puts the actual figure higher. Prejudice and discrimination have marked the relationship of Mexican Americans and whites over the years.

Puerto Ricans became citizens of the United States in 1917. Currently there are about three million Puerto Ricans living in the United States. Strong ethnic identity is maintained because over three-quarters of them continue to speak Spanish in their homes, and they are able to move between the mainland and Puerto Rico easily. Puerto Ricans have a lower social standing than other Hispanics as evidenced by more female-headed households, a fairly low median family income, and a high level of poverty.

Cubans immigrated to the United States after the 1959 socialist revolution. Currently about one million Cubans reside in the U.S. They re highly educated, have a higher median family income, and have less poverty than other Hispanics. A recent immigration of 125.000 Cuban refuges has added a poorer and less-educated component to the Cuban American population in the United States.

White Ethnic Americans

Many white Americans have traditionally been proud of their ethnic heritage. Those who are non-WASPs have been identified as *white ethnics*. Examples include German, Irish, Italian, and Jewish people. These immigrants, arriving mainly after 1840, faced hostility from WASPS, who had settled already. Overt discrimination was focused on the white ethnics during the height of immigration in the U.S.: 1880-1930. Immigration quotas restricted their entrance to the U.S. between 1921 and 1968 as a result of opposition by nativist elements. White ethnics and blacks sometimes find themselves on opposite sides of issues due to competition over valued resources in society.

RACE AND ETHNICITY: LOOKING AHEAD

Our society's great cultural diversity is the result of immigration. Immigration rates today, roughly 1,000,000 annually, at about the same level as was representative of the great immigration era of a century ago. The countries from which the people are primarily coming is changing. They face prejudice and discrimination as did immigrants before them; however, they also share the hope of opportunity, and the hope that ethnic diversity will someday be viewed as a matter of difference rather than inferiority. The *Controversy and Debate* box (pp. 234-235) reviews three points made by proponents of affirmative action and three points made by critics of affirmative action.

PART IV: KEY CONCEPTS

affirmative action
American dilemma
assimilation
authoritarian personality
Brown vs. the Board of Education of Topeka
de facto segregation
de jure segregation
discrimination
ethnicity
genocide
hypersegregation
internal colonialism
institutional discrimination
institutional prejudice
minority
miscegenation
pluralism
prejudice
race
racism
scapegoat theory
segregation
stereotype
WASP
white ethnics

PART V: IMPORTANT RESEARCHERS

Robert Merton   Emory Bogardus

T. W. Adorno   Thomas Sowell

PART VI: STUDY QUESTIONS

True-False

1. T F According to the author of our text, for sociological purposes the concepts of *race* and *ethnicity* can be used interchangeable.
2. T F A racial or ethnic *minority* is a category of people, distinguished by physical or cultural traits, who are socially disadvantaged.
3. T F The *scapegoat theory* links prejudice to frustration and suggests that prejudice is likely to be pronounced among people who themselves are disadvantaged.
4. T F In *Robert Merton's* typology of patterns of prejudice and discrimination an unprejudiced-nondiscriminator is labeled an "all-weather liberal."
5. T F According to the author, as a cultural process, *assimilation* involves changes in ethnicity but not in race.
6. T F *Native Americans* were not granted citizenship in the United States until 1924.
7. T F The *Dredd Scott* Supreme Court decision declared that blacks were to have full rights and privileges as citizens of the United States.
8. T F Though a "silent minority," *Chinese Americans* have higher poverty rates and lower average family incomes than African Americans and Hispanics.
9. T F *Cuban Americans* have the lowest average family income and highest poverty rates of all Hispanic Americans.
10. T F The highest rates of *immigration* to the United States occurred during the 1920s and 1930s.

Multiple Choice

1. Linda Brown was not permitted to enroll in the second grade at an elementary school near her home in Topeka, Kansas bcuse she was:

    (a) Jewish   (d) HIV positive
    (b) African American   (e) Iranian
    (c) blind

2. A category of men and women who share biologically transmitted traits that members of a society deem socially significant, is the definition for:

    (a) race   (c) minority group
    (b) ethnicity   (d) none of the above

3. *Minority groups* have two major characteristics:

    (a) race and ethnicity
    (b) religion and ethnicity
    (c) physical traits and political orientation
    (d) sexual orientation and race
    (e) distinctive identity and subordination

4. A *form of prejudice* that views certain categories of people as innately inferior is called:

    (a) stereotyping   (c) discrimination
    (b) racism   (d) scapegoating

5. One explanation of the origin of prejudice is found in the concept of the *authoritarian personality*. Such a personality exhibits:

    (a) an attitude of authority over others believed to be inferior
    (b) frustration over personal troubles directed toward someone less powerful
    (c) rigid conformity to cultural norms and values
    (d) social distance from others deemed inferior

6. *Robert Merton's* study of the relationship between prejudice and discrimination revealed one behavioral type that discriminates against persons even though he or she is not prejudiced. This person would be called a(n):

    (a) active bigot   (c) timid bigot
    (b) all-weather liberal   (d) fair-weather liberal

7. According to the work of W. I. Thomas, a *vicious cycle* is formed by which variables?

    (a) miscegenation and authoritarianism (d) segregation and integration
    (b) race and ethnicity   (e) prejudice and discrimination
    (c) pluralism and assimilation

8. *Pluralism* has only limited application in U.S. society because:

    (a) most Americans only want to maintain their distinctive identities to a point
    (b) society does not always allow distinctive categories to maintain separate ways of life
    (c) distinctive identities are sometimes forced on minority groups
    (d) all of the above

9. *Miscegenation* is:

    (a) the biological process of interbreeding among racial categories
    (b) the process by which minorities gradually adopt patterns of the dominant culture
    (c) a state in which all categories of people are distinct but have social parity
    (d) a condition of prejudice leading to discrimination

10. In _____ the U.S. government made Native Americans wards of the state and set out to resolve the "Indian problem."

    (a) 1770   (d) 1911
    (b) 1807   (e) 1946
    (c) 1871

128

11. Approximately what percentage of African Americans are living in poverty today?

(a) 10
(b) 19
(c) 29
(d) 41
(e) 62

12. Which category of Asian Americans has the *highest* social standing in the U.S. today?

(a) Filipino
(b) Chinese
(c) Vietnamese
(d) Korean
(e) Japanese

Matching

1. ___ A category composed of men and women who share biologically transmitted traits that members of a society deem socially significant.
2. ___ An approach contending that while extreme prejudice may characterize some people, some prejudice is found in everyone.
3. ___ Hostility toward foreigners.
4. ___ A person or category of people, typically with little power, whom people unfairly blame for their troubles.
5. ___ A theory holding that prejudice springs from frustration among people who are themselves disadvantaged.
6. ___ The process by which minorities gradually adopt patterns of the dominant culture.
7. ___ A state in which people of all races and ethnicities are distinct but have social parity.
8. ___ A shared cultural heritage.
9. ___ Non-WASPs whose ancestors lived in Ireland, Poland, Germany, Italy, or other European countries.
10. ___ A category of people, distinguished by physical or cultural traits, that is socially disadvantaged.

a. xenophobia
b. assimilation
c. minority
d. scapegoat
e. ethnicity
f. white ethnic Americans
g. cultural theory
h. pluralism
i. race
j. scapegoat theory

Fill-In

1. The term _____ refers to a category composed of men and women who share biologically transmitted traits that members of society deem socially significant.
2. The three part scheme of racial classification developed by biologists during the nineteenth century included _____, _____, and

_____.
3. While *race* is a _____ concept, *ethnicity* is a _____ concept.
4. Two major characteristics of *minorities* are that they have a _____ identity and are _____ by the social-stratification system.

5. A _____ is a set of *prejudices* concerning some category of people.
6. _____ refers to bias in attitudes or actions inherent in the operation of any of society's institutions.
7. _____ is the process by which minorities gradually adopt patterns of the dominant culture.
8. *Gunnar Myrdal* argued that the denial of basic rights and freedoms to entire categories of Americans was the _____.
9. In 1990 the *median family income* for the entire population of the U.S. was $35,225. For *Asian Americans* this figure was _____.
10. More than _____ *immigrants* have come to the U.S. each year during the 1990s.

Short-Answer and Definition

1. Identify and describe the four *explanations* of why prejudice exists.
2. Differentiate between the concepts *prejudice* and *discrimination*.
3. What are the four types of people identified by *Robert Merton's* typology of patterns of prejudice and discrimination? Provide an illustration for each.
4. What is *institutional prejudice and discrimination*? Provide two illustrations.
5. What are three criticisms of *affirmative action*? What are three reasons given by proponents of affirmative action to continue this social policy.
6. What are the four models representing the *patterns of interaction* between minority groups and the majority group? Define and discuss an illustration for each of these.
7. In what three important ways did Japanese immigration and assimilation into U.S. society differ from the Chinese?
8. How do Native Americans, African Americans, Hispanic Americans, and Asian Americans compare to whites in terms of relative social standing using the variables of *educational achievement, family income,* and *poverty rates.*
9. What was the *Dredd Scott* ruling by the Supreme Court? What was the Court's ruling in *Brown Versus the Board of Education of Topeka case*?

PART VII: ANSWERS TO STUDY QUESTIONS

True-False

1.	F	(p. 214)	6.	T	(p. 224)
2.	T	(p. 215)	7.	F	(p. 226)
3.	T	(p. 218)	8.	F	(p. 229)
4.	T	(p. 220)	9.	F	(p. 231)
5.	T	(p. 222)	10.	F	(p. 236)

Multiple Choice

1.	b	(p. 213)	7.	e	(p. 221)
2.	a	(p. 214)	8.	d	(p. 222)
3.	e	(p. 215)	9.	a	(p. 222)
4.	b	(p. 217)	10.	c	(p. 224)
5.	c	(p. 218)	11.	c	(p. 227)
6.	d	(p. 220)	12.	e	(p. 229)

Matching

1.	i	(p. 214)	6.	b	(p. 222)
2.	g	(p. 218)	7.	h	(p. 222)
3.	a	(p. 236)	8.	e	(p. 215)
4.	d	(p. 218)	9.	f	(p. 233)
5.	j	(p. 218)	10.	c	(p. 215)

Fill-In

1. race (p. 214)
2. Caucasian, Negroid, Mongoloid (pp. 214-215)
3. biological, cultural (p. 215)
4. distinctive, subordination (p. 215)
5. stereotype (p. 217)
6. institutional prejudice and discrimination (p. 220)
7. assimilation (p. 222)
8. American dilemma (p. 226)
9. $42,240 (p. 229)
10. 1,000,000 (p. 236)

PART VIII: ANALYSIS AND COMMENT

Critical Thinking

"Does Race Affect Intelligence?"

Key Points: Questions:

Controversy and Debate

"Affirmative Action: Problem or Solution?"

Key Points: Questions:

Seeing Ourselves--National Map 9-1 and 9-2

"Where the Minority-Majority Already Exists"

Key Points: Questions:

"The Concentration of Hispanics/Latinos, African Americans, and Asian Americans, by County, 1990"

Key Points: Questions:

Sex and Gender

10

PART I: CHAPTER OUTLINE

I.   Sex and Gender
    A.   Sex: A Biological Distinction
    B.   Sexual Orientation
    C.   Gender: A Cultural Distinction
    D.   Patriarchy and Sexism
II. Gender and Socialization
    A.   Gender and the Family
    B.   Gender and the Peer Group
    C.   Gender and Schooling
    D.   Gender and the Mass Media
III. Gender and Social Stratification
    A.   Working Women and Men
    B.   Gender and Education
    C.   Gender and Politics
    D.   Minority Women
    E.   Are Women a Minority?
    F.   Violence Against Women
IV. Theoretical Analysis of Gender
    A.   Structural-Functional Analysis
    B.   Social-Conflict Analysis
V.   Feminism
    A.   Basic Feminist Ideas
    B.   Variants within Feminism
    C.   Opposition to Feminism
VI. Looking Ahead: Gender in the Twenty-First Century
VII. Summary
VIII. Key Concepts
IX. Critical-Thinking Questions

PART II: LEARNING OBJECTIVES

1.   To know the distinction between sex and gender.
2.   To be able to distinguish between sex and sexual orientation.
3.   To understand the cultural component in gender and sexual orientation.
4.   To become aware of the various types of social organization based upon the relationship between females and males.

5.	To be able to describe the link between patriarchy and sexism, and to see how the nature of each is changing in modern society.
6.	To be able to describe the role that gender plays in socialization in the family, the peer group, schooling, the mass media, and adult interaction.
7.	To see how gender stratification occurs in the work world, education, and politics.
8.	To consider key arguments in the debate over whether women constitute a minority.
9.	To consider how the structural-functional and social-conflict paradigms help explain the origins and persistence of gender inequality.
10.	To begin to recognize the extent to which women are victims of violence, and to begin to understand what we can do to change this problem.
11.	To consider the central ideas of feminism, the variations of feminism and resistance to feminism.

PART III: CHAPTER REVIEW--KEY POINTS

This chapter begins with a brief account of the *beauty myth*, in which, first, women are socialized to believe that their personal importance, accomplishment, and satisfaction are to be measured in terms of physical appearance. Second, women are taught to value relationships and how their beauty is tied to them. Third, women are to be seen as objects to be possessed by men. Through all of this the positions of men and women in society are established into a social hierarchy.

SEX AND GENDER

Sex: A Biological Distinction

Sex refers to *the biological distinction between females and males.* It is determined at the moment of conception. Each fertilized egg contains 23 chromosome pairs. One of these pairs determines sex. The female always contributes the X chromosome, and the male contributes either an X or a Y chromosome. If the male contributes an X, the embryo will develop into a female. If the male contributes a Y, the embryo will develop into a male.

Two variations from male and female sexes are discussed. *Hermaphrodite*, referring to *a human being possessing some combination of female and male internal and external genitalia.* The status of such people varies cross-culturally. Another category is that of *transsexuals*, or *people who feel they are one sex though biologically they are the other.*

Sexual Orientation

Sexual orientation, is *an individual's preference in terms of sexual partners: same sex, other sex, either sex, neither sex.* The meaning of different sexual orientations varies cross-culturally, but all societies endorse *heterosexuality*, by which a person is attracted to the opposite sex. However, *homosexuality*, or attraction to members of one's own sex, is not uncommon.

Homosexuals, or *gays*, in the U.S. continue to be subjected to prejudice and discrimination. The term *lesbian* is used to refer to female homosexuals. *Homophobia*, or fear of gay people, is still quite evident in our society.

The pioneering work of Alfred Kinsey during the middle of this century showed that exclusive homosexuality represented about 4 percent of our male population and 2 percent of our female population, though 25 percent of our population has experienced at least one homosexual encounter.

Figure 10-1 (p. 241) entitled "Measuring Sexual Orientation" provides data on homosexual activity. People who have combined homosexual and heterosexual orientations are called *bisexuals*. Less than one percent of our population claim this sexual orientation. Sexual orientation is determined by a combination of factors, including biological factors present at birth, hormonal influences, and social experiences.

Gender: A Cultural Distinction

Gender refers to *the significance a society attaches to the biological categories of female and male*. Typically they are differentiated into *feminine* and *masculine* traits. Biologically, males and females reveal limited differences. The significance played by *culture* in the development of gender is illustrated by various types of research, including studies that focus on egalitarian gender role patterns in the *Israeli kibbutzim*. Other cross-cultural evidence, for example the research by anthropologist *Margaret Mead*, again uncovers the variety of ways in which masculine and feminine traits are defined and experienced by males and females. She studied three primitive societies in New Guinea--the Arapesh, the Mundugumor, and the Tchambuli. In each society very different gender-role patterns were found to have existed. Cross-cultural research by *George Murdock* in over 200 preindustrialized societies shows some consistencies in the distribution of certain tasks between females and males. However, within these general patterns, significant variation was found.

Patriarchy and Sexism

While conceptions of gender vary cross-culturally and historically, there is an apparent universal pattern of *patriarchy*, *a form of social organization in which males dominate females*.
Matriarchy, defined as *a form of social organization in which females dominate males* is not known to have ever existed. Patriarchy is based on *sexism*, or *the belief that one sex is innately superior to the other*. Some researchers argue that sexism is very similar in form to racism. *Institutionalized sexism* is also common. The *Global sociology* box (p. 244) takes a look at the case of Unity Dow, a woman from the African nation of Botswana where the tradition of patriarchy is being questioned.

The *costs of sexism* are great. It is argued that society itself, as well as men, pay a price for it. Males are more susceptible to accidents, stress, heart attacks, and other diseases that result in higher death rates for males of all ages.

Is patriarchy inevitable? Patriarchy in societies with simple technology tends to reflect biological sex differences. In industrial societies, technology minimizes the significance of any biological differences.

GENDER AND SOCIALIZATION

Males and females are encouraged through the socialization process to incorporate gender into their personal identities. *Table 10-1* (p. 245) identified the traditional gender identity characteristics along the dimensions of *masculinity* and *femininity*. Studies show that even with the cultural norms which script behavior, women and men don't exclusively exhibit gender-appropriate attributes. The pattern suggests however, that scripts may be more imposing on males than on females. *Gender roles* are *attitudes and activities that a society links to each sex*. They are the active expression of gender identity for females and males.

Gender and the Family

Jesse Bernard suggests girls and boys are born into different worlds-- the *pink* and the *blue*. The girl's world being revolving around passivity and emotion, and the boy's world placing a premium on independence and action.

Gender and the Peer Group

Janet Lever's research on peer group influences on gender suggests that the cultural lessons being taught boys and girls are very different. Boys are more likely to play in team sports with complex rules and clear objectives. Girls are more likely to be engaging in activities in smaller groups involving fewer formal rules and more spontaneity, and rarely leading to a "victory."

Carol Gilligan's has conducted research on moral reasoning that demonstrated differences between boys and girls. Girls seem to understand morality in terms of responsibility and maintaining close relationships. Boys, seem to reason more according to rules and principles.

Gender and Schooling

Research has shown that historically, males are the focus of attention in literature to a considerably greater extent than females. Further, females depicted are more typically portrayed as "objects." In the last decade this pattern has begun to change. However, at the college level, females and males still tend to select different majors and extracurricular activities.

Gender and the Mass Media

The mass media has portrayed males as dominant in U.S. culture. Women have tended to be shown as less competent than men, and often as sex objects. Children's programs also reinforce gender stereotypes. Changes in such patterns are occurring slowly. This is particularly true in advertising.

GENDER AND SOCIAL STRATIFICATION

Gender stratification refers to *the unequal distribution of wealth, power, and privilege between the two sexes*. The general conclusion is that women around the world have fewer of their society's valued resources than men.

Working Women and Men

Figure 10-2 (p. 247) presents data on labor force participation rates for women and men since 1950. The participation rate for women is increasing significantly. Several different categories of women--married, single, married with children, and divorced--are discussed. For each category, a significant majority is working. In the *Window on the World* box (p. 248), *Global Map 10-1* shows that while labor force participation of women is very high in the United States, and relatively high in other industrialized societies, the rate is very low in poor societies around the world.

Women are still positioned in the lower paying, traditionally female occupations. Almost one-half of working women fall into one of two broad occupational categories--clerical and service. *Table 10-2* (p. 249) reviews the jobs with the highest concentration of women. Men dominate virtually all other

136

job categories. Even within a given occupation category (i.e., teaching). The higher prestige jobs and higher paying jobs are usually held by males. Women working full-time earn only 75 percent of what their male counterparts earn. Research shows two-thirds of this difference to be attributed to the *type of work* in which males and females are employed, and *family-related responsibilities*. Still, one-third is attributable to discrimination. The concept of *glass-ceiling* is identified, referring to the subtle and hidden ways in which women are discriminated against in the corporate world. *Table 10-3* (p. 251) presents data on earning differences between women and men for several of occupations.

Gender and Education

Higher education was traditionally the domain of males. However, this pattern has been changing in recent decades. Over one-half of all college students today are females, and females earn 52 percent of all M.A. degrees conferred. Further, females are pursuing programs traditionally dominated by males. However, significant differences still exist, particularly in the percentage of PhDs granted, and in the areas of law and medicine.

Gender and Politics

Key events in the history of women in U.S. politics are placed in chronological order in *Table 10-4* (p. 252). While the political power of women has increased dramatically during the last century, at the highest levels of government women's roles are still minimal compared to men. In the *Seeing Ourselves* box (p. 253), *National Map 10-1* shows data concerning women in state governments across the United States.

Minority Women

Statistics indicate that minority women are doubly disadvantaged, earning less than minority men. The femininization of poverty is evident by the fact that over 50 percent of households headed by African American or Hispanic women are living in poverty.

Are Women a Minority?

Our author argues that objectively women must be viewed as a minority group given their social disadvantage and being physically distinct. However, subjectively, most women do not perceive themselves as such because of being distributed across the social-class structure of society and due to being socialized to accept their position.

Violence Against Women

It is argued that, in part, violence directed against women by men is the result of the cultural devaluing of what is feminine. One type of violence against women is sexual--violence which is fundamentally about power not sex. Another type of violence is *sexual harassment*, or *comments, gestures, or physical contact of a sexual nature that are deliberate, repeated, and unwelcome*. Currently the *effect standard* is being used to determine if sexual harassment exists. The underlying factor is the existence of a *hostile environment*. *Pornography* is another form of violence against women. The challenge of trying to define pornography is discussed, along with the surrounding *moral* and *political* issues.

THEORETICAL ANALYSIS OF GENDER

Structural-Functional Analysis

Using this perspective, gender-role patterns over history and cross-culturally are understood to be the result of the functional contributions made to the survival of society. Industrial technology has allowed greater variation in gender roles. However, gender roles still reflect long-standing institutionalized attitudes.

Talcott Parsons theorized that gender plays a part in maintaining society in industrial times by providing men and women with a set of *complimentary roles (instrumental and expressive)*. Through socialization males and females adopt these roles.

Criticisms of this approach include the lack of recognition that many women have traditionally worked outside the home, the over-emphasis on only one kind of family, and the neglect of the personal strains associated with such a family orientation.

Social-Conflict Analysis

Focus here is on inequality between women and men. This theoretical view holds that women are a minority group and men benefit by the unequal relationship which is perpetuated by sexism and sexist ideology. *Friedrich Engels* identified the historical formation of social classes to the origins of gender inequality. The creation of property and social classes were seen by Engels as the basis of male dominance over females.

One criticism of this approach is that it neglects the cooperation of females and males in the institution of the family. Another criticism is that capitalism is not the origin of gender stratification since socialist societies are patriarchal as well. And finally, critics say that this approach casts traditional families as evil.

FEMINISM

Feminism is *the advocacy of social equality for the sexes, in opposition to patriarchy and sexism.* Its *first wave* in this country occurred in the mid-nineteenth century, culminating with the right to vote for women in 1920. The *second wave* began in the 1960s and continues today.

Basic Feminist Ideas

Feminism shares at least two qualities with the sociological perspective: first, questioning of our basic assumptions about social patterns; and second, an awareness of the relationship between personal experiences and society.

There are differences in opinion among feminists, but most support five basic principles which include: *the importance of change, expanding human choice, eliminating gender stratification, ending sexual violence, and sexual autonomy. Figure 10-3* (p. 258) shows the use of contraception by married women of childbearing age. Wide variation exists. The ERA, first proposed in Congress in 1923, has had considerable support; however, the failure to formally enact the ERA seems to suggest resistance is still strong.

Variation of Feminism

Three distinct forms of feminism are identified. These include: (1) *liberal feminism*, which accepts the basic organization of society, but seeks the same rights and opportunities for women and men, (2) *socialist feminism*, which supports the reforms of liberal feminism, but believes they can be gained only through the elimination of the capitalist economy, and (3) *radical feminism*, which advocates the elimination of patriarchy altogether by organizing a gender-free society. The *Exploring Cyber-Society* box (p. 259) discusses how technological development affects gender stratification .

Opposition to Feminism

Reasons for opposition to feminism include a preference for traditional gender and family definitions, a concern that our self-identity will be subject to change, and a fear or ignorance of what feminism is in actuality. One final issue concerns opinions about how change should occur. Nationally though, only about 34 percent of all adults support a gender-based division of labor.

Looking Ahead: Gender in the Twenty-First Century

Several general observations are being made: First, the trend over the last century or so in our society has been toward greater equality between the sexes. Second, while strong opposition to the feminist movement remains, deliberate policies toward reducing patriarchy are advancing the status of women. Finally, while radical change in views about gender is not likely in the short-term, movement toward greater equality in rights and opportunities for females and males will continue to gain strength. The *Controversy and Debate* box (p. 261) concerns men's rights, asking if men are really so privileged.

PART IV: KEY CONCEPTS

bisexual
expressive qualities
femininity
feminism
gender
gender identity
gender roles
gender stratification
heterosexuality
hermaphrodite
homophobia
homosexual
instrumental qualities
kibbutzim
masculinity
matriarchy
patriarchy

pornography
sex
sexual harassment
sexual orientation
transsexuals

PART V: IMPORTANT RESEARCHERS

Alfred Kinsey   Margaret Mead

George Murdock   Talcott Parsons

Jesse Bernard   Janet Lever

PART VI: STUDY QUESTIONS

True-False

1. T   F   *Hermaphrodites* are scorned and viewed negatively in all known societies.
2. T   F   The research by *Alfred Kinsey* suggests sexual orientations may not be mutually exclusive.
3. T   F   While *gender identity* is a personality characteristic that is predominantly created culturally, *sexual orientation* is clearly rooted in biology.
4. T   F   The conclusions made by *Margaret Mead* in her research on three New Guinea societies is consistent with the sociobiological argument that "persistent biological distinctions may undermine gender equality."
5. T   F   *George Murdock's* cross-cultural research has shown some general patterns in terms of which type of activities are classified as *masculine* or *feminine*.
6. T   F   In global perspective, societies consistently define only a few specific activities as *feminine* or *masculine*.
7. T   F   Research suggests that the vast majority of young people in the United States develop consistently "masculine" or "feminine" personalities.
8. T   F   *Carol Gilligan's* research on patterns of moral reasoning suggests that boys learn to reason according to "rules and principles" more so than girls.
9. T   F   In 1995, 66.6 percent of people in the U.S. ages sixteen and over were working for income: 75 percent of men and 58.9 percent of women.
10. T   F   Women with children under the age of six years have a much smaller proportion of their number working in the labor force than married women with no children.
11. T   F   Approximately two-thirds of the *pay gap* between men and women is the result of two factors--types of work and family responsibilities.
12. T   F   *Minority females* earn more on average than minority males.
13. T   F   The *ERA* was first proposed to Congress in 1972.
14. Y   F   The ideology of *liberal feminism* respects the family as a social institution.

Multiple Choice

1. _____ refers to the biological distinction between females and males.

    (a)   sex   (c)   sexuality
    (b)   gender   (d)   sexual orientation

141

2.   Which of the following is correct?

   (a)   women always contribute the Y chromosome during conception

3.   The female embryo will develop if:

   (a)   the father contributes an X chromosome and the mother contributes an X chromosome
   (b)   the father contributes an X chromosome and the mother contributes a Y chromosome
   (c)   the mother contributes an X chromosome and the father contributes a Y chromosome
   (d)   the mother contributes a Y chromosome and the father contributes a Y chromosome

4.   A hormone imbalance before birth that results in the birth of a child with one male and female internal and external genitals is termed a(n):

   (a)   transsexual   (c)   hermaphrodite
   (b)   bisexual   (d)   aphrodisiac

5.   The social inequality of men and women has been shown to be culturally based rather than exclusively biological by which of the following studies:

   (a)   Murdock's study of preindustrial societies
   (b)   Israeli kibbutzim studies
   (c)   New Guinea studies by Margaret Mead
   (d)   all of the above

6.   Among the *Mundugumor*, Margaret Mead found:

   (a)   both females and males to be very passive
   (b)   females to be very aggressive and males to be passive
   (c)   both males and females to be aggressive and hostile
   (d)   sex roles to be very similar to what they are in the U.S.

7.   A form of social organization in which females are dominated by males is termed:

   (a)   matriarchal   (c)   patriarchal
   (b)   oligarchal   (d)   egalitarian

8.   Which sociologist suggests that, soon after birth, family members introduce infants to either a *pink* or a *blue* world, depending on whether the infant is a she or a he?

   (a)   Karl Marx   (c)   George Murdock
   (b)   Jesse Bernard   (d)   Talcott Parsons

9. Which of the following statements about women in the labor force is *inaccurate*?

   (a) most married women are in the paid labor force
   (b) most married women without children are in the paid labor force
   (c) most married women with children under the age of six are in the paid labor force
   (d) about 46 percent of all women in the paid labor force work in either clerical or service type jobs
   (e) less than one-half of all divorced women with children work in the paid labor force

10. On average, what percentage of a male's income does a female earn?

   (a) 39   (d) 75
   (b) 48   (e) 89
   (c) 57

11. *Talcott Parsons* argued that there exist two *complementary role sets* which link males and females together with social institutions. He called these:

   (a) rational and irrational   (d) residual and basic
   (b) effective and affective   (e) instrumental and expressive
   (c) fundamental and secondary

12. Which theorist suggested that the male dominance over women was linked to technological advances which led to surpluses of valued resources?

   (a) Talcott Parsons   (c) Friedrich Engels
   (b) Erving Goffman   (d) Janet Lever

Matching

1. ___ The biological distinction between females and males.
2. ___ An individual's preference in terms of sexual partners.
3. ___ The significance society attaches to the biological categories of females and male.
4. ___ The advocacy of social equality for the sexes in opposition to patriarchy and sexism.
5. ___ The belief that one sex is innately superior to the other.
6. ___ The father's chromosome that results in a male embryo.
7. ___ The unequal distribution of wealth, power, and privilege between the two sexes.
8. ___ The chromosome always contributed by the mother.
9. ___ Attitudes and activities that a society links to each sex.
10. ___ A human being with some combination of female and male internal and external genitalia.
11. ___ Did cross-cultural research on gender roles and suggested culture largely determined differences in the relative statuses and roles of females and males.
12. ___ A structural-functionalist, differentiated between instrumental and expressive roles.

a.	sexual orientation	g.	Y chromosome
b.	feminism	h.	sex
c.	Margaret Mead	i.	hermaphrodite
d.	gender	j.	gender roles
e.	gender stratification	k.	Talcot Parsons
f.	sexism	l.	X chromosome

Fill-In

1. The _____ _____ teaches women to measure their importance in terms of their physical appearance, teaches women to let men assess their beauty and significance, and primes men to seek and possess physically beautiful women.

2. *Sexual* _____ is an individual's preference in terms of sexual partners.

3. The irrational fear of gay people is known as _____.

4. _____ is a form of social organization in which *females dominate males*.

5. _____ _____ are attitudes and activities that a culture links to each sex.

6. _____ refers to the unequal distribution of wealth, power, and privilege between the sexes.

7. In 1995, 75 percent of men and _____ percent of women over the age of 16 were in the *labor force*.

8. Almost one-half of all working women fall within two broad *occupational categories*: _____ and _____.

9. In 1995, _____ percent of all associate and bachelor's degrees were granted to females.

10. The two types of *violence* against women focused on in the text include _____ and _____.

11. Basic *feminist ideas* include--the importance of _____, the expanding human _____, eliminating gender _____, ending sexual _____, and promoting sexual _____.

12. The three types of *feminism* are _____, _____, and _____.

Definition and Short-Answer

1. Briefly review the significant events in the history of the *Women's Movement* during the nineteenth century.

2. What does *Alfred Kinsey* mean by the statement that "in many cases, sexual orientations are not mutually exclusive."

3. Compare the research by *Margaret Mead* in New Guinea with the research done at the Israeli *Kibbutzim* in terms of the cultural variability of gender roles.

4. What generalizations about the linkage between *sex* and *gender* can be made based on the cross-cultural research of *George Murdock*?

5. According to the author, is *patriarchy* inevitable? Why? What roles have technological advances and industrialization played in the changes in the relative statuses of women and men in society?

6. *Table 10-1* presents lists of traits linked to the traditional gender identities of *femininity* and *masculinity*. Develop a questionnaire using the traits identified in this table to survey females and males to determine to what extent these traits differentiate between the sexes.

7. Identify five important points about *gender stratification* within the occupational domain of our society.

8. What are the explanations as to why males dominate *politics*? To what extent are the roles of women changing in this sphere of social life? What factors are influencing these changes?

9. Review the issue of *violence against women* in our society. What are the types of violence discussed? What are the demographics of violence?

10. Are women a *minority group*? What are the arguments for and against this idea?

11. Compare the analyses of gender stratification as provided through the *structural-functional* and *social-conflict* paradigms.

12. What are the five *basic principles* accepted by most *feminists*? Discuss the specific examples for each.

13. What are the three types of *feminism*? Briefly differentiate between them in terms of the basic arguments being made about gender roles in society.

14. What are the three general criticism of the conclusions being made by *social-conflict* theorists concerning gender stratification?

15. What evidence can you provide from your own experience and observations concerning the argument being made by *Jesse Bernard* about the *pink* and *blue* worlds?

PART VII: ANSWERS TO STUDY QUESTIONS

True-False

1.	F	(p. 240)	8.	T	(p. 246)
2.	T	(p. 241)	9.	F	(p. 247)
3.	F	(p. 240)	10.	F	(p. 249)
4.	F	(p. 243)	11.	T	(p. 251)
5.	T	(p. 243)	12.	F	(p. 253)
6.	T	(p. 245)	13.	F	(p. 258)
7.	F	(p. 246)	14.	T	(p. 258)

Multiple-Choice

1.	a	(p. 239)	7.	c	(p. 243)
2.	e	(pp. 239-240)	8.	b	(p. 246)
3.	a	(p. 240)	9.	e	(p. 249)
4.	c	(p. 240)	10	d	(p. 250)
5.	d	(pp. 242-243)	11.	e	(p. 256)
6.	c	(p. 243)	12.	c	(p. 257)

<u>Matching</u>

1.	h	(p. 239)	7.	e	(p. 247)
2.	a	(p. 240)	8.	l	(p. 240)
3.	d	(p. 242)	9.	j	(p. 245)
4.	b	(p. 257)	10.	i	(p. 240)
5.	f	(p. 244)	11.	c	(p. 243)
6.	g	(p. 240)	12.	k	(p. 255)

<u>Fill-In</u>

1. beauty myth (p 239)
2. orientation (p. 240)
3. homophobia (p. 241)
4. matriarchy (p. 243)
5. gender roles (p. 245)
6. gender stratification (p. 247)
7. 58.9 (p. 247)
8. clerical, service (p. 247)
9. 55 (p. 251)
10. sexual harassment, pornography (p. 254)
11. change, choice, stratification, violence, autonomy (pp. 257-258)
12. liberal, socialist, radical (pp. 258-259)

PART VIII: ANALYSIS AND COMMENT

Global Sociology

"Patriarchy Breaking Down: A Report from Botswana"

Key Points: Questions:

Controversy and Debate

"Men's Rights! Are Men Really So Privileged?"

Key Points: Questions:

146

Exploring Cyber-Society

"Is Gender Part of Virtual Reality?"

Key Points: Questions:

Window on the World--Global Map 10-1

"Women's Paid Employment in Global Perspective"

Key Points: Questions:

Seeing Ourselves--National Map 10-1

"Women in State Government across the U.S.

Key Points: Questions:

Economics and Politics

PART I: CHAPTER OUTLINE

I. The Economy: Historical Overview
  A. The Agricultural Revolution
  B. The Industrial Revolution
  C. The Information Revolution and the Postindustrial Society
  D. Sectors of the Economy
  E. The Global Economy
II. Global Economic Systems
  A. Capitalism
  B. Socialism
  C. Democratic Socialism and State Capitalism
  D. Relative Advantages of Capitalism and Socialism
  E. Changes in Socialist Countries
III. Work in the Postindustrial Economy
  A. The Changing Work Place
  B. Labor Unions
  C. Professions
  D. Self-Employment
  E. Unemployment
  F. Social Diversity in the Work Place
  G. Technology and Work
IV. Corporations
  A. Economic Concentration
  B. Conglomerates and Corporate Linkages
  C. Corporation and Competition
  D. Looking Ahead: The Economy of the Twenty-First Century
V. Politics: Historical Overview
VI. Comparative Political Systems
  A. Monarchy
  B. Democracy
  C. Authoritarianism
  D. Totalitarianism
  E. A Global Political System?

148

PART II: LEARNING OBJECTIVES

1.   To be able to identify the elements of the economy.
2.   To be able to review the history and development of economic activity from the Agricultural Revolution through to the Postindustrial Revolution.
3.   To be able to identify and describe the three sectors of the economy.
4.   To be able to compare the economic systems of capitalism, state capitalism, socialism, and democratic socialism.
5.   To be able to explain the difference between socialism and communism.
6.   To be able to describe the general characteristics and trends of work in the U.S. postindustrial society.
7.   To begin to see the impact of multinational corporations on the world economy.
8.   To recognize the difference between power and authority.
9.   To be able to compare the four principal kinds of political systems.
10.   To be able to describe the nature of the American political system of government, and discuss the principal characteristics of the political spectrum of the U.S.
11.   To be able to compare the pluralist and power-elite models of political power.
12.   To be able to describe the types of political power that exceed, or seek to eradicate, established politics.
13.   To be able to identify the factors which increase the likelihood of war.
14.   To recognize the historical pattern of militarism in the United States and around the world, and to consider factors which can be used in the pursuit of peace.

PART III: CHAPTER REVIEW--KEY POINTS

This chapter focuses on two major social institutions of society--the economy and politics. A *social institution* is being defined as *organized spheres of social life, or societal subsystem, designed to meet human needs.*

THE ECONOMY: HISTORICAL OVERVIEW

The *economy* is *the social institution that organizes a society's production, distribution, and consumption of goods and services. Goods* ar commodities that range from basic necessities to luxury items. *Services* include various activities that benefit others.

The Agricultural Revolution

The harnessing of animals to plows some five thousand years ago produced revolutionary change. The four factors of *agricultural technology, productive specialization, permanent settlements,* and *trade* have been important in the development of economy. Economic expansion has also created greater inequalities.

The Industrial Revolution

Five revolutionary changes are identified as resulting in the Industrial Revolution of Europe. These include: *new forms of energy, the spread of factories, manufacturing and mass production, specialization,* and *wage labor.* Greater productivity steadily raised the standard of living.

The Information Revolution and the Postindustrial Society

By 1950, further changes created the beginning of the *postindustrial society, a productive system based on service work and high technology.* Most jobs in our society are service related and not part of industrial production. A critical part of the postindustrial economy is the *Information Revolution.* Three key changes unleashed by the Information Revolution include: (1) *From tangible products to ideas,* (2) *From mechanical skills to literacy skills,* and (3) *The decentralization of work away from factories.*

Sectors of the Economy

The *primary sector* is *the part of the economy that generates raw materials directly from the natural environment.* In the *Window on the World* box, (p. 270), *Global Map 11-1* places agricultural employment in global perspective. Agriculture is included in the primary sector. The *secondary sector* is *the part of the economy that transforms raw materials into manufactured goods.* The *tertiary sector* is *the part of the economy involving services rather than goods.* About 70 percent of our labor force is employed in such work today. In the *Window on the World* box (p. 270) *Global Map 11-2* shows the scope of industrial employment worldwide. *Figure 11-1* (p. 268) shows the relative sizes of the three sectors of the economy for low, middle, and high-income countries.

The Global Economy

The *global economy* is *economic activity across national borders*. There are three main consequences of a global economy. These include: *products pass through many national economies, national governments no longer control their economies,* and *large companies control more economic activity.*

GLOBAL ECONOMIC SYSTEMS

Capitalism

Capitalism is *an economic system in which natural resources and the means of producing goods and services are privately owned.* This system has four distinctive features: *private ownership of property, pursuit of personal profit, free competition,* and *consumer sovereignty.* However, even the leading capitalist society of the U.S., the government affects our economy very significantly. The government owns and operates specific parts of the economy. It also assumes economic responsibility in bailout situations.

Socialism

Socialism is *an economic system in which natural resources and the means of producing goods and services are collectively owned.* Its distinguishing characteristics include: *collective ownership of property, pursuit of collective goals,* and *government control of the economy.* The extent of socialism in the word has declined in recent years.

Democratic Socialism and State Capitalism

Several western European democracies have introduced socialist policies through elections. *Democratic socialism* is *an economic and political system that combines significant government control of the economy with free elections.* Sweden and Italy are examples. These societies have high taxes and less extremes of social inequality.

Yet another variant of this economic form is *state capitalism,* in which privately owned companies cooperate closely with the government. Japan, South Korea, and Singapore are examples.

Relative Advantages of Capitalism and Socialism

Precise objective comparisons are not possible. Many factors affect a society's economic performance, including historical and cultural patterns, variations in the size and composition of the labor force, available natural resources, different levels of technological development, and trade alliances. One domain of comparison is in terms of *productivity*. Using GDP as a measure, the average figure for the capitalist systems was 2.7 times greater than for socialist systems. Another domain for comparison is *economic inequality*. Capitalist economies produce a higher overall standard of living but with greater income disparity than socialist systems. One final domain for comparison is in *civil liberties*. Broader political freedoms exist in the capitalist systems.

151

Changes in Socialist Countries

Economic reform in the socialist world has been very significant. The reasons for the changes are broad and complex. The rate of market reform varies among the old socialist countries.

WORK IN THE POSTINDUSTRIAL ECONOMY

In 1995 there were 132 million people, or two-thirds of those over the age of fifteen in the labor force. A larger proportion of men (75 percent) than women (58.9 percent) had income-producing jobs, but the gap is getting smaller. In the *Seeing Ourselves* box (p. 274), *National Map 11-1* shows labor force participation across the United States.

The Changing Work Place

Currently, less than 3 percent of the U.S. labor force is involved in farming. *Figure 11-2* (p. 275) shows the changing pattern of work in the U.S. In 1996, more than two-thirds of employed women and men held white-collar jobs. Most of these people held service jobs that afford workers only a modest standard of living.

Labor Unions

In recent years there has been a significant decline in labor union, or organizations of workers seeking to improve wages and working conditions. Today, only 15 percent of the non-farm labor force is unionized. Compared to other industrialized societies the U.S. has relatively low union membership. Several factors are related to this decline. First, the blue-collar sector of the economy has been experiencing massive layoffs in recent decades. Second, most newly created jobs are found in the service tertiary sector (service jobs), which is far less likely to be unionized.

Professions

A *profession* is *a prestigious, white-collar occupation that requires extensive formal education.* Professions share the following characteristics: *theoretical knowledge, self-regulating practice, authority over clients,* and *an orientation to community rather than to self-interest.*

Self-Employment

Self-employment refers to earning a living without working for a large organization. In the early nineteenth century, about 80 percent of the labor force was self-employed. By 1870, only about one-third, and by 1940 only one in five. Today, about 8 percent of the labor force is classified as self-employed--9 percent of men and 6 percent of women.

Unemployment

Some unemployment is found in all societies. Currently, about 5.6 percent of the people in the U.S. over the age of 16 are unemployed. *Figure 11-3* (p. 277) illustrates unemployment patterns for various categories of adults in 1995.

Social Diversity in the Work Place

The proportion of women, racial minorities, and ethnic minorities in the labor force is dramatically increasing. The *Social Diversity* box (p. 278) takes a closer look at the increasing diversity of the U.S. labor force.

Technology and Work

The increasing role of the computer in the postindustrial age is discussed. The issues of the *deskilling* of labor, work as becoming more *abstract*, the *limiting of workplace interaction*, and the *increasing supervision and control* of workers. given the computer revolution, are discussed.

CORPORATIONS

A *corporation* is *an organization with a legal existence, including rights and liabilities, apart from those of its members*. Of some 20 million businesses in the United States, 4 million are incorporated. There are two primary benefits of incorporating, including protection of owners from personal liability, and providing advantages under tax laws which increase profits.

Economic Concentration

While one-half of U.S. corporations are small, with assets of under 100,000, the largest corporations dominate the U.S. economy. Over this century there has been a tremendous concentration of national and international economic power.

Conglomerates and Corporate Linkages

A *conglomerate* is a giant corporation composed of many smaller corporations. Another type of linkage between corporations is called an *interlocking directorate*, or social networks made up of people who simultaneously serve on the boards of directors of many corporations. This is an important part of the U.S. economic system. It tends to concentrate power.

Corporations and Competition

Monopoly, or *domination of a market by a single producer*, was declared a century ago by the government to be against the public welfare. Monopolies have been limited, but *oligopoly*, or *domination of a market by a few producers*, persists.

Corporations and the Global Economy

Advantages and disadvantages of multinational corporations for rich and poor nations ar discussed. Foreign corporations own more of the U.S. than U.S. corporations own abroad. *Figure 11-4* (p. 280) illustrates how labor costs are less expensive in poor countries.

153

Looking Ahead: The Economy of the Twenty-First Century

Three important societal transformations are identified and discussed, including the *Information Revolution*, the growth of the *global economy*, and rethinking of conventional *economic models*. Two conclusions are drawn--the economic future of the U.S. and other nations will be played out around the world, and we will all confront the ever-pressing issue of global inequality.

POLITICS: HISTORICAL OVERVIEW

Politics refers to *the social institution that distributes power, sets a society's agenda, and makes decisions.* Max Weber defined *power* as *the ability to achieve desired ends despite opposition.* **Authority**, said Weber, is *power people perceive as legitimate rather than coercive.* Weber identified three general contexts in which power is commonly defined as authority.

Traditional authority is power legitimated by respect for long-established cultural patterns. This type of power is very common in preindustrialized societies. It has a scared character. *Rational-legal authority*, or bureaucratic authority, is power legitimated by legally enacted rules and regulations. It stresses achievement over ascribed characteristics, and underlies most authority in the U.S. today. *Charismatic authority* is power legitimated through extraordinary personal abilities that inspire devotion and obedience. Charismatic movements are very dependent on their leader. The long-term persistence of such a movement requires ***routinization of charisma***, or *the transformation of charismatic authority into some combination of traditional and bureaucratic authority.* Christianity is an example of this process.

COMPARATIVE POLITICAL SYSTEMS

Government refers to *a formal organization that directs the political life of a nation.* The 191 nations of the world manifest many different types of governments, but they virtually all bear close resemblance to one of four types of political systems.

Monarchy

A ***monarchy*** is *a type of political system that transfers power from generation to generation within a single family.* It is legitimated primarily through tradition. *Absolute monarchies* dominated from England to China, and remained widespread until early in the twentieth century. Today, several countries, such as Great Britain, Sweden, and the Netherlands, have *constitutional monarchies*, in which monarchs are merely symbolic heads of state.

Democracy

Democracy refers to *a political system giving power to the people as a whole.* A representative democracy places authority in the hands of elected officials who are accountable to the people. This type of system is most common in the relatively rich industrial societies of the world. They are characterized by rational-legal patterns of authority and function as bureaucracies.

Political *freedom* in the "West" has meant *liberty.* In socialist societies freedom has traditionally meant *freedom from basic want.* In the ***Window on the World*** box (p. 282), *Global Map 11-3* puts political freedom into global perspective. Only 20 percent of the world's population is "politically free."

154

Authoritarianism

Authoritarianism refers to *a political system that denies popular participation in government.* While to some degree this is true for all political systems, as used here, authoritarianism characterizes political systems that are indifferent to people's lives.

Totalitarianism

A more severe political control characterizes **totalitarianism**, *a highly centralized political system that extensively regulates peoples lives.* Such systems have emerged only within this century as technological means have enabled such leaders to rigidly regulate citizen's lives. Such systems bridge the political continuum from the far right, like Nazi Germany, to the far left, like the People's Republic of China. Socialism, an economic system, is not to be confused with totalitarianism, a political system.

A Global Political System?

Multidimensional corporations and the Information Revolution are identified as forces that are changing the nature of global politics.

POLITICS IN THE UNITED STATES

As a democracy, the U.S. system is distinctive given certain historical events, economic forces, and cultural traits.

POLITICS IN THE UNITED STATES

U.S. Culture and the Growth of Government

Our tradition of valuing individualism is guaranteed in the Bill of Rights, and the self-reliance and competition which emerges supports our capitalist economy. While Americans do not like "too much" government, almost everyone thinks that government is necessary. Federal spending today is 1.6 trillion dollars annually. It was a mere 4.5 million dollars in 1789. *Figure 11-5* (p. 285) illustrates though that as big as our government is, most high income countries have higher taxes than we do here in the U.S.

The Political Spectrum

The *political spectrum* ranges from the extreme liberals on the left to the extreme conservatives on the right. Historically the Republican Party has been more conservative and the Democratic party more liberal.

Attitudes in the U.S. differ on two kinds of issues--*economic* and *social*. Democrats tend to support more extensive government involvement in the economy than the Republicans would support. The Democratic Party is more liberal on social issues than the Republican party. Political attitudes vary by race also.

155

Political party identification in the U.S. is relatively weak compared to European democracies. *Table 11-1* (p. 287) reviews the political party identification in the U.S. for 1994.

Special-Interest Groups

A *special-interest group* refers to political alliances of people interested in a particular economic or social issue. Many such groups employ lobbyists who represent their concerns to the government. *Political Action Committees* (PACS) are organizations formed by special-interest groups, independent of political parties, to pursue political aims by raising and spending money.

Voter Apathy

Despite socialization influences, formal and informal, many people express indifference concerning politics. Voter apathy has recently been found to be worse in the United States than in most other industrialized democracies. The likelihood of voting increases with age and varies by race, ethnicity, and sex.

There are many causes for this apathy--registration rules, physical disabilities, and illiteracy are three examples. Being satisfied with social conditions as they are can also reduce voter participation. Conservatives believe *indifference* is the cause of voter apathy. For liberals, the cause is seen as *alienation*.

THEORETICAL ANALYSIS OF POLITICS

The Pluralist Model: Structural-Functional Analysis

The *pluralist model* is *an analysis of politics that views power as dispersed among many competing interest groups*. Politics is seen as mediating between many competing organizational interests. Organizations then operate as *veto groups*. Negotiating alliances and compromises are believed to be crucial in this process.

The Power-Elite Model: Social-Conflict Analysis

The *power-elite model* is *an analysis of politics that views power as concentrated among the rich*. The term was introduced by C. Wright Mills in 1956. He perceived the U.S. society, its economy, government, and military, as being dominated by a coalition of families. Research by Robert and Helen Lynd suggests that this was true in the typical U.S. city. They studied Muncie, Indiana and referred to it as Middletown.

How these models help us answer certain questions concerning the distribution and operation of power in our society is reviewed in *Table 11-2* (p. 288). The debate between the pluralists and "elitists" will not be resolved soon as there is evidence to support each view. However, the balance of the research seems to provide support for the power-elite model. In the *Global Snapshot* box (p. 290), *Figure 11-6* provides public opinion survey data supporting the power-elite model.

POWER BEYOND THE RULES

Political Revolution

Political revolution is *the overthrow of one political system in order to establish another.* While reform involves change within a system, revolution means change of the system itself. Several general patterns characterize revolutions. These include: *rising expectations, unresponsive government, radical leadership by intellectuals,* and *establishing a new legitimacy.*

Terrorism

Terrorism, or *violence or the threat of violence employed by an individual or group as a political strategy,* characterized the decade of the 1980s. Three insights are offered about terrorism. First, it elevates violence to a legitimate political tactic. Second, it is especially compatible with totalitarian governments as a means of sustaining widespread fear and intimidation. Third, extensive civil liberties make democratic societies vulnerable to terrorism. While many societies are target, one-fourth of all acts of terrorism worldwide are directed against the United States.

An additional form of terrorism is *state terrorism,* or the use of violence without support of law against individuals or groups by a government or its agents.

WAR AND PEACE

War is *armed conflict among the people of various societies, directed by their governments. Figure 11-7* (p. 293) shows data on deaths of Americans in ten U.S. wars.

The Causes of War

War, according to research, is not the result of some natural human aggressive tendency. It is a product of society. The following factors are identified by Quincy Wright as promoting war: *perceived threats, social problems, political objectives, moral objectives,* and *the absence of alternatives.*

The Costs and Causes of Militarism

The cost of militarism runs far greater than actual war. To fund it, governments must divert resources away from social needs. Seventeen percent of our federal budget goes to fund our military. The *arms race,* a mutually reinforcing escalation of military might, has developed. The *military-industrial complex* refers to *a close association among the government, the military, and defense industries.*

Nuclear Weapons and War

Nuclear proliferation refers to the acquisition of nuclear weapons technology by more and more societies. The current list of nations possessing nuclear capability are identified, as well as those which are close to having such capability.

The Pursuit of Peace

Several approaches are identified as means of reducing the danger of nuclear war. These include: *maintaining the status quo, high-technology defense, diplomacy and disarmament,* and *resolving underlying conflict.*

Looking Ahead: Politics in the Twenty-First Century

Three critically important dilemmas and trends are identified and discussed--*the growth of global politics, the broader range of political systems,* and *the looming danger of war.* The **Controversy and Debate** box (p. 295) looks at how new information technology is likely to affect political democracy.

PART IV: KEY CONCEPTS

Economics:

capitalism
communism
conglomerates
corporation
democratic socialism
economy
interlocking directorate
labor unions
monopoly
oligopoly
postindustrial economy
primary sector
profession
secondary sector
socialism
tertiary sector

Politics:

arms race
authoritarianism
authority
charismatic authority
democracy
government
military-industrial complex
monarchy
peace
pluralist model
political Action Committees
politics

power
power-elite model
rational-legal authority
revolution
routinization of charisma
special-interest group
state terrorism
totalitarianism
traditional authority
voter apathy
war

PART V: IMPORTANT RESEARCHERS

Max Weber   C. Wright Mills

Robert and Helen Lynd   Quincy Wright

PART VI: STUDY QUESTIONS

True-False

1.   T   F   The *economy* includes the production, distribution, and consumption of both goods and services.
2.   T   F   *Agriculture*, as a subsistence strategy, emerged some five thousand years ago.
3.   T   F   The *primary sector* of the economy is the part of the economy that generates raw material directly from the natural environment.
4.   T   F   The terms *primary, secondary,* and *tertiary* referring to sectors in the economy, imply a ranking in importance for our society.
5.   T   F   *Socialism* is being defined as both a political and economic system.
6.   T   F   Per capita GDP tends to be significantly higher in capitalist as compared to socialist economies.
7.   T   F   More than two-thirds of employed men and women in the U.S. hold *white-collar jobs*.

8.	T	F	In 1995, less than 4 percent of the civilian labor force was officially classified as being *unemployed*.
9.	T	F	Transformations occurring as a result of the *Information Revolution* include computers deskilling labor and computers making work more abstract.
10.	T	F	An *oligopoly* refers to domination of a market by a few producers.
11.	T	F	While the *global economy* is becoming more important, still, U.S. corporations currently own about 35 percent more overseas than foreign companies own in the United States.
12.	T	F	*Authority* is power people perceive as legitimate rather than coercive.
13.	T	F	*Authoritarianism* refers to a political system that denies popular participation in government.
14.	T	F	For every 14 U.S. citizens there is one government employee.
15.	T	F	Most U.S. adults claim identification with the *Republican Party*.
16.	T	F	*Political Action Committees* are organizations formed by special-interest groups, independent of political parties, to pursue political aims.
17.	T	F	*Voter apathy* is a problem, as evidenced by the fact that citizens in the U.S. are less likely to vote today than they were a century ago.
18.	T	F	Research by *Robert* and *Helen Lynd* in Muncie, Indiana (the Middletown study) supported the *power-elite* model concerning how power is distributed in the United States.
19.	T	F	One of the five insights offered concerning *terrorism* is that democracies are especially vulnerable to it because these governments afford extensive civil liberties to their people and have limited police networks.
20.	T	F	In recent years, defense has been the largest single expenditure by the U.S. government, accounting for 17 percent of federal spending.

Multiple Choice

1. The *sector* of the economy that transforms raw materials into manufactured goods is termed the:

   (a) primary sector
   (b) secondary sector
   (c) manifest sector
   (d) competitive sector
   (e) basic sector

2. Which of the following is *not a sector* of the modern economy?

   (a) primary
   (b) secondary
   (c) manifest
   (d) tertiary

3. Which of the following is *not* an example of *democratic socialism*?

   (a) Sweden
   (b) Italy
   (c) Canada
   (d) none are examples

4. A political and economic system that combines significant government control of the economy with free elections is:

    (a) socialism
    (b) market communism
    (c) world economy
    (d) democratic socialism
    (e) oligarchy

5. *Capitalist* economies have about _____ times the er capita GDP as *socialist* economies.

    (a) 2.7
    (b) 8.2
    (c) 1.3
    (d) 12.9
    (e) .75

6. What percentage of women in the U.S. had *income-producing jobs* in 1995?

    (a) 31.7
    (b) 44.6
    (c) 58.9
    (d) 67.5
    (e) 81.5

7. Currently, what percentage of our non-farm labor force is *unionized*?

    (a) 25
    (b) 39
    (c) 8
    (d) 15
    (e) 4

8. In 1940, one-fifth of all U.S. workers were *self-employed*. Currently, that figure is:

    (a) 1
    (b) 3.1
    (c) 8
    (d) 12.5
    (e) 20

9. Which of the following is most accurate?

    (a) African American teens have an unemployment rate of about 35 percent
    (b) a much higher proportion of African American females are unemployed than African American males
    (c) in 1995 about one-third of employed people in the U.S. held white-collar jobs
    (d) the unemployment rate in the U.S. stood at about 3 percent in 1995
    (e) all of the above are accurate statements

10. Giant corporations that are clusters of many smaller corporations are called:

    (a) megacorporations
    (b) multinational corporations
    (c) oligarchies
    (d) monopolies
    (e) conglomerates

161

11. Who defined *power* as the ability to achieve desired ends despite opposition?

(a) C. Wright Mills   (c) Max Weber
(b) Alexis de Tocqueville   (d) Robert Lynd

12. Which of the following is *not* one of the general contexts in which power is commonly defined as authority?

(a) traditional   (c) charismatic
(b) rational-legal   (d) democratic

13. Power that is legitimated by respect for long-established cultural patterns is called:

(a) traditional   (d) sacred
(b) political   (e) charismatic
(c) power-elite

14. According to *Max Weber*, the survival of a charismatic movement depends upon _____.

(a) pluralism   (c) political action
(b) routinization (d) assimilation

15. Which idea below represents the *pluralist model* of power?

(a) power is highly concentrated
(b) voting cannot create significant political changes
(c) the U.S. power system is an oligarchy
(d) wealth, prestige, and political office are rarely combined

16. With which general sociological paradigm is the *power-elite model* associated?

(a) social-conflict   (c) symbolic-interaction
(b) structural-functional (d) social-exchange

17. In which stage of *revolution* does the danger of counter-revolution occur?

(a) rising expectations
(b) nonresponsiveness of the old government
(c) establishing a new legitimacy
(d) radical leadership by intellectuals

18. *Quincy Wright* has identified which of the following circumstances as conditions which lead humans to go to war?

(a) perceived threat   (d) political objectives
(b) social problems   (e) all are identified
(c) moral objectives

162

19. Which of the following was *not* listed as a means of reducing the danger of nuclear war?

    (a) maintaining the status quo
    (b) high-technology defense
    (c) diplomacy and disarmament
    (d) resolving underlying conflict
    (e) all were identified

20. Together, the world's nations spend some _____ *trillion* annually for military purposes.

    (a) 1   (d) 4
    (b) 5   (e) 8
    (c) 2

Matching

Economy

1. ___ A productive system based on service work and high technology.
2. ___ An organized sphere of social life, or societal subsystem, designed to meet human needs.
3. ___ An economic system in which natural resources and the means of producing goods and services are collectively owned.
4. ___ The social institution that organizes a society's production, distribution, and consumption of goods and services.
5. ___ The part of the economy involving services rather than goods.
6. ___ Economic activity spanning many nations of the world with little regard for national borders.
7. ___ The part of the economy that transforms raw materials into manufactured goods.
8. ___ An organization with a legal existence, including rights and liabilities, apart from those of its members.
9. ___ Giant corporations composed of many smaller corporations.
10. ___ An economic form in which privately owned companies cooperate closely with the government.

    a. socialism   f. state capitalism
    b. conglomerates   g. economy
    c. secondary sector   h. postindustrial economy
    d. tertiary sector   i. global economy
    e. social institution   j. corporation

163

Politics

1. ___ Random acts of violence or the threat of such violence by an individual or group as a political strategy.
2. ___ A highly centralized political system that extensively regulates people's lives.
3. ___ The ability to achieve desired ends despite opposition.
4. ___ An analysis of politics that views power as dispersed among many competing interest groups.
5. ___ The percentage adults in the U.S. who identify with the Republican party.
6. ___ Tax revenues as a share of the gross domestic product for Sweden in 1993.
7. ___ A political system that denies popular participation in government.
8. ___ An analysis of politics that views power as concentrated among the rich.
9. ___ Power people perceive as legitimate rather than coercive.
10. ___ Tax revenues as a share of the gross domestic product for the U.S. in 1993.

a.	power-elite model	f.	37.5
b.	29.1	g.	plural model
c.	authoritarianism	h.	power
d.	authority	i.	49.9
e.	terrorism	j.	totalitarianism

Fill-In

1. _____ range from necessities like food to luxuries like swimming pools, while _____ include various activities that benefit others.
2. A _____ _____ is a productive system based on service work and high technology. As part of this system, the Information Revolution unleashed three key changes, including: From tangible products to _____, from mechanical skills to _____ skills, and the _____ of work away from factories.
3. The _____ _____ is the part of the economy generating raw materials directly from the natural environment.
4. The _____ is the part of the economy generating services rather than goods.
5. Most of the world's nations have economies that are largely _____.
6. A comparison of economic performance between *capitalist* and *socialist* economies supports the conclusion that capital economies produce a _____ overall standard of living but with _____ income disparity.
7. *Socialist* systems in Eastern Europe prior to the great transformations of 1989 and 1990 did do way with _____ *elites*, but expanded the clout of _____ *elites*.
8. While _____ percent of males over the age of 16 in the U.S. have income-producing jobs, _____ of the females do.
9. _____ are giant corporations comprised of many smaller corporations.
10. _____ refers to domination of a market by a few producers.
11. _____ is the social institution that distributes power, sets a social agenda, and makes decisions.
12. *Power* people perceive as legitimate rather than coercive is referred to as _____.

13. _____ *authority* is power legitimated through extraordinary personal abilities that inspire devotion and obedience.

14. _____ is a political system that denies popular participation in government.

15. One major cluster of attitudes related to the *political spectrum* concerns _____ issues, while another concerns _____ issues.

16. The _____ *model*. closely allied with the *social-conflict paradigm*, is an analysis of politics that views power as concentrated among the rich.

17. The _____ *complex* refers to a close association among government, the military, and defense industries.

18. *Quincy Wright* cites five factors that promote *war*, including: perceived _____ , social _____ , _____ objectives, _____ imperatives, and the absence of _____ .

Definition and Short-Answer

1. What were the five revolutionary changes brought about by the *Industrial Revolution*?
2. Define the concept *postindustrial society*, and identify three key changes unleashed by the *Information Revolution*.
3. What are the three basic characteristics of *capitalism*?
4. What are the three basic characteristics of *socialism*?
5. What is *democratic socialism*?
6. Comparing productivity and economic equality measures for *capitalist* and *socialist* economic systems, what are the relative advantages and disadvantages of each? Make comparisons in terms of *productivity, economic inequality,* and *civil liberties*.
7. What are the three main consequences of the development of a *global economy*?
8. What are the three major *sectors* of the economy? Define and illustrate each of these.
9. What are the basic characteristics of a *profession*?
10. Differentiate between the concepts *power* and *authority*.
11. Differentiate between *Max Weber's* three types of *authority*.
12. Four types of *political systems* are reviewed in the text. Identify and describe each of these systems.
13. What are the general patterns in attitudes among U.S. citizens concerning *social* and *economic issues* as reviewed in the text?
14. What is the evidence that *voter apathy* is a problem in our society? What are its causes?
15. Discuss the *changing work place* using demographic data presented in the text. What are three changes that you think are positive? What are three changes you think are negative?
16. Differentiate between the *pluralist* and *power-elite* models concerning the distribution of power in the United States.
17. What are the five general patterns identified in the text concerning *revolutions*?
18. What are the five factors identified in the text as promoting *war*?
19. Several approaches to reducing the chances for *nuclear war* are addressed in the text. Identify these approaches.
20. In what three ways has politics gone global?
21. What are the five insights presented in the text concerning *terrorism*?

PART VII: ANSWERS TO STUDY QUESTIONS

True-False

1.	T	(p. 266)	11.	F	(p. 280)
2.	T	(p. 266)	12.	T	(p. 281)
3.	T	(p. 268)	13.	T	(p. 284)
4.	F	(p. 268)	14.	T	(p. 286)
5.	F	(p. 271)	15.	F	(p. 287)
6.	T	(p. 272)	16.	T	(p. 287)
7.	T	(p. 273)	17.	T	(p. 287)
8.	F	(p. 276)	18.	T	(p. 289)
9.	T	(pp. 276-277)	19.	T	(p. 291)
10.	T	(p. 279)	20.	T	(p. 292)

Multiple Choice

1.	b	(p. 268)	11.	c	(pp. 280-281)
2.	c	(p. 268)	12.	d	(p. 281)
3.	c	(p. 271)	13.	b	(p. 281)
4.	d	(pp. 271-272)	14.	d	(p. 282)
5.	a	(p. 272)	15.	d	(p. 288)
6.	c	(p. 273)	16.	a	(p. 289)
7.	a	(p. 274)	17.	d	(p. 290)
8.	c	(p. 275)	18.	e	(p. 292)
9.	a	(p. 277)	19.	e	(pp. 293-294)
10.	e	(p. 277)	20.	b	(p. 293)

Matching

Economy

1.	h	(p. 267)	6.	i.	(p. 269)
2.	e	(p. 266)	7.	c	(p. 269)
3.	a	(p. 271)	8.	j	(p. 277)
4.	g	(p. 266)	9.	b	(p. 277)
5.	d	(p. 268)	10.	f	(p. 272)

Politics

1.	e	(p. 290)	6.	i.	(p. 285)
2.	j.	(p. 284)	7.	c	(p. 284)
3.	h	(p. 281)	8.	a	(p. 289)
4.	g	(p. 288)	9.	d	(p. 2281)
5.	f	(p. 287)	10.	b	(p. 285)

<u>Fill-In</u>

1. goods, services (p. 266)
2. postindustrial economy, ideas, literacy, decentralization (p. 267)
3. primary sector (p. 268)
4. tertiary sector (p. 268)
5. capitalist (p. 269)
6. higher, greater (p. 272)
7. economic, political (p. 273)
8. 75, 58.9 (p. 273)
9. conglomerates (p. 277)
10. oligopoly (p. 279)
11. politics (p. 280)
12. authority (p. 281)
13. charismatic (p. 281)
14. authoritarianism (p. 284)
15. economic, social (p. 286)
16. power-elite (p. 289)
17. military-industrial (p. 291)
18. threat, problems, political, moral, alienation (p. 292)

PART VIII: ANALYSIS AND COMMENT

Controversy and Debate

"Here Comes On-Line Democracy"

Key Points: Questions:

Social Diversity

"The Work Force of the Twenty-First Century"

Key Points: Questions:

167

Window on the World--Global Map 11-1, 11-2, 11-3

"Agricultural Employment in Global Perspective"

Key Points: Questions:

"Industrial Employment in Global Perspective"

Key Points: Questions:

"Political Freedom in Global Perspective"

Key Points: Questions:

Seeing Ourselves--National Map 11-1

"Labor Force Participation across the United States"

Key Points: Questions:

Family and Religion

12

X.   Religion and Social Change
     A.   Max Weber: Protestantism and Capitalism
     B.   Liberation Theology
XI. Church, Sect, and Cult
XII. Religion in History
XIII. Religion in the United States
     A.   Religious Commitment
     B.   Religion and Social Stratification
XIV. Religion in a Changing Society
     A.   Secularism
     B.   Civil Religion
     C.   Religious Revival
     D.   Looking Ahead: Religion in the Twenty-First Century
XV. Summary
     A.   Family
     B.   Religion
XVI. Key Concepts
     A.   Family
     B.   Religion
XVII. Critical-Thinking Questions

PART II: LEARNING OBJECTIVES

1.   To be able to define and illustrate basic concepts relating to the social institutions of kinship, family, and marriage.
2.   To gain a cross-cultural perspectives of the social institutions of kinship, family, and marriage.
3.   To be able to analyze the social institutions of kinship, family, and marriage using the structural-functional, social-conflict, and symbolic-interaction perspectives.
4.   To be able to describe the traditional life course of the U.S. family.
5.   To be able to recognize the impact of social class, race, ethnicity, and gender socialization on the family.
6.   To be able describe the problems and transitions that seriously affect family life.
7.   To be able to describe the composition and prevalence of alternative family forms.
8.   To become aware of the impact, both technologically and ethically, of new reproductive techniques on the family.
9.   To be able to identify four sociological conclusions about the family as we enter the twenty-first century.
10. To be able to define basic concepts relating to the sociological analysis of religion.
11. To be able to identify and describe the three functions of religion as developed by Emile Durkheim.
12. To be able to discuss the view that religion is socially constructed.
13. To be able to discuss the role of religion in maintaining social inequality.
14. To be able to describe how industrialization and science affect religious beliefs and practices.
15. To be able to review the basic demographic patterns concerning religious affiliation, religiosity, secularization, and religious revival in the U.S. today.

170

PART III: CHAPTER REVIEW--KEY POINTS

The chapter opens with a discussion concerning an important issue in Japanese society today--the declining birth rate. One reason for this is that Japanese women are delaying marriage.

THE FAMILY: BASIC CONCEPTS

Kinship refers to *a social bond, based on blood, marriage, or adoption, that joins people into families.* The *family* is *a social institution that unites individuals into cooperative groups that oversee the bearing and rearing of children.* A *family unit* is *a social group of two or more people, related by blood, marriage, or adoption, who usually live together.* Families form around *marriage, a legally sanctioned relationship involving economic cooperation, as well as normative sexual activity and childbearing, that people expect to be enduring.* People without legal or blood ties who feel they belong together may identify themselves as *families of affinity.*

THE FAMILY: GLOBAL VARIATIONS

While all societies recognize families there are great cross-cultural variations in the structures and functions of this institution. One general pattern is the *extended family*, or *a social unit including parents and children, but also other kin.* Such a family form is common in preindustrialized societies. It is also referred to as the *consanguine family*, meaning based on blood ties. Industrial societies are represented by the *nuclear family*, or *a social unit containing one, or more commonly, two adults and any children.* Typically based on marriage it is also known as the *conjugal family.*

Marriage Patterns

Norms identify categories of people suitable for marriage for particular individuals. *Endogamy* refers to *marriage between people of the same category.* It is differentiated from the norm of *exogamy*, or *marriage between people of different categories.* All societies enforce varying degrees of each type. *Monogamy* means *marriage involving two partners.* *Polygamy* is defined as *marriage that unites three or more people.* Polygamy takes one of two forms. One type is called *polygyny*, by far the more common, referring to marriage that joins one male with more than one female. The second type is called *polyandry*, referring to marriage that joins one female with more than one male. In the *Window on the World* box (p. 302) *Global Map 12-1* looks at marital form in global perspective. Three-fourths of the societies in the world endorse some form of marriage in addition to monogamy. However, most marriages in the world are monogamous.

Residential Patterns

Neolocality, a residential pattern in which a married couple lives apart from the parents of both spouses, is the most common form in industrial societies. *Patrilocality* is a residential pattern in which a married couple lives with or near the husband's family. *Matrilocality* is a residential pattern in which a married couple lives with or near the wife's family.

Patterns of Descent

Descent refers to *the system by which members of a society trace kinship over generations.* Industrial societies follow the *bilateral descent* system of tracing kinship through both males and females. Preindustrial societies typically follow one of two patterns of unilineal descent. The more common, *patrilineal descent* is a system tracing kinship through males. *Matrilineal descent* refers to a system of descent tracing kinship though females.

Patterns of Authority

The universal presence of patriarchy is reflected in the predominance of polygyny, patrilocality, and patrilineal descent. No known society is clearly matriarchal. Egalitarian family patterns are beginning to evolve, particularly in societies in which women are becoming more involved in the labor force.

THEORETICAL ANALYSIS OF THE FAMILY

Functions of the Family: Structural-Functional Analysis

The structural-functionalists focus on four important social functions served by the family. These include: The family serves as the primary agent in the *socialization* process during the entire life course of an individual.

Another function involves the *regulation of sexual activity.* Some restrictions on sexual behavior are characteristics of every culture. Every society has some type of **incest taboo**, *a norm forbidding sexual relations or marriage between certain kin.* It minimizes sexual competition, creates alliances between families through exogamous marriages, and establishes specific linkages of rights and obligations between people.

Many ascribed statuses are determined at birth through the family. Transmission of social standing through the family is universal. This is referred to as the *social placement function.*

Families are to provide for the *material and emotional security* for its members. Self-worth and security are established within the intense and enduring relationships characteristic of the family. Structural-functionalists tend to underemphasize problems in families, and underestimate the great diversity of family forms.

Inequality and the Family: Social-Conflict Analysis

The focus of the social-conflict approach to the study of the family is how this institution perpetuates patterns of social inequality. The forms this takes includes *property* and *inheritance, patriarchy, race* and *ethnicity.*

Constructing Family Life: Micro-Level Analysis

The structural-functional and social-conflict paradigms provide a macro-level perspective from which to understand the institution of the family. Symbolic-interaction analysis is used to study how specific realities are *socially constructed* within specific families. Social-exchange theory draws attention to the power of negotiation, and *family life as exchange.*

STAGES OF FAMILY LIFE

Courtship and Romantic Love

Preindustrial societies typically are characterized by *arranged marriages* where the kinship group determines marriage patterns. Marriages are viewed as alliances between different kinship groups for economic and political purposes. In industrial societies personal choice in mate selection dominates, with tremendous emphasis on *romantic love*--or the feeling of deep affection and sexual passion toward another person as the basis for marriage. Romantic love is a less stable foundation for marriage than are social and economic consideration. In the *Global Snapshot* box (p. 306), *Figure 12-1* presents global data concerning college students willingness to marry without romantic love. We in the U.S. tend to believe in the ideal of romantic love. However, **homogamy**, or *marriage between people with the same social characteristics*, is very common.

Settling In: Ideal and Real Marriages

Marriage and family life tends to be idealized by most people, with real life experiences never quite meeting expectations. Changing patterns of sexual experiences and norms have affected courtship and marriage as well. Research on extramarital sex suggests that this phenomenon is a reality in a fairly significant percentage of marriages.

Child Rearing

Child rearing creates major transitions for families. *Table 12-1* (p. 307) presents data concerning U.S. adults' ideas about the ideal number of children for a family. Several factors have brought about a decline in the birth rate in the United States, including economic costs, birth control technology, and the employment of women. The issue of *latchkey kids* is discussed.

The Family in Later Life

With life expectancy increasing, the number of years a couple lives together without children during what is known as the "empty-nest" stage is increasing. Many new challenges are faced by couples during these years.

U.S. FAMILIES: CLASS, RACE, AND GENDER

Social Class

Social class has a major impact on the family, including determining a family's standard of living, economic security, and likelihood of unemployment. Further, research by Lillian Rubin suggests that differences in the lifestyles of working-class and middle-class families affect relationships within a family.

173

Ethnicity and Race

Ethnicity and race of families affect the kinds of norms that families follow, the amount of assimilation families experience, and the amount of poverty experienced. The concept *machismo* among Hispanic communities is reviewed.

African American families have a poverty rate three times that of whites. In 1994, 48 percent of African American families were headed by single-parent women. This compares with 25 percent for Hispanic families and 14 percent for white families. More than half of African American children today grow up in poverty. *Figure 12-2* (p. 310) shows the percentage of different family forms in 1994 for different racial and ethnic categories.

Gender

Cultural views regarding gender in U.S. society significantly affect the family. Jesse Bernard suggests every marriage is actually two separate ones--*his* and *hers*. Cultural values tend to promote the idea that marriage is more beneficial for women than for men. Empirical research supports the very opposite.

TRANSITIONS AND PROBLEMS IN FAMILY LIFE

Divorce

The divorce rate in the U.S. during this century has fluctuated dramatically with changing conditions in society. The United States has the highest marriage rate in the world. However, while the marriage rate has remained stable over the century, the divorce rate has risen significantly. *Figure 12-3* (p. 311) illustrates the changes in the divorce rate in the U.S. between 1890-1995. Societal factors affecting the divorce rate include *individualism rising, romantic love often fades, women are less dependent on men, many of today's marriages are stressful, divorce is more socially acceptable,* and *divorce is legally easier to accomplish.*

Who divorces? People at greater risk include: young spouses, women in stressful careers, couples who marry because of an unexpected pregnancy, marrying after a brief courtship, couples with alcohol or other substance-abuse problems, geographically mobile couples, and couples with few financial resources. Also, people who have divorced once are more likely to divorce again than people in their first marriages.

Remarriage

About 80 percent of people who divorce in the U.S. remarry. Remarriage rates are higher for men than for women. Remarriage often creates a *blended family* consisting of a biological parent and stepparent, along with children of their respective first marriages and any children of the blended marriage. This provides a context in which stress and conflict is often greater than in other families. In the *Seeing Ourselves* box (p. 312), *National Map 12-1* provides data on the geographic location of divorced people across the United States.

Family Violence

Many families are characterized by *family violence*, or emotional, physical, or sexual abuse of one family member by another. The family has been characterized as one of the most violent institutions in our society.

Violence transcends the boundaries of social class. Common stereotypes of abusers are brought into question using empirical data. Low reporting rates deflates the official statistics. One-sixth of all couples have relationships characterized by at least some violence each year. The argument is made that the seriousness of abuse is greater for wives than for husbands. The issue of *marital rape* is discussed.

About two million children are victims of abuse each year, though this is only a rough estimate. Abuse is both physical and emotional. These children often feel guilt, self-blame, and psychological problems as a result of abuse. Most abusers are men. Their abusive behaviors are often learned during their childhoods.

ALTERNATIVE FAMILY FORMS

One-Parent Families

The impact of new reproductive technology on the family in recent years has been dramatic, with many benefits having been realized. However, the new technology has brought with it many difficult ethical problems. One method, *in vitro fertilization*, involves the union of the male sperm and the female ovum on glass rather than in the woman's body. The benefits are twofold. First, about 20 percent of couples who otherwise could not conceive are able to using this technique. Second, the genetic screening of sperm and eggs reduces the incidence of birth defects.

One ethical issue raised concerns the fact that the benefits are expensive and only available to those who can afford them. Another issue involves the control medical experts have over who the technology is made available to. Finally, the is the issue of *surrogate motherhood*. Moral and cultural legal standards to guide this option remain ambiguous.

Cohabitation

Cohabitation is *the sharing of a household by an unmarried couple*. There has been a five-fold increase in cohabitation over the last twenty years. This household structure is discussed in terms of cross-cultural comparisons. Most cohabitating coupes do not marry, and only a small percentage have children. Commitment tends not to be as strong as in marriage.

Gay and Lesbian Couples

In 1989 Denmark because the first country to legalize homosexual marriages. However, even there, legal option is still not allowed for such couples. A few legal benefits of marriage for gays exist in some metropolitan areas in the U.S. Many gay couples form long-term relationships. Some of these couples are raising children. Their interpersonal relationships parallel heterosexual relationships in terms of communication, finances, and domestic division of labor. Many feel they must keep their relationships a secret to avoid prejudice and discrimination. This situation can place considerable strain on relationships.

175

Singlehood

Singlehood is increasing in the United States. About one in four households contain a single adult. Singlehood is still primarily a transitory stage, although financially independent women now comprise a fast-growing component that choose singlehood as a lifestyle. As women reach their 30s and 40s unmarried, the availability of men relative to themselves decreases significantly.

New Reproductive Technology

Over the last twenty years these has been a dramatic increase in the percentage of *one-parent* families. Women are four times more likely than men to head a single-parent family. Distributions for whites, African Americans, and Hispanics are discussed. Single-parent families are not by themselves detrimental to children's development; however, economic hardships often occur in female-headed, single-parent families.

Looking Ahead: The Family in the Twenty-First Century

Family life as dramatically changed in recent decades. This transformation has generated controversy. The **Critical Thinking** box (pp. 316-317) reviews some of the issues underlying the place of the traditional family in contemporary society. Five general conclusions are proposed looking ahead to the next century. First, the divorce rate will likely remain high. Second, family life will be highly variable. Third, in most families, men will continue to play a limited role in child rearing. Fourth, with more two-earner families, family-time will be squeezed out even more. And fifth, new reproductive technology will continue to grow in importance.

RELIGION: BASIC CONCEPTS

Religion primarily concerns the purpose and meaning of life. Emile Durkheim distinguished between the ***profane***, meaning *an ordinary element of everyday life*, and the **sacred**, or *that which people define as extraordinary, inspiring a sense of awe and reverence, and even fear*. **Religion** is *a social institution, involving beliefs and practices, that distinguishes the sacred from the profane*. Religion is a matter of ***faith***, or *belief anchored in conviction rather than scientific evidence*. The sacred is approached through *ritual*, or formal, ceremonial behavior. Sociology investigates the *social consequences* of religion, but cannot assess its *validity*.

THEORETICAL ANALYSIS OF RELIGION

Functions of Religion: Structural-Functional Analysis

Emile Durkheim argued society has an existence of its own, beyond the lives of the people who create it. Society and the sacred are inseparable in Durkheim's view. Durkheim believed that the power of society was understood by people through their creation of sacred symbols. In technologically simple societies a ***totem*** is *an object collectively defined as sacred*. Ritual behavior with the totem provided unity for the community. He saw religion as providing major functions for society, including *social cohesion, social control,* and *providing meaning and purpose*. A weakness in the structural-functional view is that it downplays the dysfunctions of religion, particularly its role in producing destructive social conflict.

Constructing the Sacred: Symbolic-Interaction Analysis

Peter Berger, operating from the symbolic-interaction view, theorized that religion is a socially constructed reality much as the family and the economy are. The sacred can provide a permanence for society as long as society's members ignore the recognition that the sacred is socially constructed.

Religion and Inequality: Social-Conflict Analysis

The social-conflict view of religion draws attention to the social ills perpetuated by the existence of religion. Karl Marx theorized that the powerful in society benefit by religion because it defines the present society as morally just. Advocates of this view also argue that major world religions support patriarchy.

RELIGION AND SOCIAL CHANGE

Max Weber: Protestantism and Capitalism

According to Max Weber, religion is not merely the conservative force as portrayed in the work of Karl Marx. Rather, Weber saw religion as a force which can promote dramatic social change. Weber's work points out that industrial capitalism in Europe paralleled the rise of Calvinism. The doctrine of *predestination*, central to this religion, was a key variable in causing people to seek material success as a sign that God favored them. Weber believed that the "spirit of capitalism" emerged from the "protestant ethic."

Liberation Theology

Liberation theology is *a fusion of Christian principles with political activism, often Marxist in character.* Adherents believe that as a matter of faith and justice greater social equality must be promoted.

CHURCH, SECT, AND CULT

A *church* is *a formal religious organization well integrated into the larger society.* Two types of church organization are the *ecclesia--a church that is formally allied with the state--*and a *denomination, or a church, not linked to the state, that accepts religious pluralism.*

A *sect*, is *a type of religious organization that stands apart from the larger society.* Sects tend to lack the formal organization of a church. Leaders are often those people who manifest *charisma--or extraordinary personal qualities that can turn an audience into followers. Proselytizing* is an important to obtain new members through *conversion,* a personal transformation resulting from new religious beliefs. Sects tend to reject the established society.

A *cult* is *a religious organization that is substantially outside the cultural traditions of a society.* It represents something almost completely new. Cults often arise from the diffusion of religious ideas cross-culturally. They tend to be more extreme than sects, requiring members to change their entire lifestyle and self-concepts.

RELIGION IN HISTORY

Archaeological research suggests religious ritual has existed for at least 40,000 years. Among hunting and gathering societies religion typically takes the form of *animism*, or *the belief that natural objects are conscious forms of life that affect humanity*. In such cultures, a shaman, or religious leader, may be recognized, however, not occupying a full-time position as a specialist. With industrialization, science begins as a force which diminishes the scope of religious power and thinking. But, science cannot answer certain fundamental questions related to the *spiritual* dimension of human existence.

RELIGION IN THE UNITED STATES

Religious Commitment

About 90 percent of U.S. adults identify with a specific religion, and some two-thirds have formal affiliation with one. *Table 12-2* (p. 324) outlines the religious identifications in the U.S. which is described as religiously pluralistic. *Religiosity* is *the importance of religion in a person's life*. This concept can be measured in a number of different ways. In the *Global Snapshot* box (p. 325) *Figure 12-5* puts religiosity in global perspective. The U.S. ranks very high. In the *Seeing Ourselves* box (p. 326), *National Map 12-2* illustrate the residential distribution of people according to their religious affiliation, with definite patterns being shown.

Religion and Social Stratification

Jews, Episcopalians, and Presbyterians have the highest *social class* standing in our society. Catholics, Lutherans, and Baptists are more representative of the lower social strata. Religion is also closely related to *ethnicity* and *race*, with certain religions predominating in particular geographic regions.

RELIGION IN A CHANGING SOCIETY

Secularization

An important and controversial pattern of social change is *secularization*, or *the historical decline in the influence of religion*. Advances in science have significantly influenced our relationship with the world of ideas and the world of nature. Yet, religion is still an important part of society and a very significant part of many people's lives.

Civil Religion

Secularization has brought about a decline in certain traditional religious beliefs, but has also affected the advancement of new forms. *Civil religion, a quasi-religious loyalty based on citizenship*, is strong in the U.S. For example, our flag serves as a sacred symbol of national identity.

Religious Revival

Membership in established religions may be declining; however, membership in other religious organizations is increasing. The human need for security seems to always give rise to some form of religious activity and commitment.

Religious fundamentalism, or *a conservative doctrine that opposes intellectualism and worldly accommodation in favor of restoring traditional, other-worldly religion*, has been increasing in the U.S. over the last decade or so. Five characteristics identity Christian fundamentalists: *the literal interpretation of Scripture, less tolerance for religious diversity, an emphasis on personal experience of religion, an opposition to secular humanism,* and *an endorsement of conservative political goals.* Fundamentalists have heavily used the mass media, particularly television and radio--*electronic churches,* to attract and maintain followers.

Looking Ahead: Religion in the Twenty-First Century

Science, it seems, is both unable to answer certain questions, and with tremendous leaps of technological advances in recent history, increases our anxiety about our future. The *Controversy and Debate* box (pp. 328-329) takes a look at the relationship between religion and science. Names of interest mentioned include Pope John Paul II, Galileo, Charles Darwin, and John Scopes.

PART IV: KEY CONCEPTS

Family:

bilateral descent
cohabitation
consanguine family
descent
endogamy
endogamy
extended family
family
family violence
homogamy
incest taboo
in vitro fertilization
kinship
marriage
matrilineal descent
matrilocality
monogamy
neolocality
nuclear family
patrilineal descent
patrilocality

polyandry
polygamy
polygyny

Religion:

animism
charisma
church
civil religion
conversion
creationism
creation science
cult
denomination
ecclesia
liberation theology
profane
religion
religious fundamentalism
religiosity
ritual
sacred
sect
secularism
totem

PART V: IMPORTANT RESEARCHERS

Lillian Rubin   Jessie Bernard

Emile Durkheim   Karl Marx

Max Weber

PART VI: STUDY QUESTIONS

True-False

1. T   F   Norms of *endogamy* relate to marriage between people of the same social category.
2. T   F   *Matrilocality* occurs more commonly in societies that engage in distant warfare or in which daughters have greater economic value.
3. T   F   Every known culture has some type of *incest taboo*.
4. T   F   While the actual number is smaller, the "ideal" number of children to have for most married U.S. adults is three or more.
5. T   F   *Jessie Bernard's* research on marriage suggests that this institution is more beneficial for men than it is for women.
6. T   F   The *divorce rate* in the U.S. during the twentieth century has actually only increased by less than 30 percent.
7. T   F   According to the text, most *child abusers* are men.
8. T   F   The percentage of households with *single adults* has actually been decreasing over the last two decades.
9. T   F   *Test-tube babies* are, technically speaking, the result of the process of *in vitro fertilization*.
10. T   F   A major component of *Emile Durkheim's* approach to the study of religion was to determine whether a divine power exists or not.
11. T   F   Two types, or forms, of churches identified in the text are the *ecclesia* and the *denomination*.
12. T   F   Whereas a *cult* is formed by a schism from established religious organizations, a *sect* represents something almost entirely new.
13. T   F   *Animism* is the belief that natural objects are conscious life forms that affect humanity.
14. T   F   According to research cited in the text, *religiosity* among Catholics is higher than among Protestants.
15. T   F   By global standards, *North Americans* are relatively nonreligious people.
16. T   F   A quasi-religious loyalty based in citizenship is called a *civil religion*.
17. T   F   In a recent national survey, over one-third of U.S. adults described their religious upbringing as *fundamentalist*.
18. T   F   Science and new technologies are reducing the relevance of religion in modern society as many moral dilemmas and spiritual issues are resolved or are diminishing in significance.

Multiple Choice

1. The *consanguine family* is also known as the:

    (a)   conjugal family
    (b)   nuclear family
    (c)   extended family
    (d)   family of orientation
    (e)   family of procreation

181

2.   *Exogamy* and *endogamy* are cultural norms relating to:

   (a)   marriage patterns   (d)   residence patterns
   (b)   descent regulations   (e)   authority patterns
   (c)   beliefs about romantic love

3.   The predominant *family form* in the U.S. has long been the:

   (a)   nuclear family   (c)   exogamous family
   (b)   consanguine family   (d)   matriarchal family

4.   A *marriage form* that unites one woman with two or more men is termed:

   (a)   monogamy   (c)   polyandry
   (b)   polygyny   (d)   endogamy

5.   Industrial societies typically show the _____ *residence pattern.*

   (a)   patrilocal   (c)   avunculocal
   (b)   matrilocal   (d)   neolocal

6.   The type of sociological analysis of the family that holds that the family serves to perpetuate social inequality is:

   (a)   social-exchange analysis   (c)   structural-functional analysis
   (b)   social-conflict analysis   (d)   symbolic-interaction analysis

7.   Sociologists have noted that *romantic love* as a basis for marriage:

   (a)   is reinforced by cultural values
   (b)   acts as a strong incentive to leave one's original family of orientation to form a new family of procreation
   (c)   is not as stable a basis for marriage as social and economic bases
   (d)   all of the above

8.   Remarriage often creates families composed of both biological parents and stepparents and children. These are called:

   (a)   second families   (c)   focal families
   (b)   blended families   (d)   families of orientation

9. Which of the following is a function of religion according to *Emile Durkheim*?

   (a) social cohesion
   (b) social control
   (c) providing meaning and purpose
   (d) all are functions identified by Durkheim
   (e) none are as he saw religion as having negative consequences for society

10. The view that religion is completely *socially constructed* by a society's members is espoused by:

   (a) Max Weber   (c) Peter Berger
   (b) Karl Marx   (d) Emile Durkheim

11. *Liberation theology* advocates a blending of religion with:

   (a) the family   (c) the economy
   (b) education   (d) politics

12. Which of the following is *not* a feature of a *sect*:

   (a) charismatic leaders   (c) animism
   (b) membership through conversion (d) proselytizing

13. Which of the following is the largest *Protestant denomination*?

   (a) Baptist   (d) Presbyterian
   (b) Methodist   (e) Episcopalian
   (c) Lutheran

14. Which of the following statements is *most accurate*:

   (a) religious affiliation in the U.S. does not seem to vary much by race, social class, or ethnicity
   (b) North Americans are a relatively nonreligious people compared to the Japanese and Europeans
   (c) less than one-half of the population of the U.S. is affiliated with a Protestant denomination
   (d) about 20 percent of U.S. adults claim they attend religious services on a weekly or almost weekly basis
   (e) the religious diversity of the United States stems from two key factors: a Constitutional ban on any government-sponsored religion and a high rate of immigration

15.   In the *Scopes trial* of 1925, the state of Tennessee prosecuted a man for:

(a)   polygamy   (c)   profanity
(b)   cohabitation   (d)   teaching evolution

<u>Matching</u>

Family

1. ___   The system by which members of a society trace kinship over generations.
2. ___   People with or without legal or blood ties who feel they belong together and want to define themselves as a family.
3. ___   Marriage between people of the same social category.
4. ___   Families composed of children and some combination of biological parents and stepparents.
5. ___   A social unit including parents, children, and other kin.
6. ___   A couple living apart from parents of both spouses.
7. ___   A form of marriage uniting one female with more than one male.
8. ___   Tracing kinship through both men and women.
9. ___   The experience of affection and sexual passion toward another person as the basis of marriage.
10. ___   A form of marriage uniting one male with more than one female.

a.   endogamy   f.   neolocality
b.   extended family   g.   family of affinity
c.   blended families   h.   polygyny
d.   bilateral decent   i.   polyandry
e.   descent   j.   romantic love

Religion

1. ___   Extraordinary personal qualities that can turn an audience into followers.
2. ___   A type of religious organization that stands apart from the larger society.
3. ___   A formal religious organization well integrated into the larger society.
4. ___   A church that is formally allied with the state.
5. ___   A social institution involving beliefs and practices based on a conception of the sacred.
6. ___   The belief that natural objects are conscious forms of life that affect humanity.
7. ___   That which people define has extraordinary, inspiring a sense of awe and reverence.
8. ___   A religious organization that is substantially outside the cultural traditions of a society.
9. ___   A natural object--or its representation--collectively defined as sacred.
10. ___   A formal ceremonial behavior.

a.	ecclesia	f.	church
b.	animism	g.	sect
c.	ritual	h.	totem
d.	religion	i.	sacred
e.	charisma	j.	cult

Fill-In

1. The _____ *family* is based on blood ties.
2. _____ is a normative pattern referring to marriage between people of the same social group or category.
3. _____ is a marriage that joins one female with more than one male.
4. Cultural norms that forbid sexual relationships or marriage between specified kin are called _____ _____.
5. _____ refers to the system by which members of a society trace kinship over generations.
6. _____ refers to marriage between people with the same social characteristics.
7. _____ is the sharing of a household by an unmarried couple.
8. *Emile Durkheim* labeled the ordinary elements of everyday life the _____.
9. A _____ is a natural object--or its representation--collectively defined as sacred.
10. According to *Max Weber*, industrial capitalism developed in the wake of _____.
11. _____ *theology* is a fusion of Christian principles with political activism.
12. A(n) _____ is a church that is formally allied with the state.
13. _____ refers to extraordinary personal qualities that can turn audiences into followers.
14. _____ is the belief that natural objects are conscious forms of life that can affect humanity.
15. The historical decline in the influence of religion is referred to as _____.
16. A _____ religion is a quasi-religious loyalty based on citizenship.
17. Science and religion embody two different levels of understanding that respond to different kinds of questions. *Science* focusing on _____ the natural world operates, and *religion* addressing questions of _____.

Definition and Short-Answer

1. What are the four basic *functions* of the family according to structural-functionalists?
2. Define and describe the three patterns of *descent*.
3. Why has the *divorce rate* increased in recent decades in the United States? What are the basic demographic patterns involving divorce in our society today?
4. What are the four *stages* of the family life cycle outlined in the text? Describe the major events occurring during each of these stages.
5. In what ways are *middle-class* and *working-class* marriages different?

6. What are the arguments being made about the family by *social-conflict* theorists?
7. What are four important points made in the text concerning *family violence*?
8. Five *alternative family forms* are discussed in the text. Identify these and review the data concerning three of them. What are your opinions concerning these changes in the family?
9. What are the five conclusions being made about marriage and family life into the twenty-first century?
10. According to *structural-functional* analysis, what are three major functions of religion? Provide an example for each from U.S. society.
11. Discuss *Max Weber's* points concerning the historical relationship between Protestantism and capitalism.
12. How do theorists operating from the *social conflict* perspective understand religion and how it operates in society? Provide two examples to illustrate.
13. In a one-page written discussion, debate the issue of whether science threatens or strengthens religion in society.
14. Discuss the issue concerning the extent of *religiosity* in the United States today.
15. Briefly describe the position of religious *fundamentalism* in our society today.
16. Discuss the relationship between *religion* and *social stratification* in the United States today.

PART VII: ANSWERS TO STUDY QUESTIONS

True-False

1.	T	(p. 301)	10.	F	(p. 319)
2.	T	(p. 303)	11.	T	(p. 322)
3.	T	(p. 303)	12.	F	(p. 322)
4.	F	(p. 307)	13.	T	(p. 323)
5.	F	(p. 310)	14.	T	(p. 324)
6.	F	(p. 311)	15.	F	(p. 324)
7.	T	(p. 313)	16.	T	(p. 326)
8.	F	(p. 315)	17.	T	(p. 327)
9.	T	(p. 315)			
10.	F	(p. 319)			

Multiple Choice

1.	c	(p. 301)	9.	d	(p. 312)
2.	a	(p. 301)	10.	c	(p. 319)
3.	a	(p. 301)	11.	d	(p. 321)
4.	c	(p. 301)	12.	c	(p. 323)
5.	d	(p. 303)	13.	a	(p. 324)
6.	b	(p. 304)	14.	e	(pp. 324-325)
7.	d	(p. 306)	15.	d	(p. 328)
8.	b	(p. 312)			

Matching

Family

1.	e	(p. 303)
2.	g	(p. 300)
3.	a	(p. 301)
4.	c	(p. 312)
5.	b	(p. 301)

6.	f	(p. 303)
7.	i.	(p. 301)
8.	d	(p. 303)
9.	j	(p. 306)
10.	h	(p. 301)

Religion

1.	e	(p. 323)
2.	g	(p. 323)
3.	f	(p. 321)
4.	a	(p. 322)
5.	d	(p. 318)

6.	b	(p. 323)
7.	i	(p. 318)
8.	j	(p. 323)
9.	h	(p. 319)
10.	c	(p. 318)

Fill-In

1. consanguine (p. 301)
2. endogamy (p. 301)
3. polyandry (p. 301)
4. incest taboos (p. 303)
5. descent (p. 303)
6. homogamy (p. 307)
7. cohabitation (p. 314)
8. profane (p. 318)
9. totem (p. 319)
10. Calvinism (p. 321)
11. liberation (p. 321)
12. ecclesia (p. 322)
13. charisma (p. 323)
14. animism (p. 323)
15. secularization (p. 325)
16. civil (p. 326)
17. how, why (p. 328)

PART VIII: COMMENT AND ANALYSIS

Critical Thinking

"Should We Save the Traditional Family?"

Key Points: Questions:

Controversy and Debate

"Does Science Threaten Religion?"

Key Points: Questions:

Window on the World--Global Map 12-1

"Marital Form in Global Perspective"

Key Points: Questions:

Seeing Ourselves--National Map 12-1 and 12-2

"Divorced People across the U.S."

Key Points: Questions:

"Religious Diversity across the U.S."

Key Points: Questions:

Education 13 and Medicine

PART I: CHAPTER OUTLINE

IX. The Medical Establishment
     A.   The Rise of Scientific Medicine
     B.   Holistic Medicine
     C.   Paying the Costs: A Global Survey
     D.   Medicine in the United States
 X. Theoretical Analysis of Medicine
     A.   Structural-Functional Analysis
     B.   Symbolic-Interaction Analysis
     C.   Social-Conflict Analysis
     D.   Looking Ahead: Medicine in the Twenty-First Century
XI. Summary
     A.   Education
     B.   Medicine
XII. Key Concepts
     A.   Education
     B.   Medicine
XIII. Critical-Thinking Questions

PART II: LEARNING OBJECTIVES

1.   To be able to describe the different role of education in low-income and high-income countries.
2.   To compare education in Japan to that provided in the United States.
3.   To be able to identify and describe the functions of schooling.
4.   To consider how education supports social inequality.
5.   To be able to discuss the major issues and problems facing contemporary education in the United States today.
6.   To be able to identify and evaluate alternatives to the current structure of the institution of education in our society.
7.   To be able to identify and describe how the health of a population is shaped by a society's cultural patterns, technology, social resources, and social inequality.
8.   To recognize the health challenges that are faced in none industrialized countrics.
9.   To be able to discuss how age, sex, race, and social class affect the level of health of individuals in our society.
10. To be able to discuss the health problems related to eating disorders, cigarette smoking, and sexually transmitted diseases.
11. To consider ethical issues related to dying and death.
12. To be able to distinguish between health care and medicine.
13. To be able to compare and contrast scientific medicine and holistic medicine.
14. To begin to evaluate various approaches to providing health care to members of our society.
15. To be able to identify and describe the three sociological paradigms in terms of their relevance to health and health care.

PART III: CHAPTER REVIEW--KEY POINTS

We are introduced to the Masuo family of Yokohama, Japan. Education in Japan is very competitive, and rigorous application of oneself to its demands is critical for success. Many children go to the *Juru*, or "cram school," several days a week after their regular day at school.

EDUCATION: A GLOBAL SURVEY

Education refers to *the social institution through which society provides its members with important knowledge, including basic facts, job skills, and cultural values.* An important kind of education in industrial societies is **schooling**, or *formal instruction under the direction of specially trained teachers.*

Schooling in Low-Income Countries

The English word school is derived from the Greek word for "leisure." In preindustrial societies specialized skills are taught in families; schooling is only available to the wealthy. Among low-income countries there is a marked diversity in schooling. One trait in common though is limited access to schooling. Illiteracy is a serious problem in these countries. *Global Map 12-1* illustrates in the *Window on the World* box (p. 335).

Schooling in High-Income Countries

Industrial societies embrace the principle of mass education, though how formalized schooling is provided varies. *Mandatory education laws,* or legal requirements that children receive a minimum of formal education, began to be enacted in the 1850s. The median number of years of schooling was 8.1 in 1910 and rose to 12.7 in 1995. *Table 13-1* (p. 336) summarizes the educational achievement levels in the U.S. (by decade) 1910-1995.

In Japan, mandatory education laws began in 1872. The cultural values of tradition and family are stressed in the early grades. In their early teens, students begin to face the rigorous and competitive exams of the Japanese system. Some 90 percent of Japanese students graduate from high school, compared with 76 percent in the U.S. However, only 40 percent go on to college, compared to 62 percent in the U.S. Japanese mothers of school-age children participate in the labor force at considerably lower rates than mothers in the U.S. in order to focus on the educational success of their children.

Schooling in the United States

Democratic ideals have characterized our system, though the ideal of *equal opportunity* has not been fully achieved. Still, the U.S. has a higher proportion of its population attending college than any other industrialized society.

People in the U.S. value *practicality*, and this fact has influenced the types of studies emphasized in schools. Earlier in this century, John Dewey was a foremost proponent of *progressive education*. *Figure 13-1* (p. 337) shows that the U.S. has an outstanding record of higher education relative to other countries.

THE FUNCTIONS OF SCHOOLING

Structural-functionalists analysis focus our attention on the functions which educational systems have for society. Education must become involved in the process of *socialization* in order to ensure members become functioning adults. Important lessons on cultural values and norms are

191

learned in schools.

Through the teaching of certain cultural values and norms, people become more unified. This function of *social integration* is particularly critical in culturally diverse societies.

Schooling serves as a screening and selection process. *Social placement* then becomes a key role of educational systems. Performance is evaluated on the basis of achievement. It provides an opportunity for upward mobility; however, ascribed statuses still influence people in terms of their success in our educational system.

Education is not merely the transmission of culture; it is also a factor in the creation of culture through critical inquiry and research. This function then relates to the process of *cultural innovation*.

Schools also serve several *latent functions*, such as providing child care. Lasting relationships are also established in school.

The structural-functional perspective helps us to see how schools support the operation of an industrialized society. But this perspective neglects a critical examination of how social inequality operates within the educational system.

SCHOOLING AND SOCIAL INEQUALITY

Social-conflict analysis views schooling as a perpetuation of social stratification. *Social control* is viewed as an outcome of schooling because youth are socialized to accept the status quo.

Testing and *social inequality* are also seen as problems in our educational system. The argument is that standardized tests favor upper middle class backgrounds. The validity of such texts are therefore brought into question.

Further, *tracking* and *social inequality* are viewed as problems. Standardized tests are used for the basis of *tracking--the division of a school's students into different educational programs*.

Public and Private Education

In 1995, eighty-nine percent of the 51 million U.S. students in primary and secondary levels were in public schools. Most students in private educational institutions at these levels attend *parochial* schools. Desegregation policies have caused some parents to place their children in private, more racially homogeneous schools. Higher levels of academic achievement are found among students attending private schools than among students attending public schools. Funds available for public schools varies greatly across the United States.

The 1966 *Coleman Report* revealed that racially segregated schools, officially illegal since 1954, provided inferior education. This report helped initiate *busing* policies. Coleman, however found only a weak relationship between funding and academic qualities of schools. Families and peer groups, and the attitudes of teachers, seemed to be most highly correlated with academic achievement.

Access to Higher Education

Approximately 62 percent of high-school graduates enroll in college. The *Seeing Ourselves* box (p. 336), *National Map 13-1* shows where in the U.S. people are more or less likely to reach college. The most crucial factor affecting access to higher education is *money*. In some respects, however, equal access has improved in recent decades. *Figure 13-2* (p. 340) shows educational achievement rates for various racial and ethnic categories. Differences remain significant.

Table 13-2 (p. 341) shows the differences in lifetime earnings and educational levels for males and females. At all levels males earn significantly more than females.

Credentialism

Randall Collins refers to the U.S. as a *credential society*, meaning degrees and diplomas are used as a sign of a person's ability to perform a specialized occupational role. *Credentialism*, then, amounts to *evaluating people on the basis of educational degrees*. Social-conflict theorists are very critical of it as a gatekeeping strategy, arguing credentials often bear little relation to the skills and responsibilities of specific jobs.

Privilege and Personal Merit

Social conflict analysis links formal education to inequality by contending that schooling is unequal for different categories of people, resulting in a process whereby *schooling transforms social privilege into personal merit*. This approach, however, minimizes the value of schooling for both individuals and the society as a whole. It underestimates the value of education for individual achievement and upward mobility.

PROBLEMS IN THE SCHOOLS

Discipline and Violence

Estimates on the extent of violence against teachers and students in U.S. schools suggests a serious problem exists. The key to overcoming this problem appears to be firm disciplinary policies in schools, with support from parents and law enforcement agencies.

Bureaucracy and Student Passivity

There is perceived to be a lack of active student participation in the learning process, known as *student passivity*. Theodore Sizer argues that our bureaucratic structure in school, while necessary, causes five serious problems. These include: *rigid conformity, numerical ratings, rigid expectations, specialization,* and *little individual responsibility*.

Suggested changes in the bureaucratic system include smaller classes, more broadly trained teachers, elimination of rigid class schedules, and basing graduation on what is learned rather than on the amount of time spent in school.

College: The Silent Classroom

Research by David Karp and William Yoels suggests that patterns of interaction in the college classroom tend to be very predictable and involve little student initiative or creative thinking. Smaller classes seem to generate more student participation.

Dropping Out

Dropping out is defined as quitting school before graduating high school. Currently 13 percent of people aged 15-24 are *dropouts*. Lack of support by parents of these young people for education, who themselves have little education, is cited as a key factor related to dropping out.

Academic Standards

A 1983 report by the National Commission on Excellence in Education entitles *A Nation At Risk* found that education in the U.S. had deteriorated during the previous decade. This report pointed out lower SAT scores as a major indicator of this decline. Further, it noted the extent of *functional illiteracy*, or *reading and writing skills inadequate for everyday living*. About one in eight U.S. students complete secondary school without learning to read or write. The **Critical Thinking** box (p. 344) elaborates on this problem. The 1983 report recommends more stringent educational requirements, including raising standards, requiring certain courses, keeping students in school until they reach certain levels of achievement, increasing the salaries of teachers, and professional training.

RECENT ISSUES IN U.S. EDUCATION

School Choice

The key issue focused on in this section is making schools more competitive. One alternative to the current system is to provide *vouchers* to families, allowing them to choose which school their children attend. Another recent development is *schooling for profit*, or schools that operate as profit-making companies.

Schooling People with Disabilities

Our educational system requires our society to provide basic educational opportunities for everyone. However, in our bureaucratized system many physically and mentally handicapped children receive little if any services. Several obstacles are discussed which makes providing educational service to these children difficult.

One recent trend has been toward *mainstreaming* or the integration of disabled students into the educational program as a whole. An alternative approach, which works best for the physically impaired students, is termed *inclusive education*. Such programs are very expensive. The benefits for all students can be tremendous.

Adult Education

Over twenty-five million adults are currently enrolled in educational programs. Most are from the middle and upper classes. The motivation for them to return to school is generally work related.

Looking Ahead: Schooling in the Twenty-First Century

Our society is struggling with many educational dilemmas which are *social problems*. Schools alone cannot fix these problems. Further, technology and the Information Revolution are changing reshaping education. The **Exploring Cyber-Society** box (p. 347) discusses the issue of on-line instruction for college credit--even degrees!

MEDICINE AND HEALTH

Medicine refers to *the social institution that focuses on combating disease and improving health*. The World Health Organization describes the ideal of **health** as *a state of complete physical, mental, and social well-being*.

Health and Society

Health in any society is shaped by several important factors. These include: *cultural patterns define health, technology and resources affect health,* and *social inequality affects health*.

HEALTH: A GLOBAL SURVEY

Health in Low-Income Countries

Health as a social issue is demonstrated by the significant increase in well-being over the course of history. The simple technology of hunting and gathering societies made it difficult to maintain a healthful environment. A many a one-half of the people in such societies died by age twenty, and few lived past the age of forty. Health in poor societies, due to poverty, is much worse than in industrial societies. The World Health Organization (WHO) estimates 1 billion people worldwide to be in poor health, mostly due to hunger. Infectious disease is very widespread.

Health in High-Income Countries

The agricultural revolution increased surpluses, but also inequality, so only the elite enjoyed better health. Urbanization during medieval times created horrible health problems. Initially, there was little improvement in health due to industrialization. It was not until the second half of the nineteenth century that medical advances had any significant impact on health.

Table 13-3 (p. 349) shows the ten leading causes of death in the U.S. for the years 1900 and 1995. Significant differences appear. Medical advances and lifestyle changes have affected the changes. About 60 percent of the deaths in the U.S. are attributable to heart disease, cancer, and cerebrovascular diseases. Chronic illnesses, rather than infectious diseases, are the major threat today.

HEALTH IN THE UNITED STATES

Social Epidemiology: Who Is Healthy?

Social epidemiology is *the study of how health and disease are distributed throughout a society's population*. Health in the U.S. of all age groups has improved during this century, with the exception of young adults, who are victims of more accidental deaths. *Gender* distinctions explain significant differences in longevity. There is also a strong relationship between *social class* and health. *Table 13-4* (p. 350) shows the assessment of personal health by different family income levels. *Table 13-5* (p. 350) shows the life expectancy for U.S. children by *race* and *sex*. Significant differences emerge. factors related to these differences are economic, with African Americans being overrepresented among the poor, placing many of them in conditions of poorer diet and greater stress. Further, the homicide rate among African Americas, particularly for males, is extremely high.

Eating Disorders

An *eating disorder* is a dangerous and intense striving to become thin, is widespread in the United States. Eating disorders have a strong cultural component. Ninety-five percent of people who suffer from anorexia nervosa or bulimia are women.

Cigarette Smoking

Cigarette smoking is the leading preventable cause of illness and death in the United States. Evidence of the health risks of smoking first appeared in the 1930s. It was not for another thirty years that the government actually began systematic research. Currently, about 450,000 people die prematurely each year as a result of the effects of cigarette smoking.

Today, 25 percent of our adult population smokes. The figure was almost 45 percent in 1960. A further reduction over the next decade is expected. Smoking is difficult to quit because nicotine is physically addictive. Smoking varies by social class, with blue-collar workers more likely to smoke than white-collar workers. A greater percentage of males smoke than females. As sales in the U.S. and other industrialized societies drop, tobacco companies have begun to sell more products in poor countries.

Sexually Transmitted Diseases

Sexually transmitted diseases (STDs) represent an exception to the general decline in infectious diseases during this century. About 1 million cases of *gonorrhea* are reported each year in the United States, although the actual number is probably much higher. Approximately 78 percent of the cases reported involve African Americans.

Syphilis is much more serious. It can lead to damage of major organs, and result in blindness, mental disorders, and death. About 76 percent of the reported cases in the U.S. involve African Americans. Both diseases can be easily cured with penicillin.

It is estimated that one-eighth of U.S. adults arc carriers of the *genital herpes* virus. The infection rate among African Americans is about three times higher than it is for whites. Although not as serious as gonorrhea or syphilis, there is currently no cure available.

AIDS, or *acquired immune deficiency syndrome*, is a health problem which could become the most serious epidemic of modern times. AIDS is caused by a human immunodeficiency virus (HIV). The virus attacks white blood cells, the core of our immune system. The presence of the virus does not necessarily generate AIDS.

Transmission of HIV almost always occurs through blood, semen, or breast milk. AIDS is not spread through casual contact. There are specific behaviors identified which put people at high risk for getting AIDS. The first is *anal sex*. Another is *sharing needles*. Yet another is *using any drug*. *Figure 13-3* (p. 354) shows the proportions for type of transmission for reported AIDS cases in 1996. Two-thirds of the people with AIDS are homosexual or bisexual males. By mid-1996, 548,000 people in the U.S. had been diagnosed with the disease, with 330,000 of these people already having died. In global perspective, as many as 15 million people are infected with HIV. In the *Window on the World* box (p. 353), *Global Map 13-2* illustrates the distribution of IIIV infected people around the world.

Ethical Issues: Confronting Death

Ethical issues permeate health and medical concerns. Questions addressed include: When is a person dead? Do people have a right to die? And, what about *mercy killing*? Medical and legal experts presently define as an *irreversible* state involving no response to stimulation, no movement or breathing, no reflexes, and no indication of brain activity.

Euthanasia, commonly known as mercy killing, is *assisting in the death of a person suffering from an incurable disease*. The "suicide machine" developed by Jack Kevorkian is discussed. Financial concerns are involved in making decisions about euthanasia.

THE MEDICAL ESTABLISHMENT

Today, *scientific medicine*, meaning the logic of science applied to research and treatment of disease and injury, dominates. In colonial America, medicine was the domain of herbalists, druggists, midwives, and ministers. Medical care was plagued by unsanitary conditions and ignorance.

During the early nineteenth century, medicine came under the control of medical societies. By 1900 there were 400 medical schools in the United States. Licensing became the order in the second half of the nineteenth century. Medical standards were established and directed by the American Medical Association (AMA), which was founded in 1847.

Holistic Medicine

Holistic medicine is *an approach to health care that emphasizes prevention of illness and takes account of the person's entire physical and social environment*. It is critical of scientific medical specialists for being focused on symptoms and diseases rather than with people. The major concerns of this approach include: *patients are people, responsibility, not dependency,* and *personal treatment*. The goal of holistic medicine is optimum health for all.

Paying the Costs: A Global Survey

In societies like the People's Republic of China and the new Russian Federation, the government directly controls medical care. Medical costs are paid for by public funds, and medical care is distributed equally among all. In the new Russian Republic, 70 percent of the physicians are women. In the U.S. 16 percent of physicians are women.

The People's Republic of China is still a relatively poor agrarian society which is just beginning to industrialize. With over 1 billion people, reaching everyone within one system is virtually impossible. Barefoot doctors, equivalent to paramedics in the U.S., bring modern methods to millions of rural residents in China. Traditional healing arts remain strong in China.

In capitalist societies, citizens provide for themselves based on their own resources and preferences. Government assistance is provided to varying degrees. In Sweden there exists a compulsory, comprehensive system of government medical care. The program is paid for through taxes. This system is known as *socialized medicine, a medical-care system in which the government owns most facilities and employs most physicians*. Great Britain has a dual system in which socialized medicine exists, but for those who wish, and can afford it, private care is available. The Canadian system does not offer a true socialized medicine. The government reimburses citizens for medical care according to set fees. Physicians operate privately. In Japan, a combination of private insurance and government programs pays for medical costs. Large Japanese corporations cover their employees well. Physicians and hospitals operate privately.

Medicine in the United States

While European governments pay about 80 percent of their citizen's medical costs, the U.S. government pays only 42 percent. For the most part, the U.S. medical system is a private, profit-making industry. It is identified as a *direct-fee system*, or *a medical system in which patients pay directly for the services of physicians and hospitals*. Poor people in the U.S. have less access to medical care than their counterparts in Europe. Overall, the relative health of our people is worse than is found in European societies.

The U.S. has not developed a national health-care program for several reasons. Americans have traditionally not been open to government intervention in the economy. There is little support for such programs by the public. Also, the AMA has worked hard against dismantling the direct-fee system.

The technological advances in medicine have caused tremendous increases in the cost of medical care. Currently, medical care absorbs over 14 percent of our GNP. In 1994, 60 percent of the U.S. population received some medical-care benefits from a family member's employer or purchased coverage on their own (*private insurance programs*). *Public insurance programs* also exist. Medicare and Medicaid were created in 1965.

HMOs, or *health maintenance organizations*, are *associations that provide comprehensive medical care for a fixed fee*. Eighteen percent of the U.S. population is covered by such programs. In all, 85 percent of people in our society have some medical-care coverage. Still, over 30 million people in the U.S. have no medical coverage. The recent debate concerning universal health-care coverage, especially President Clinton's "managed competition" plan, is reviewed.

THEORETICAL ANALYSIS OF HEALTH AND MEDICINE

Structural-Functional Analysis

The key concept in structural-functional analysis of illness is the *sick role*, or *patterns of behavior defined as appropriate for those who are ill*. As developed by Talcott Parsons, the sick role has four characteristics, including: a sick person is exempted from routine responsibilities; a person's illness is not deliberate; a sick person must want to be well; and a sick person must seek competent help. Another key concept is the *physician's role*. The physician is expected to cure illness. according to Parsons, a hierarchy exists in which physicians expect compliance from their patients.

Criticism of the structural-functional view of society includes a failure to recognize the inequalities in medical care services in the U.S. Also, Parson's physicians role concept fits contemporary scientific medicine, but not holistic medicine.

Symbolic-Interaction Analysis

Symbolic-interactionists focus on the subjective dimension of illness, or how illness is *socially constructed*. The concept of *psychosomatic disorder*, referring to how a person's state of mind affects physical well-being, relates to this issue. *Socially constructed treatment* is also addressed. The gynecological exam conducted by a male doctor is used to illustrate. A problem with this approach is that it minimizes an objective sense of health and illness.

Social-Conflict Analysis

The *access issue* regarding medical care is the central concern of the proponents of this perspective. Inequality for social-conflict theorists is rooted in the capitalist-class system, which doe not equitably distribute its resources. The *profit motive* dominates. They point out that three-fourths of all surgery in the U.S. is elective, not prompted by medical emergencies. Objections to this approach include the fact that it minimizes the improvements in medical care brought about by scientific medicine. The *Global Sociology* box (p. 361) takes a look at the issue of female genital mutilation, a common practice in many African nations.

Looking Ahead: Health in the Twenty-First Century

The advances in medicine that have been occurring over this century are expected to continue. There are many encouraging trends. Yet, health problems will continue, especially for the poor.

PART IV: KEY CONCEPTS

Education:

A Nation At Risk
Coleman Report
credentialism
education
functional illiteracy
juku
mainstreaming
mandatory education laws
schooling
student passivity
tracking

Medicine:

AIDS
anorexia nervosa
direct-fee system
euthanasia
health
health care
HIV
HMO
holistic medicine
living will
psychosomatic disorder
scientific medicine
sick role

social epidemiology
socialized medicine
WHO

PART V: IMPORTANT RESEARCHERS

David Karp and William Yoels   Randall Collins

James Coleman   Jonathan Kozol

Christopher Jencks   John Dewey

Theodore Sizer   Erving Goffman

Talcott Parsons

PART VI: STUDY QUESTIONS

<u>True-False</u>

1. T   F   The United States was among the first nations to enhance the principle of *mass education*.
2. T   F   About twenty-five percent of adults in the U.S. have a *college degree*.

3. T F More students in the U.S. who graduate high school go on to college than do students in Japan.

4. T F *John Dewey* was a foremost advocate of the idea that schooling should have practical consequences.

5. T F Roughly seventy-five percent of primary and secondary school children in the U.S. attend *public schools*.

6. T F The *Coleman Report* determined that the amount of educational funding was the most important factor in determining education achievement.

7. T F About 80 percent of high-school graduates in the U.S. enroll in college the following fall.

8. T F Male college graduates can expect in their lifetime to earn about 45 percent more than female college graduates.

9. T F The argument is being made that an emphasis on *credentialism* in our society leads to a condition of undereducation as people seek the status of a career and its earnings over the completion of degree programs at college.

10. T F The work *A Nation At Risk* focuses on the deteriorating health care in the U.S. due to rising health-care costs and increasing poverty levels.

11. T F The World Health Organization defines *health* as simply the absence of disease.

12. T F The top five *causes of death* int he U.S. have changed very little since 1900.

13. T F Sex is a stronger predictor of health than race.

14. T F *Venereal diseases* first appeared during the colonialization of Africa and Asia by European nations.

15. T F The *American Medical Association* was founded in 1945.

16. T F Approximately 70 percent of *physicians* in the new Russian Federation are women.

17. T F The U.S. is unique among industrialized societies in lacking government programs that ensure basic medical care to every citizen.

18. T F Only about 25 percent of the U.S. population has some private or company-paid medical insurance coverage.

19. T F Most surgery in the U.S. is *elective*, or not prompted by a medical emergency.

20. T F One criticism of the *symbolic-interaction* paradigm is that this approach seems to deny that there are any objective standards of well-being.

Multiple Choice

1. The extra, intensive schooling received by *Japanese* elementary school children in the afternoon takes place within the:

    (a) huanco   (c) taruku
    (b) mitchou   (d) juku

2. *Mandatory education* laws were found in every state in the U.S. by:

    (a) 1781   (c) 1850
    (b) 1822   (d) 1918

3. Who advocated the idea that schooling should have *practical* consequences and promoted *progressive education*?

    (a)   James Coleman   (c)   John Dewey
    (b)   Daniel Moynihan   (d)   Christopher Jencks

4. According to *structural-functionalists*, which of the following functions of formal education helps forge a population into a single, unified society?

    (a)   socialization   (c)   social placement
    (b)   social integration   (d)   cultural innovation

5. The *Coleman Report* and research by *Christopher Jencks* concluded that:

    (a)   social inequality is not a problem in public education within our society
    (b)   the simple answer to qualify education is more funding for schools
    (c)   minority schools are actually better than schools that are predominately white in terms of their student achievement
    (d)   education is the great equalizer and stressing the importance of differences between families is not particularly important for educational achievement
    (e)   schools alone cannot overcome social inequality

6. The National Commission on Excellence in Education (1983) issued a report called *A Nation At Risk*, in which it recommended:

    (a)   ending student passivity
    (b)   increasing credentialism
    (c)   more stringent educational requirements
    (d)   reducing the length of time students spend in school to allow more students to learn practical skills through employment
    (e)   reducing our educational focus on reading, writing, and arithmetic

7. *Functional illiteracy* refers to:

    (a)   an inability to read and write at all
    (b)   an inability to read at the appropriate level of schooling based on one's age
    (c)   an inability to write
    (d)   reading and writing skills inadequate for everyday living

8. The *health* of any population is shaped by:

    (a)   the society's cultural patterns
    (b)   the society's technology
    (c)   the society's social inequality
    (d)   all of the above

9. The study of how health and disease are distributed throughout a society's population is called:

(a) scientific medicine
(b) social epidemiology
(c) holistic medicine
(d) epistemology

10. The improvement in health in the nineteenth century was mainly due to:

(a) the rising standard of living
(b) medical advances
(c) changes in cultural values toward medicine
(d) increases in the number of medical personnel
(e) none of the above

11. Which of the following were the *leading causes of death* in the U.S. in 1900?

(a) accidents and heart disease
(b) cancer and diphtheria
(c) influenza and pneumonia
(d) lung disease and kidney disease
(e) homicide and diabetes

12. The institutionalization of *scientific medicine* by the AMA resulted in:

(a) expensive medical education
(b) domination of medicine by white males
(c) an inadequate supply of physicians in rural areas
(d) all of the above
(e) none of the above

13. *Holistic medicine* is a reaction to scientific medicine. Which of the following is *not* an emphasis advocates of holistic medicine share?

(a) an emphasis upon the environment in which the person exists
(b) an emphasis upon the responsibility of society for health promotion and care
(c) an emphasis upon optimum health for all
(d) an emphasis upon the home setting for medical treatment

14. *European* governments pay about ____ percent of medical costs, whereas in the *United States*, the government pays about ____ percent of medical costs.

(a) 80/42
(b) 25/50
(c) 100/10
(d) 40/60

15. Approximately what percentage of our GNP is related to health care?

    (a) 2   (c) 14
    (b) 6   (d) 24

16. An association that provides comprehensive medical care for a fixed fee is termed a(n):

    (a) WHO   (c) DFS
    (b) AMA   (d) HMO

17. Which of the following *theoretical paradigms* in sociology utilizes concepts like *sick role* and *physician's role* to help explain health behavior?

    (a) social-conflict   (d) social-exchange
    (b) symbolic-interaction   (e) structural-functional
    (c) materialism

18. Which of the following *theoretical paradigms* in sociology focuses on the issues of *access* and *profits* in the study of health care?

    (a) social-conflict   (c) structural-functional
    (b) symbolic-interaction   (d) social-exchange

Matching

Education

1. ___ Evaluating people on the basis of education degrees.
2. ___ A 1983 study on the quality of schooling.
3. ___ The Assignment of students to different types of educational programs.
4. ___ The percentage of high-school graduates who attend college the same year as receiving their high-school diploma.
5. ___ The percentage of the 51 million primary and secondary school children attending state-funded public schools.
6. ___ The percentage of students bused outside their neighborhoods.
7. ___ Schooling in the U.S. reflects the value of _____.
8. ___ The percentage of U.S. adults aged 25-64 with a college degree.
9. ___ Confirmed that predominately minority schools suffer problems, but cautioned that money alone will not magically improve academic quality.
10. ___ Championed progressive education.

    a. tracking   f. 5
    b. 62   g. James Coleman
    c. equal opportunity   h. John Dewey
    d. credentiaism   i. A Nation at Risk
    e. 24   j. 89

Medicine

1. ___ The number one cause of death in the U.S. today.
2. ___ The study of how health and disease are spread throughout a society's population.
3. ___ An approach to health care that emphasizes prevention of illness and takes account of the person's entire physical and social environment.
4. ___ The social institution that focuses on combating disease and improving health.
5. ___ A medical-care system in which the government owns most facilities and employs most physicians.
6. ___ The percentage of health expenditures paid by the government in the U.S. today
7. ___ Patterns of behavior defined as appropriate for those who are ill.
8. ___ The number two cause of death in the U.S. today.
9. ___ Percentage of physicians in the new Russian Federation who are women.
10. ___ The percentage of health expenditures paid by European governments today.

a. sick role   f. 80
b. cancer   g. medicine
c. socialized medicine   h. heart disease
d. 70   i. 42
e. social epidemiology   j. holistic medicine

Fill-In

1. The social institution through which society provides its members with important knowledge, including basic facts, job skills, and cultural values is termed _____.
2. While in Japan _____ percent of its population graduates from high school, in the U.S. the rate is _____ percent.
3. According to *structural-functionalists* _____ enhances the operation of society by providing socialization, social integration, social placement, and other latent functions.
4. _____ refers to the division of a school's students into different educational programs.
5. In the U.S., the most crucial factor affecting *access* to higher education is _____.
6. The average *annual earnings* for a male with a high-school education is about $ _____, while the average earnings for a woman with a college education is about $ _____.
7. *Theodore Sizer* identified through his research five ways in which large, _____ schools undermine education, including rigid conformity, numerical rating, rigid expectations, specialization, and little individual responsibility.
8. The 1983 report by the National Commission on Excellence in Education was entitled
   _____.
9. Researchers *David Karp* and *William Yoels* studied the problem of _____ in the college classroom.
10. _____ refers to the integration of disabled students into the educational program as a whole.
11. About _____ million adults in the U.S. are now enrolled in college.
12. _____ is the study of how health and disease are distributed throughout a society's population.

205

13. The leading cause of death today in the U.S. is _____, while in 1900 it was _____ and _____.

14. Consumption of *cigarettes* has fallen since 1960, when almost _____ percent of U.S. adults smoked. Today, only about _____ percent of U.S. adults are smokers.

15. AIDS, acquired immune deficiency syndrome, is caused by HIV or, a _____.

16. _____ is assisting in the death of a person suffering from an incurable disease.

17. _____ *medicine* is an approach to health care that emphasizes prevention of illness and takes account of the person's entire physical and social environment.

18. About _____ percent of U.S. physicians are *women*.

19. While *European* governments pay for about eighty percent of their people's medical costs, in the *United States* the government pays for about _____ percent.

20. The _____ _____ refers to patterns of behavior defined as appropriate for those who are ill.

21. *Social-conflict* analysis focuses attention on the _____ issue, the _____ motive, and medicine as _____ in helping us understand health and medical care in our society.

Definition and Short-Answer

1. Describe the four basic *functions* of education as reviewed in the text.
2. What were the basic findings of the *Coleman Report*?
3. How do *annual earnings* differ for men and women given different levels of education achievement?
4. What are the five serious problems with the *bureaucratic* nature of the our educational system?
5. What recommendations were made in the report *A Nation At Risk*?
6. Differentiate between the educational systems of the U.S. and Japan.
7. What are the major *problems* in U.S. education? Identify the specific factors involved in each problem identified. What is one recommendation you have to solving each of the problems?
8. It is pointed out in the text that the *health* of any population is shaped by important characteristics of the society as a whole. What are three general characteristics and an example of each?
9. How have the *causes of death* changed in the U.S. over the last century?
10. What is *social epidemiology*? Provide two illustrations of patterns of health found using this approach.
11. What is *AIDS*? How is it transmitted?
12. What is meant by the *sick role*?
13. Describe the three basic characteristics of *holistic medicine*.
14. In what ways does the health-care system of the U.S. differ from health-care systems in other capitalist systems?
15. What are *social-conflict* analysts' arguments about the health care system in the United States?
16. What factors are identified as reasons for why the U.S. does not have a *national health-care system*?
17. What do *symbolic-interactionists* mean by *socially constructing illness* and *socially constructing treatment*?

PART VII: ANSWERS TO STUDY QUESTIONS

<u>True-False</u>

1.	T	(p. 334)
2.	T	(p. 336)
3.	T	(p. 336)
4.	T	(p. 336)
5.	F	(p. 338)
6.	F	(p. 339)
7.	F	(p. 340)
8.	T	(p. 341)
9.	F	(p. 341)
10.	F	(p. 343)

11.	F	(pp. 346-347)
12.	F	(p. 349)
13.	T	(p. 350)
14.	F	(p. 351)
15.	F	(p. 355)
16.	T	(p. 356)
17.	T	(p. 357)
18.	F	(p. 357)
19.	T	(p. 359)
20.	T	(p. 360)

<u>Multiple Choice</u>

1.	d	(p. 333)
2.	d	(p. 334)
3.	c	(p. 336)
4.	b	(p. 337)
5.	e	(p. 339)
6.	c	(p. 343)
7.	d	(p. 344)
8.	d	(p. 347)
9.	b	(p. 349)
10.	a	(p. 349)

11.	c	(p. 349)
12.	d	(p. 355)
13.	b	(p. 356)
14.	a	(p. 357)
15.	c	(p. 357)
16.	d	(p. 358)
17.	e	(p. 358)
18.	a	(pp. 359-360)

<u>Matching</u>

Education

1.	d	(p. 341)
2.	i	(p. 343)
3.	a	(p. 338)
4.	b	(p. 340)
5.	j	(p. 338)

6.	f	(p. 339)
7.	c	(p. 336)
8.	e	(p. 337)
9.	g	(p. 339)
10.	h	(p. 336)

Medicine

1.	h	(p. 349)
2.	e	(p. 349)
3.	j	(p. 356)
4.	g	(p. 346)
5.	c	(p. 356)

6.	i	(p. 357)
7.	a	(p. 358)
8.	b	(p. 356)
9.	d	(p. 356)
10.	f	(p. 357)

1.   education (p. 334)
2.   90, 82 (p. 336)
3.   schooling (p. 337)
4.   tracking (p. 338)
5.   money (p. 340)
6.   29, 510, 32,051 (p. 341)
7.   bureaucratic (p. 342)
8.   A Nation At Risk (p. 343)
9.   passivity (p. 343)
10.   mainstreaming (p. 345)
11.   25 (p. 346)
12.   social epidemiology (p. 349)
13.   heart disease, influenza, pneumonia (p. 349)
14.   45, 25 (p. 351)
15.   human immunodeficiency virus (p. 352)
16.   euthanasia (p. 354)
17.   holistic (p. 356)
18.   16 (p. 356)
19.   42 (p. 357)
20.   sick role (p. 358)
21.   access, profit, politics (p. 359)

PART VIII: ANALYSIS AND COMMENT

Critical Thinking

"Functional Illiteracy: Must We Rethink Education?"

Key Points: Questions:

Global Sociology

"Female Genital Mutilation: When Medicine is Politics"

Key Points: Questions:

Exploring Cyber-Society

"Welcome to "Cyber-College"!"

Key Points: Questions:

Seeing Ourselves--National Map 13-1

"College Attendance across the United States"

Key Points: Questions:

Window on the World--Global Maps 13-1 and 13-2

"Illiteracy in Global Perspective"

Key Points: Questions:

"HIV Infection of Adults in Global Perspective"

Key Points: Questions:

Population and Urbanization

14

PART I: CHAPTER OUTLINE

PART II: LEARNING OBJECTIVES

1. To learn the basic concepts used by demographers to study populations.
2. To be able to compare Malthusian theory and demographic transition theory.
3. To be able to recognize how populations differ in industrial and nonindustrial societies.
4. To gain an understanding of the worldwide urbanization process, and to be able to put it into historical perspective.
5. To be able to describe demographic changes in the U.S. throughout its history.
7. To consider urbanism as a way of life as viewed by several historical figures in sociology.
8. To consider the idea of urban ecology.

PART III: CHAPTER REVIEW--KEY POINTS

This chapter begins with a brief review of Cortes' discovery and destruction of the great Aztec city of Tenochtitlan in the early sixteenth century. In its place he began to build Mexico City, which is expected to have a population of almost thirty million by the year 2000. The triple burden of rising population, urban sprawl, and desperate poverty plagues much of today's world.

DEMOGRAPHY: THE STUDY OF POPULATION

Demography is *the study of human population*. It is a quantitative discipline; however, crucial questions about the consequences of population variables are analyzed and have great qualitative significance.

Fertility

Fertility is *the incidence of childbearing in a society's population*. A female's childbearing years last from the beginning of menstruation to menopause. But, *fecundity*, or potential childbearing, is greatly reduced by health, financial constraints, and cultural norms.

A typical measurement used for fertility is the *crude birth rate*, or *the number of live births in a given year for every thousand people in a population*. In 1995 about 3.9 million live births occurred in the U.S. (population 260.4 million) for a crude birth rate of 14.9.

Mortality

Mortality is *the incidence of death in a society's population*. The *crude death rate* refers to *the number of deaths in a given year for every thousand people in a population*. There were about 2.3 million deaths in the U.S. in 1995, for a crude death rate of 8.8.

The *infant mortality rate*, refers to *the number of deaths among infants under one year of age for each thousand live births in a given year*. The infant mortality rate in the U.S. in 1995 was 7.8. *Table 14-1* (p. 367) compares fertility, mortality, and infant mortality rates for countries around the world. Significant differences exist between industrialized and poor nations.

Life expectancy, or *the average life span of a society's population*, is negatively correlated with a society's infant mortality rate. For males born in the U.S. in 1996 life expectancy is 72 years and for females 79 years. In poor societies life expectancy is more than twenty years less.

Migration

Migration refers to *the movement of people into and out of a specified territory*. Some is involuntary, such as the historical existence of slave trading, while most is voluntary and based on various "push-pull" factors. Movement into a territory, commonly termed *immigration* is also known as *in-migration*. Movement out of an area, or *emigration*, is typically termed *out-migration*. The difference between the two figures is termed the *net-migration rate*.

Population Growth

Migration, fertility, and mortality each affect a society's population size. The *natural growth rate* of a society is determined by subtracting the crude death rate from the crude birth rate. This figure for the U.S. in 1995 was 6.1 per thousand, or 0.61 percent annually. In the *Window on the World* box (p. 367), *Global Map 14-1* shows the projected rates for different world regions during the 1990s. Industrialized regions--Europe, North America, and Oceania--have very low rates, while in Asia, Africa, and Latin America--relatively high rates exist. In the *Seeing Ourselves* box (p. 368), *National Map 14-1* shows data on population change across the United States.

Dividing a society's growth rate into the number seventy yields the *doubling time* for a society's population. In Latin America, for example, where the annual growth rate is 2 percent, the doubling time is thirty-five years. Africa, with a 3 percent growth rate, has a doubling time of twenty-four years.

Population Composition

The *sex ratio* refers to *the number of males for every hundred females in a given population*. In the U.S. in 1995 the sex ratio was 95.2. A more complicated descriptive device is the *age-sex pyramid* which is *a graphic representation of the age and sex of a population*. *Figure 14-2* (p. 370) presents the age-sex pyramids for the U.S. and Mexico. Dramatic differences exist. Two birth cohorts identified and discussed are the *baby boom* and *baby bust* cohorts.

HISTORY AND THEORY OF POPULATION GROWTH

Until relatively recently in human history, societies desired high birth rates as they meant more human resources for productivity. High birth rates were needed to offset high death rates. Birth control was very unreliable. A crucial point in world population growth occurred in the middle of the eighteenth century as the earth's population began a sharp increase (reaching 1 billion in 1850), resulting more from a drop in the mortality rate than from a rise in the birth rate. In the twentieth century alone the world's population has increased four-fold. *Figure 14-3* (p. 371) illustrates actual and projected world population growth 1700-2100. There are almost 6 billion people in the world today, and by 2025 it is estimated there may be 8 billion.

Malthusian Theory

In the late eighteenth century Thomas Malthus developed a theory of population growth in which he warned of disaster. He predicted population would increase according to a *geometric progression*, while food production would only increase in *arithmetic progression*. Several reasons why his projections have not been realized are discussed. Technology has caused problems for the environment, and population growth in poor nations remains very high.

Demographic Transition Theory

Demographic transition theory has now replaced Malthusian theory and is *a thesis linking population patterns to a society's level of technological development. Figure 14-4* (p. 372) illustrates three stages of technological change, and the related birth and death rates associated with each. Stage 1 is represented by the preindustrial agrarian society with high birth rates and high death rates. Stage 2, represented by industrialization, marks the beginning of the demographic transition, with high birth rates continuing, but death rates dropping significantly. In stage three, the fully industrialized society, birth rates begin to drop significantly and death rates remain stable and low. A higher standard of living is found in stage 3. This view is more optimistic than Malthusian theory.

WORLD POPULATION: A SURVEY

The Low-Growth North

Using demographic transition theory important differences between industrialized and nonindustrilized societies can be noted in terms of population patterns. Europe and the U.S. are near population replacement level of 2.1 births per woman, a point known as *zero population growth*, or the level of reproduction that maintains population at a steady state. In certain European societies, a fourth stage may have even been reached where there is actually a population decline. Several factors, including the increasing cost of raising children, a high percentage of women and men in the labor force, abortion, contraceptives, and delaying marriage, are reasons for low birth rates in industrial societies.

The High-Growth South

Few societies are still represented by stage 1. Most poor nations, having a combination of agrarian and industrial economies, fall in stage 2. *Figure 14-3* (p. 371) shows the population distribution, past and projected, in rich and poor societies from 1700-2100. The decreasing death rates in poor societies has resulted in a population explosion.

Birth rates are high for age-old reasons--the economic asset of children to the family and high infant mortality rates. The cultural norm of patriarchy also is a factor. The social status of women is therefore a critical issue in this demographic picture. The *Critical Thinking* box (p. 374) takes a closer look at this point.

URBANIZATION: THE GROWTH OF CITIES

Urbanization is *the concentration of humanity into cities.* World history has been characterized by three urban revolutions.

The Evolution of Cities

The *first urban revolution* occurred about 10,000 years ago with the emergence of permanent settlements. Two factors are discussed as *preconditions of cities*, a *favorable ecology* and a *changing technology*.

The *first city* is argued to have been Jericho, just north of the Dead Sea, coming into existence about 8000 B.C.E. By 4000 B.C.E. there were several cities within the Fertile Crescent in present day Iraq and along the Nile in Eqypt. Cities emerged independently in at least three other areas of the world--in present-day Pakistan (about 2500 B.C.E.), in China (about 2000 B.C.E.), and in Central and South America (about 1500 B.C.E.).

Preindustrial European cities began to emerge in about 1800 B.C.E. Urbanization began in Europe on Crete and spread throughout Greece in the form of hundreds of city states. Athens is the most well known. As Greek civilization faded, the city of Rome grew to almost 1 million by the first century C.E. The militaristic Roman Empire had expanded throughout Europe and Northern Africa. The fall of the Roman Empire started a period of urban decline. The Dark Ages followed, and lasted 600 years. Cities became smaller and were usually surrounded by walls. By the eleventh century medieval cities began to remove their walls to facilitate trade. These cities in Europe were categorized by "quarters," or areas where particular occupational groups were represented.

Industrial European cities emerged as a result of the increasing commerce created by the *bourgeoisie*, or affluent middle class. By 1750 the *second urban revolution* was under way, triggered by the Industrial Revolution.

The Growth of U.S. Cities

Native Americans established few permanent settlements. The Spanish made their first settlement in St. Augustine in Florida in 1565. The English founded Jamestown in Virgina in 1607. Today, more than three-quarters of the U.S. population lives in urban areas. *Table 14-3* (p. 377) shows the change in the number and percentage of the U.S. population living in urban areas between 1790 and 1990.

The first period discussed is referred to as *colonial settlement: 1624-1800*. The changing face of settlements in the northeastern U.S. during the seventeeth century is discussed. *Figure 14-4* (p. 376) contrasts the different urban devlopment patterns of early colonial cities, showing how the traditional European shape of winding and narrow roads were replaced by grid-like patterns.

The second period discussed is referred to as *urban expansion: 1800-1860*. Important transportation developments influenced the development of cities in the East and Midwest. By 1860 about one-third of the U.S. population lived in cities.

The third period discussed is referred to as the *metropolitan era: 1860-1950*. *Table 14-4* (p. 377) illutrates the rapid growth of cities in the late nineteenth century. The growth between 1860-1900 marked the beginning of the era of the *metropolis*. By the end of World War I most people in the U.S. lived in cities.

The fourth period discussed is referred to as *urban decentralization: 1950-present*. Since 1950, people have been moving away from the central cities in the U.S. *Table 14-4* (p. 377) also illustrates how many Northeastern and Midwestern cities have been experiencing either stable or declining populations. Urbanization continues, however, with growth of suburbs.

The Rise of Suburbs

Suburbs, the urban areas beyond the political boundaries of a city, have been expanding in recent decades. The post-World War II economic boom, more affordable cars, and an increased birth rate all were factors in the rapid growth of suburbia. By 1970, more people lived in the suburbs than in central cities. Tax revenues in cities declined, causing many cities to decay. The government responded with *urban renewal*, or government progams intended to revitalize cities.

Postindustrial Sunbelt Cities

In 1940 the "Snowbelt" contained 60 percent of the U.S. population. In 1996 the "Sunbelt" contained 60 percent of the U.S. population. Six of the ten largest cities (by population) are now in the Sunbelt. This shift in population is linked to the postindustrial economy.

Megalopolis: Regional Cities

Decentralization has created regional cities. The Census Bureau officially recognizes 253 urban regions in the U.S. These are claled *metropolitan statistical areas* (MSAs). They must include a city with a population of at least 50,000, plus densely populated surrounding counties. The largest MSAs are called *consolidated metropolitan statistical areas* (CMSAs). Eighteen of these exist in the United States. When several of the CMSAs geographically meet, like the east coast from Boston to northern Virgina, a *megalopilis*, or vast urban region containing a number of cities and their surrounding suburbs, is created.

URBANISM AS A WAY OF LIFE

Ferdinand Toennies: Gemeinschaft and Gesellschaft

Ferdinand Toennies, a German sociologist of the late nineteenth century differentiated between two types of social organization. The first, **Gemeinschaft**, refers to *a type of social organization by which people are bound closely together by kinship and tradition*. It describes social settings dominated by primary groups and small villages. In contrast, **Gesellschaft** is *a type of social organization by which people stand apart based on self-interest*. This represents city dwellers.

Emile Durkheim: Mechanical and Organic Solidarity

Emile Durkheim, a French sociologist of the late nineteenth and early twentieth centuries, saw the spread of urbanization in much the same way as Toennies. His concept **mechanical solidarity** refers to *social bonds based on collective conformity to tradition*. In contrast, his concept **organic solidarity** refers to *social bonds based on specialization and interdependence*. Durkheim was more optimistic than Toennies about this historical transformation.

Georg Simmel: The Blase' Urbanite

Georg Simmel, another German sociologist of the same time period, used a micro-level analysis of how urban life shaped the behavior and attitudes of people. He argued city dwellers needed to be selective in what they respond to because of the social intensity of such a life. They then develop a *blase' attitude* out of necessity.

Robert Park: Walking the Streets

The first major sociology progam in the U.S. to focus on urban development was at the University of Chicago. Robert Park is perhaps the most famous urban researcher to have worked at Chicago. He saw the city as a highly ordered mosaic of distinctive regions. Cities were viewed as

215

complex social organism by Park.

Louis Wirth: Urbanism as a Way of Life

As another of the Chicago urban researchers, Louis Wirth identified three factors that define urbanism: large population, dense settlement, and social diversity. He saw cities as impersonal, superficial, and tansitory.

Support for Park's and Wirth's views of city life have been mixed. While a greater sense of community exists in rural areas, the difference compared to cities can be exaggerated. So, early sociologists were incorrect in their projection that urban life would neutralize the effects of class, race, and sex.

Urban Ecology

Urban ecology is *the study of the link between the physical and social dimensions of cities.* One issue concerns where cities are located. Another issue concerns the physical design of cities. Models discussed include the *concentric zone* model of Ernest Burgess, the *Wedge-shaped sector* model of Homer Hoyt, the *multi-centered* model of Chauncy Harris and Edward Ullman, the *social area* model, and an integrated analysis developed in the late 1960s.

URBANIZATION IN POOR SOCIETIES

Previously described were the first and second urban revolutions. A third urban revolution began about 1950. In 1950, about 25 percent of the low-income countries' population was urbanized; by the year 2000 this figure is expected to exceed 50 percent (it is currently 42 percent). In the *Window on the World* box (p. 383), *Global Map 14-2* puts urbanization into global perspective. *Table 14-3* (p. 384) compares the world's ten largest cities in 1980 and the projected sizes of certain cities for the year 2000. By 2000 only four of the largest cities are expected to be in industrial societies.

Looking Ahead: Population and Urbanization in the Twenty-First Century

Modernization and underdevelopment theories provide different answers to what is needed in order to stabilize and nurture the urban growth patterns in poor countries. Throughout history cities have improved people's living standards; Can this occur in poor societies? The answer affects all of us.

PART IV: KEY CONCEPTS

Population:

age-sex pyramid
crude birth rate
crude death rate
demographic transition theory
demography
emigration
fecundity

fertility
immigration
infant mortality rate
life expectancy
Maltusian theory
migration
mortality
natural growth rate
net-migration
sex ratio
zero population growth

Urbanization:

Gemeinschaft
Gesellscaft
megalopolis
suburbs
urbanization
urban ecology
urban renewal

PART V: IMPORTANT RESEARCHERS

Ferdinand Toennies

Emile Durkheim

Robert Park

Louis Wirth

Georg Simmel

Thomas Malthus

PART VI: STUDY QUESTIONS

True-False

1. T F Demorgaphers using what is known as the *crude birth rate* only take into account women of childbearing age in the calculation for this figure.
2. T F The U.S., using the demographer's *natural growth rate* measure, is experiencing a decline in population during the 1990s.
3. T F A significantly larger percentage of the U.S. population over the next two decades will be comprised of *childbearing aged women* than at any other period in our nation's history.
4. T F The world's population reached 1 billion in 1800, 2 billion in 1930, 3 billion in 1963, 4 billion in 1974, and 5 billion in 1987.
5. T F According to *demographic ttransition theory*, population patterns are linked to a society's level of technological development.
6. T F The *first urban revolution* occurred about ten thousand years ago.
7. T F *Urbanization* in Europe began about 1800 B.C.E.
8. T F In the mid-eighteenth century, the *Industrial Revolution* triggered a *second urban revolution*.
9. T F Most of the ten *largest cities* in the U.S. (by population) are in the *Sunbelt*.
10. T F Compared to *Louis Wirth, Robert Park* had a relatively negative view of urban life.
11. T F The *third urban revolution* begam around 1950 and continues to this day.
12. T F The population growth of urban areas in poor societies located in Latin America, Asia, and Africa is *twice* the rate for their societies as a whole.

Multiple-Choice

1. *Hernando Cortes'* reached the Aztec capital of _____ in 1519.

    (a) Cuzco   (c) Montezuma
    (b) Tikal   (d) Tenochititlan

2. The *sex ratio* in the U.S. is:

    (a) 85.4   (d) 100
    (b) 90.3   (e) 105
    (c) 95.2

3. *Demographic transition theory* links population patterns to a society's:

    (a) religious beliefs and practices
    (b) technological development
    (c) natural resources
    (d) sexual norms

4. The *first city* to have ever existed is argued to be:

   (a) Athens   (d) Cairo
   (b) Tikal   (e) Jericho
   (c) Rome

5. According to the text, the *second urban revolution* was triggered by:

   (a) the fall of Rome   (d) the post-World War II baby boom
   (b) the Industrial Revolution (e) the discovery of the New World
   (c) the fall of Greece

6. The period of *1950 to the present* is described in the text as:

   (a) urban decentralization   (c) the metropolitan era
   (b) urban expansion   (d) the second urban revolution

7. *Ferdinand Toennies'* concept referring to the type of social organization by which people stand apart based on self-interest is:

   (a) megalopolis   (d) sector model
   (b) Gesellschaft   (e) multi-nucei model
   (c) Gemeinschaft

8. The link between the *physical* and *social* dimensions of cities is known as:

   (a) Gesellschaft   (d) urban ecology
   (b) organic solidarity   (e) mechanical solidarity
   (c) demography

9. What percentage of the populations livng in *poor societies* is expected to be living in *urban areas* in the year 2000?

   (a) 82   (d) 50
   (b) 25   (e) 67
   (c) 37

10. Which of the following is expected to be the *largest urban area* (by population) in the year 2000?

    (a) Tokyo-Yokohama   (d) Shanghai
    (b) New York   (e) Buenos Aires
    (c) Mexico City

Matching

1. ___ Saw the city as a living organism, truly a human kaleidoscope.
2. ___ Developed the concepts Gemeinschaft and Gesellschaft.
3. ___ Developed the concepts of mechanical and organic solidarity.
4. ___ 1860-1950.
5. ___ Potential childbearing in a given population.
6. ___ A type of social organization by which people stand apart from one another in pursuit of self-interest.
7. ___ A theory claiming that population would soon rise out of control.
8. ___ Social bonds based on collective conformity to tradition.
9. ___ Argued that urbanites develop a blase' attitude, selectively tuning out much of what goes on around them.
10. ___ The incidence of childbearing in a society's population.
11. ___ The concentration of humanity into cities.
12. ___ A thesis linking population patterns to a society's level of technological development.

a. Ferdinand Toennies
b. mechanical solidarity
c. fertility
d. Gesellschaft
e. demographic transition theory
f. metropolitan era
g. Robert Parks
h. Malthusian theory
i. Emile Durkheim
j. fecundity
k. urbanization
l. Georg Simmel

Fill-In

1. _____ is the incidence of childbearing in a society's population.
2. *Thomas Malthus* saw population increasing according to _____ progression, and food production increasing in _____ progression.
3. _____ *theory* is the thesis that population patterns are linked to a society's level of technological development.
4. The two factors which set the stage for the development of the first cities were a *favorable* _____ and a *changing* _____.
5. The term _____ is from the Greek meaning "mother city."
6. The *metropolitan era* is characterized in the text as existing from _____ to _____.
7. The *Bureau of the Census* recognizes 253 urban areas in the U.S. which they call MSAs, or
   _____.
8. _____ refers to a type of social organization by which people are bound closely together by kinship and tradition.
9. By 1990, _____ cities had more than 5 million residents, and _____ were in *poor societies*.
10. Throughout history, _____ have *improved* people's standard of living more than any other settlement pattern.

Definition and Short-Answer

1.   What are the three basic factors which determine the *size* and *growth rate* of a popualtion? Define each of these concepts.
2.   Differentiate between *Malthusian theory* and *demoraphic transition theory* as perspectives on population growth.
3.   What are the three stages in the *demographic transition theory*? Describe each.
4.   Identify and describe the five *periods of growth* of U.S. cities.
5.   Differentiate between the concepts *metropolis* and *megalpolis*.
6.   Differentiate between the perspectives of *Louis Wirth* and *Robert Park* concerning urbanization.
7.   Describe how *urbanization* patterns are changing around the world.
8.   Compare the fiews of *Ferdinand Toennies* and *Emile Durkhein* concerning urbanization.
9.   What are three factors that are causing *urban growth* in poor societies?
10.   What is *urban ecology*? What are two criticism of this approach?
11.   Briefly review the *evolution of cities* as described in the text.
12.   Discuss significant points made in the text about the *low-growth north* and the *high-growth south*.
13.   What is the perspective offerred by *Georg Simmel* urbanism?
14.   What are three factors in the U.S. that helped cause the rise of suburbs in the U.S. after World War II?
15.   What are the three *urban revolutions*? Briefly describe each.

PART VII: ANSWERS TO STUDY QUESTIONS

True-False

1.	F	(p. 366)	7.	T	(p. 375)
2.	F	(p. 368)	8.	T	(p. 375)
3.	F	(p. 370)	9.	T	(p. 378)
4.	T	(p. 370)	10.	F	(p. 381)
5.	T	(p. 371)	11.	T	(p. 384)
6.	T	(p. 375)	12.	T	(p. 385)

Multiple-Choice

1.	d	(p. 365)	6.	a	(p. 377)
2.	c	(p. 368)	7.	b	(p. 379)
3.	b	(p. 371)	8.	d	(p. 381)
4.	e	(p. 375)	9.	d	(p. 384)
5.	b	(p. 375)	10.	a	(p. 384)

Matching

1.	g	(p. 381)	7.	h	(p. 370)
2.	a	(p. 381)	8.	b	(p. 379)
3.	i	(pp. 379-380)	9.	i	(p. 380)
4.	f	(p. 377)	10.	c	(p. 366)
5.	j	(p. 366)	11.	k	(p. 374)
6.	d	(p. 379)	12.	e	(p. 371)

Fill-In

1. fertility (p. 366)
2. geometric, arithmetic (p. 371)
3. demographic transition (p. 371)
4. ecology, technology (p. 375)
5. metropolis (p. 377)
6. 1860, 1950 (p. 377)
7. metropolitan statistical area (p. 379)
8. Gemeinschaft (p. 379)
9. 33, 25 (p. 384)
10. cities (p. 386)

PART VIII: ANALYSIS AND COMMENT

Critical Thinking

"Empowering Women: The Key to Controlling Population Growth"

Key Points: Questions:

Controversy and Debate

"Apocalypse Soon?: Will People Overwhelm the Earth?"

Key Points: Questions:

Seeing Ourselves--National Map 14-1

"Population Change across the United States"

Key Points: Questions:

Window on the World--Global Maps 14-1 and 14-2

"Population Growth in Global Perspective"

Key Points: Questions:

"Urbanization in Global Perspective"

Key Points: Questions:

Environment and Society

15

PART I: CHAPTER OUTLINE

I.   Ecology: The Study of the Natural Environment
    A.   The Role of Sociology
    B.   The Global Dimension
    C.   The Historical Dimension
    D.   Population Increase
    E.   Cultural Patterns: Growth and Limits
II. Environmental Issues
    A.   Solid Waste: The "Disposable Society"
    B.   Preserving Clean Water
    C.   Clearing the Air
    D.   Acid Rain
    E.   The Rain Forests
III. Society and the Environment: Theoretical Analysis
    A.   Structural-Functional Analysis
    B.   Cultural Ecology
    C.   Social-Conflict Analysis
    D.   Environmental Racism
IV. Looking Ahead: Toward a Sustainable Society and World
V.   Summary
VI. Key Concepts
VII. Critical-Thinking Questions

PART II: LEARNING OBJECTIVES

1.   To gain an appreciation for the global dimension of the natural environment.
2.   To develop an understanding of how sociology can help us confront environmental issues.
3.   To be able to discuss the dimensions of the "logic of growth" and the "limits to growth" as issues and realities confronting our world.
4.   To be able to identify and discuss major environmental issues confronting our world today.
5.   To be able to identify and discuss the three contrasting theories concerning the relationship between society and the environment.
6.   To begin to develop a sense about the ingredients for a sustainable society and world in the century to come.

PART III: CHAPTER REVIEW--KEY POINTS

The tiny island of Nauru in the South Pacific is the world's smallest and most isolated country. Nauruans are rich, but even there the environment is being depleted.

ECOLOGY: THE STUDY OF THE NATURAL ENVIRONMENT

Ecology is *the study of the interaction of living organisms and the natural environment.* The **natural environment** refers to *the earth's surface and atmosphere, including living organisms as well as air, water, soil, and other resources necessary to sustain life.* Like all living species, humans are dependent on the natural environment. However, humans are unique in a capacity for culture which allows us to remake the world according to our own interests and desires.

The Role of Sociology

Sociologists offer three major contributions to the exploration of ecological matters: (1) insights into what the environment means to people of varying social backgrounds, (2) the monitoring of the public pulse on many environmental issues, (3) an ability to demonstrate how human social patterns have placed mounting stress on the natural environment.

The Global Dimension

Our planet consists of one **ecosystem**, or *the system composed of the interaction of all living organisms and their natural environment.* The Greek meaning of "eco" is house. All living things in the natural environment are *interrelated.* The use of chloroflurocarbons is used to illustrate.

The Historical Dimension

Culture, specifically *technology* poses a threat to the natural environment. High energy use is a major problem in the industrial and postindustrial world. *Environmental deficit*, meaning *a situation in which our relationship to the environment, while yielding short-term benefits, generates negative long-term consequences* is a critical issue. Three important ideas are implied in this concept: (1) the state of the environment is a *social issue*, (2) the damage done to the environment is often *unintentional*, and (3) in some, but not all instances, the damage done to the environment is *reversible*.

Population Increase

As the Industrial Revolution progressed, rising living standards in Europe sent death rates down dramatically. In 1850 the world's population reached one billion people. Today, in 1997, we number 5.9 billion. The net gain of people each day worldwide is 250,000. The highest growth rates are found in the poorest countries. Issues related to rapid population growth are discussed.

Cultural Patterns: Growth and Limits

The point is being made that the planet suffers not just from economic *under*development in some parts of the world but also from economic *over*development in others. The core values in our society of *material comfort, progress,* and *science* underlie the **logic of growth** view. This is an optimistic view, one seeing productive technology improving over time. But, as many of the earth's resources are *finite*, this view helps create many environmental problems.

Environmentalists argue that the logic of growth view has contributed to the deterioration of the natural environment. They argue that humanity must implement policies to control the growth of population, material production, and use of resources in order to avoid environmental collapse. The is known as the **limits of growth** view. Projections are provided in *Figure 15-1* (p. 394).

ENVIRONMENTAL ISSUES

Solid Wast: The "Disposable Society"

For our nation as a whole, over one billion pounds of solid waste are generated every day. *Figure 15-2* (p. 395) shows data on the composition of household trash in the U.S. Fifty percent is comprised of paper products. We have been labeled the *disposable society*. We *recycle* on 10 percent of our waste materials. In comparison, Japan recycles one-third of their waste materials. The **Global Sociology** box (pp. 396-397) looks at a recycling success story from Egypt. The focus is on a people called the Zebaleen. Barred from many jobs due to religious discrimination, they haul and recycle much of the city's trash.

Preserving Clean Water

While the earth naturally recycles water and refreshes land through a process known as the *hydrological cycle,* two key concerns exist--supply and pollution. Concern for the *water supply* is actually an issue which dates back to ancient times in civilizations of Egypt, China, and Rome. Current and projected problems in Asia and North Africa are discussed. Increasing population and complex technology are major factors. Industry draws 25 percent of all global water usage. Households account for 10 percent of usage. *Water pollution* is a major problem as well. Even in the U.S., 500 million pounds of toxic waste is absorbed into rivers and streams each year.

Cleaning the Air

Industrialization has impacted negatively on air quality. Factories and automobiles are major sources of this problem. Strides are being made to improve the situation. Laws helping to reduce pollution are discussed. In the **Seeing Ourselves** box (p. 399), *National Map 15-1* shows information on the level of air pollution for all states in the U.S.

Acid Rain

Acid Rain refers to *precipitation made acidic by air pollution that destroys plant and animal life.* *Figure 15-3* (p. 400) illustrates how acid rain is formed. One phenomenon which is demonstrated is how one form of pollution causes another. The global scope of the problem is clear.

The Rain Forests

Rain forests are *regions of sense forestation, most of which circle the globe close to the equator.* In the **Window on the World** box (p. 398), *Global Map 15-1* shows the location of rain forests around the world. Today, approximately 7 percent of the earth's land surface is covered by rain forests. The largest is in South America, primarily in Brazil. The world's rain forests are being deforested at the rate of 1 percent each year.

Rain forests play an important role in removing carbon dioxide from the atmosphere. Today the atmospheric concentration of carbon dioxide is 10-20 percent higher than it was 150 years ago. *Global warming* is one result of this change. What is being created is a ***greenhouse effect***, or *a rise in the earth's average temperature due to an increasing concentration of carbon dioxide in the atmosphere.*

There is also the serious problem of *declining biodiversity*. The *biodiversity,* or the array of plant and animal life, is decreasing around the globe. Rain forests hold approximately one-half of all living species in the world. Why should we be concerned? First, biodiversity provides a varied source of food. Second, it provides a vital genetic resource. Third, the beauty and complexity of our natural environment is diminished. Finally, it is important to remember that extinction is irreversible.

SOCIETY AND THE ENVIRONMENT: THEORETICAL ANALYSIS

Structural-Functional Analysis

The structural-functionalists offer three important insights about the natural environment. These include: (1) the fundamental importance of *values* and *beliefs* to the operation of a social system, (2) the interconnectedness of various dimensions of social life, and (3) strategies for responding to environmental problems.

Cultural Ecology

Closely aligned with structural-functionalism is ***cultural ecology***, or *a theoretical paradigm that explores the relationship between human culture and the natural environment.* An illustration using Marvin Harris' study of India's sacred cow provides insight into this perspective.

Critics of these two views stress that they overlook issues of inequality and power. Further, many environmentalists are skeptical about the optimism held by proponents of these views, particularly the structural-functionalists. Further, in critic of cultural ecology, the relationship between the natural environment and culture is greater in societies with limited technologies.

Social-Conflict Analysis

This view directs us to see problems in the natural environment being the result of social arrangements favored by elites. Capitalism is seen as a major contributor to environmental crisis. They further stress the significance of inequality between nations as a major factor in the exploration of the natural world.

Environmental Racism

Environmental racism refers to *the pattern by which environmental hazards are greatest in proximity to poor people and especially minorities.* For example, factories and toxic waste dumps are often near poor neighborhoods.

Critics of these last two views argue that capitalism is no more hostile to the natural environment than other systems. Poor countries are also putting stress on the natural environment, particularly given their high population growth rates.

LOOKING AHEAD: TOWARD A SUSTAINABLE SOCIETY AND WORLD

An environmental deficit exists anywhere humans live. An *ecologically sustainable culture* refers to *a way of life that meets the needs of the present generation without threatening the environmental legacy of future generations*. Three basic strategies for achieving such an existence are identified. These include: (1) conservation of finite resources, (2) reducing waste, and (3) bringing world population growth under control.

Environmental strategies are not enough. Four changes in terms of how we perceive ourselves and our world are also needed. These include: (1) seeing the present as being tied to the future, (2) seeing humans are linked in countless ways to all other species of life, (3) the need for global cooperation, and (4) a critical reevaluation of the logic of growth view. The *Controversy and Debate* box (p. 407) focuses on the issue of what we are willing to give up to help out the environment. We seem to want more government action to protect the environment, but don't want to pay higher taxes for it.

PART IV: KEY CONCEPTS

acid rain
biodiversity
cultural ecology
disposable society
ecologically sustainable culture
ecology
environmental deficit
environmental racism
greenhouse effect
natural environment
rain forest
recycling

PART V: IMPORTANT RESEARCHERS

Marvin Harris

PART VI: STUDY QUESTIONS

True-False

1.   T   F   The cultural values of material comfort, progress, and science form the foundation for the *logic of growth* thesis.
2.   T   F   The *limits of growth* thesis, stated simply, is that humanity must implement policies to restrain the growth of population, cut back on production, and use fewer natural resources in order to head off environmental collapse.

3.	T	F	The limits to growth theorists are also referred to as *neo-Malthusians*.
4.	T	F	The Japanese recycle over three times more solid waste per capita than people in the U.S.
5.	T	F	Households around the world account for more *water use* than does industry.
6.	T	F	*Texas* and *Alabama* are two of the least polluted states in the U.S.
7.	T	F	*Biodiversity* tends to be relatively low in rain forest environments.
8.	T	F	The *greenhouse effect* is the result of too little carbon dioxide in the atmosphere.
9.	T	F	One criticism of the *structural-functional* paradigm is that it fails to take account of the interconnectedness of various dimensions of social life.
10.	T	F	According to *social-conflict* theorists, rich nations are overdeveloped and consume too much of the world's natural resources.

Multiple Choice

1. The Greek meaning of the word *eco* is:

    (a) weather
    (b) house
    (c) material

    (d) satisfaction
    (e) work

2. Riddle: A pond has a single water lily growing on it. The lily doubles in size each day, In thirty days, it covers the entire pond. On which day did it cover half the pond?

    (a) 5
    (b) 8
    (c) 15

    (d) 21
    (e) 29

3. How many pounds of *solid waste* are generated in the U.S. each day?

    (a) 15 million
    (b) 100 million
    (c) 250 million

    (d) 1 billion
    (e) 8 billion

4. Which is not a projection for the next century using the *limits of growth* thesis?

    (a) a stabilizing, then declining population
    (b) declining industrial output per capita
    (c) declining resources
    (d) increasing, then declining pollution
    (e) increasing food per capita

5. What percentage of the solid waste in the U.S. is either *recycled* or *burned*?

    (a) 2
    (b) 35
    (c) 11

    (d) 35
    (e) 50

6. Which type of solid waste represents about *one-half* of all household trash in the U.S?

   (a) metal products   (d) yard waste
   (b) paper   (e) plastic
   (c) glass

7. According to the Sierra Club, U.S. rivers and streams absorb _____ pounds of toxic waste each year.

   (a) 10,000   (c) 50 billion
   (b) 500 million   (d) 25 million

8. *Rain forests* cover approximately _____ percent of the earth's land surface.

   (a) .01   (c) 7
   (b) 2   (d) 11

9. The world's *largest rain forest* is found in:

   (a) South America   (d) Indonesia
   (b) North America   (e) Asia
   (c) Africa

10. The *structural-functional* paradigm offers three important insights about the natural environment. These include:

    (a) the importance of values and beliefs to the operation of a social system
    (b) the interconnectedness of various dimensions of social life
    (c) some strategies for responding to environmental problems
    (d) all of the above
    (e) none of the above

11. Strategies recommended for creating a sustainable ecosystem include:

    (a) conservation   (c) bringing population under control
    (b) reducing waste   (d) all of the above

12. A collection of environmental strategies alone will not succeed without some fundamental changes in the ways in which we think about ourselves and our world. Important points to consider include:

    (a) the present is tied to the future
    (b) humans are linked in countless ways to all other species of life
    (c) achieving an ecologically sustainable culture is a task that requires global cooperation
    (d) a critical reevaluation of the "logic of growth" thesis is required
    (e) all of the above

Matching

1. ___ The system composed of the interaction of all living organisms and their natural environment.
2. ___ The pattern by which environmental hazards are greatest in proximity to poor people and especially minorities.
3. ___ People living on a remote South Pacific island.
4. ___ The number of gallons of water consumed by a person in the U.S. over a lifetime.
5. ___ The study of the interaction of living organisms and the natural environment.
6. ___ The number of people added to the world's population each year (net gain).
7. ___ A religious minority living in Cairo.
8. ___ The earth's surface and atmosphere, including living organisms as well as the air, soil, and other resources necessary to sustain life.
9. ___ Regions of dense forestation most of which circle the globe close to the equator.
10. ___ A situation in which our relationship with the environment, while yielding short-term benefits, generates negative long-term consequences.

a.	natural environment	f.	ecology
b.	Zebaleen	g.	environmental deficit
c.	10 million	h.	rain forests
d.	Nauruans	i.	environmental racism
e.	90 million	j.	ecosystem

Fill-In

1. An _____ is defined as the system composed of the interaction of all living organisms and their natural environment.
2. The concept of *environmental deficit* implies three important ideas. First, the state of the environment is a _____ _____. Second, much environmental damage is _____. And third, in some respects environmental damage is _____.
3. Our planet gains an additional _____ people each day.
4. Core values that underlie cultural patterns in the U.S. include progress, material comfort, and science. Such values form the foundation for the _____ *thesis*.
5. The _____ *thesis* states that humanity must implement policies to control the growth of population, material production, and the use of resources in order to avoid environmental collapse.
6. While in Japan at least _____ of waste is recycled, in the U.S. only about _____ percent is recycled.
7. The earth naturally recycles water and refreshes the land through what scientists call the _____ *cycle*.
8. It is estimated that fifty percent of household trash is _____.
9. Experts estimate the atmospheric concentration of *carbon dioxide* is now _____ to _____ percent higher than it was 150 years ago.
10. *Structural-functional* analysis is criticized for overlooking the issues of _____ and _____ and how these affect our relationship with the natural environment.

11. Strategies for creating an *ecologically sustainable culture* include _____,
    _____ _____, and bringing _____ _____
    under control.

12. Environmental strategies alone won't succeed without fundamental changes in the way we
    think about ourselves and our world. We must see that the present is tied to the _____,
    humans are linked in countless ways to all other _____ of life, achieving an
    ecologically sustainable culture is a task that requires _____ _____,
    and a critical reevaluation of the logic of _____ thesis is necessary for a sustainable
    society.

Definition and Short-Answer

1. Differentiate between the concepts *ecology* and *natural environment*.
2. What three important ideas are implied by the concept *environmental deficit*?
3. Briefly describe the pattern of word *population growth* prior to an after the Industrial
   Revolution.
4. Critically differentiate between the *logic of growth* and the *limits to growth* views concerning
   the relationship between human technology and the natural environment.
5. What is meant by the term *disposable society*? What evidence is being presented to support
   this view of the U.S?
6. Review the global research concerning either *water pollution* or *air pollution*.
7. Discuss the connection between the depletion of the rain forest and global warming and
   declining biodiversity.
8. Differentiate between the *structural-functional, cultural ecology,* and *social-conflict* views on
   the relationship between human society and the natural world. What are three important
   insights offered by each view? What is one criticism of each view?
9. What are the three strategies identified for creating an *ecologically sustainable culture*?
10. What are the fundamental changes in the ways we think about ourselves and the world which
    are being suggested in the text? What other changes in our thinking would you suggest be
    made?

PART VII: ANSWERS TO STUDY QUESTIONS

True-False

1.	T	(p. 393)	6.	F	(p. 399)
2.	T	(p. 393)	7.	F	(p. 400)
3.	T	(p. 394)	8.	F	(p. 401)
4.	T	(p. 395)	9.	F	(p. 402)
5.	F	(p. 397)	10.	T	(p. 404)

Multiple-Choice

1.	b	(p. 390)
2.	e	(p. 392)
3.	d	(p. 394)
4.	e	(p. 394)
5.	c	(p. 395)
6.	b	(p. 395)

7.	b	(p. 399)
8.	c	(p. 400)
9.	a	(p. 400)
10.	d	(pp. 402-403)
11.	d	(p. 406)
12.	e	(pp. 407-408)

Matching

1.	j	(p. 390)
2.	i	(p. 405)
3.	d	(p. 389)
4.	c	(p. 397)
5.	f	(p. 389)

6.	e	(p. 392)
7.	b	(p. 396
8.	a	(pp. 389-390)
9.	h	(p. 400)
10.	g	(p. 391)

Fill-In

1. ecosystem (p. 390)
2. social issue, unintended, reversible (p. 391)
3. 250,000 (p. 292)
4. logic of growth (p. 393)
5. limits of growth (p. 393)
6. one-third, 10 (p. 395)
7. hydrological (p. 395)
8. paper (p. 395)
9. 10-20 (p. 400)
10. inequality, power (p. 404)
11. conservation, reducing waste, population growth (p. 406)
12. future, species, global cooperation, growth (p. 406)

PART VIII: ANALYSIS AND COMMENT

Global Sociology

"Turning the Tide: A Report from Egypt"

Key Points: Questions:

Controversy and Debate

"Reclaiming the Environment: What Are We Willing to Give Up?"

Key Points: Questions:

Window on the World--Global Map 15-1

"Water Consumption in Global Perspective"

Key Points: Questions:

Seeing Ourselves--National Map 15-1

"Air Pollution Across the United States"

Key Points: Questions: